PARIS ABC SCHOOL OF ART

DRAWING AND PAINTING COURSE

PRINTED IN FRANCE 1983   © ECOLE ABC DE PARIS 1971   ENGLISH TRANSLATION © LINGUAPHONE INSTITUTE LIMITED, LONDON 1982
                                         (new edition 1982)

TECHNIQUES

Contents

Original French text by
Georges Dayez
Artist, member of the *Comité du Salon de Mai.*
Teacher, head of the lithography studio at the *École Nationale Supérieure des Beaux-Arts* in Paris.

Basic techniques

THE PENCIL

Everyone has used a pencil for drawing. A visit to any museum will show you what masterpieces have been created with this medium.

Modern pencils are of excellent quality, whether they are the traditional wooden kind or propelling pencils, which exist in several diameters.

Pencils are graduated from very hard to very soft:

1. 7H, 6H and 5H are very hard and are used for "geometrical" drawings.
   4H, 3H, 2H and 1H are hard.
   HB is medium.
   1B, 2B, 3B and 4B are soft.

2. The former system of graduation, which is hardly ever used today, went from 00, 1, 2, 3, 4 . . . that is, from the softest to the hardest.

The lead in pencils was originally natural graphite, which is a carbon derivative, but the lead is now manufactured by using a bonding material with graphite powder.

Lead pencils can only be used to produce weaker or stronger shades of black.

In old catalogues you can find "black stone" mentioned. This is natural graphite cut into sticks of varying hardness. It produces a grey colour.

Generally speaking, lead pencils can be used on all non-shiny papers. To obtain good results, especially with advanced work, you should use Ingres paper or paper which contains a great deal of glue.

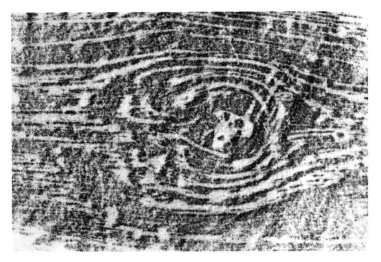

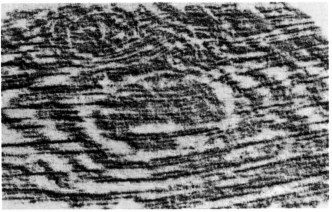

Rubbing on oak.

Of course, sketches can be done on thinner paper, even paper such as brown wrapping paper, which can give the work a certain charm.

It is practical to use sketch books if you are working outside. These can be bought in various sizes and qualities.

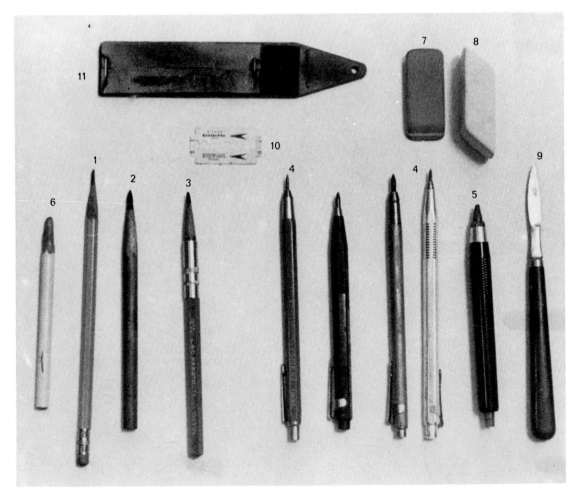

1. Pencil.
2. Conté pencil.
3. Pencil in holder (enables you to use up small ends of pencil).
4. Propelling pencil.
5. Propelling pencil for thick leads.
6. Ink rubber in pencil form.
7. Ink rubber or eraser.
8. Pencil rubber or eraser.
9. Scraping knife.
10. Razor blade.
11. Sandpaper (fine & medium) attached to board.

I-3

Rubbing on canvas, fine grain.

TRACING

Repeated pencil strokes and rubbings out can rapidly spoil the surface of the paper.

Once you have completed your sketch, you can, if you wish, make a more or less final copy of it on a new sheet of paper. For this you will need tracing paper.

The procedure is as follows: on a piece of fairly thin tracing paper, trace the shapes in as much detail as you wish. Then, take a piece of tracing paper of the same size, which you cover by rubbing all over it with a soft pencil. The covering should be quite thick, and should be spread to a regular consistency with the finger or a piece of wadding. (This sheet of paper can be used several times.) The treated paper and the tracing paper should be placed over the paper which will receive the definitive drawing. They should be held in place with drawing pins, clips, a heavy object, or sellotape.

You then go over the lines of the tracing with a tracing pencil. You should check the drawing from time to time by lifting both papers to ensure that the tracing is clear, but not too heavy, so that you can rub it out easily if necessary.

Instead of using two sheets of tracing paper, you could simply cover the reverse side of the paper on which you do the tracing with lead pencil.

Method of holding a pencil.

ERASERS

Everyone is familiar with the ink rubber and the pencil rubber. The latter should be of good quality and should be kept clean. If the rubber is not used for some time, it develops a hard surface and this must be cut off with a sharp knife.

The pencil eraser is made from rubber with various additives.

The ink eraser contains an abrasive (pumice powder).

Apart from drawings done with hard pencils, all others should be protected with a fixative, unless they are immediately put under glass.

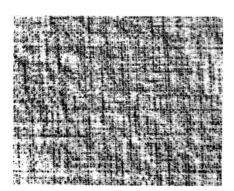

Rubbing on canvas, coarse grain.

COLOURED PENCILS, COLOURED CRAYONS, HARD PASTELS, CONTÉ STICKS

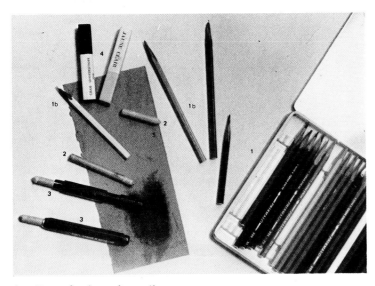

1. Box of coloured pencils.
1b. Coloured pencils.
2. Coloured crayons.
3. Coloured crayons in special crayon holders.
4. Coloured chalks (unsuitable for fixing).
5. Sandpaper.

Coloured pencils are obtainable in a wide variety of colours. We would particularly recommend those made by Derwent and by Caran d'Ache. The latter produce a range which are water soluble, allowing the work to be softened and the colours merged if a wet sable brush is passed over them.

They do not need any fixative and can be scraped, so as to allow the colour below to appear, even in the case of white. They are difficult to erase.

When you use coloured pencils, you should press hard on the paper, in order to give a full rich colour. This is what children do, which gives their drawings part of their charm.

Also available are coloured crayons — round sticks of colour like hard pastels. These can be bought individually or in boxes containing from a dozen to several dozen shades.

There are also Conté crayons, known usually as Conté sticks, which come in black, white and a range of browns.

We should also mention oil pastels. They can be used in thick layers, resulting in very rich colours. They may be used by themselves or to finish off oil paintings on canvas or paper. They are soluble in turpentine.

CHARCOAL

1. Extra large charcoal stick.
2. Large charcoal stick.
3. Medium charcoal stick.
4. Fine charcoal stick.
5. Compressed charcoal.
6. Paper wrapped charcoal.
7. Cotton wool.
8. Rag.
9. Chamois leather.
10. Razor blade.
11. Scraping knives.
12. Chalk.
13. Sandpaper.
14. Mouth-operated fixative diffuser.
15. Fixative aerosol spray.

Because it is associated with students in art schools, charcoal has been rather looked down on. It can, however, provide an extraordinarily rich texture. It can be used both in the most meticulous or the most spontaneous work (Seurat, Odilon Redon, Matisse). As it can be easily erased by simply wiping it off, charcoal is often used to make the preliminary sketch for paintings, even water-colours.

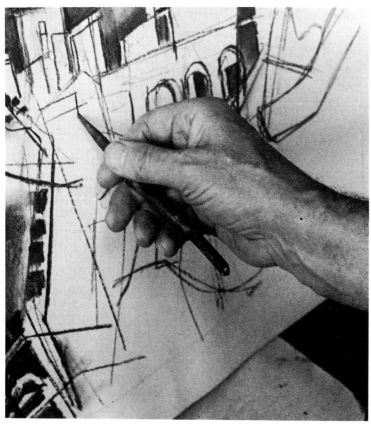

Method of holding charcoal.

The charcoal is held flat on the paper along its entire length in order to cover large areas.

The paper used with charcoal is usually cream or white Ingres paper. The fact that charcoal can be erased so easily is both an advantage and a disadvantage. Whilst it can be erased with a rag or, preferably, chamois leather or cotton wool, it is also easy to spoil a section of a drawing by a clumsy movement. Consequently, when working with charcoal, the paper should be placed on an easel, or against the back of a chair. When you have freely made your first sketch, you can eliminate the parts which are wrong or too black by flicking them with a rag, then knocking the back of the board, or blowing on it, to remove the loosened dust. (Rubbing the surface of the paper only succeeds in spreading a uniform grey colour.) Then you can carry on.

You must not scratch the surface of the paper, but you can create highlights by using either a putty rubber or stale breadcrumbs. (There are special erasers available, known as bread rubbers). When you do this, however, you always leave a greasy film on the paper, which you can't draw over. Consequently, you should only erase when the work is finished.

Charcoal is made from willow or limes, which are semi-carbonised in sealed containers. It should be light and of an intense black. Charcoal is graded as H (extra hard), HB (semi-hard) and B (soft). They should be used in this order as far as possible. They exist in different thicknesses: the small stick, which is 3mm in diameter; the medium 8mm stick, which is the most frequently used; and the large or Venetian stick, from 10 to 20mm in diameter.

The large stick is generally only used for sketching out compositions on canvas or on large surfaces. When cut with a bevelled edge, it can be used to fill in large areas of colour.

Charcoal is held either directly in the hand or with a charcoal holder. It can also be applied along its entire edge. It can be given a sharp point with a knife or razor blade.

We will offer only a few words of advice: do not be too hasty in applying the more intense degrees of black, and be very careful not to spoil the surface of the paper. Different means of shading off can be used: edges can be softened or blurred with pieces of blotting paper or chamois leather; pale grey shades can be spread with the finger or, preferably, with a piece of cloth; white areas can be created with a rubber. However, these techniques are not entirely advisable as they give rather smudgy results.

How to use a chair as an easel.

FIXING

This is delicate work. It consists of covering the fine particles of carbon on the paper with as fine a covering as possible of lacquer. The fixative is a solution of gum lac in alcohol, the latter evaporating when applied. The best method of application is to rub the fixative rapidly over the back of the paper with a piece of cotton wool. This, however, can only be done if the paper contains a small amount of glue. (This can be checked by licking a corner of the paper, which should have a slightly blotting paper texture.)

The most general method, however, is spraying. There are some very good simple vaporisers, both pliable and rigid, which are mouth operated. There are also aerosols available, which use synthetic resin with a solvent instead of gum lac and alcohol. It is important they should be kept away from any naked flame.

When fixing, one must avoid producing large droplets or shiny areas.

If insufficient fixative is used, the drawing will not last, while if too much is used, a varnished surface will result. It is important to hold the vaporiser or aerosol far enough away from the drawing. One should spray evenly, and the operation should be carried out several times, using only a little fixative on each occasion.

Charcoal can be fixed by applying a coat of water or alcohol with a brush. However, this process changes the appearance completely. The work can be finished off with black Indian ink, using a brush or different types of pens.

RED OCHRE AND CHALK

Ochre is a natural mineral and is normally used commercially in the form of compressed sticks or lead for propelling pencils. Also available in a similar form is white chalk, which is harder than school chalk; the latter should not be used, as fixing makes it almost invisible.

"South of Toledo". (Pure and diluted Indian ink.)

1. Natural graphite.
2. Conté graphite stick.
3. Conté red ochre stick.
4. Natural red ochre stick.
5. White conté stick.
6. Paper stumps.
7. Leather stumps.
8. Pencil rubber.
9. Ink rubber.
10. Scraping knives.
11. Razor blade.
12. Sandpaper (fine and medium) attached to board for crayon sharpening.
13. File mounted on board (same use).

USING THREE CRAYONS

Ochre, used alone or with a black medium and chalk, has often been used by the masters. If you use chalk, you will obviously need coloured paper. Chalk, which loses its whiteness when fixed, is often replaced by white gouache or white conté stick.

THE PEN

We will only mention a few uses of the pen here, as these are endless and can be suited to the technique of the individual.

The following are basic points:

Paper This must be bonded paper, otherwise the pen strokes will spread, as on blotting paper. Water-colour paper, paper for wash-drawings, Canson paper, tracing paper, vellum, Bristol board, etc., are commonly used.

Ink Indian ink is normally used. Although it is not normally diluted, the ink can be thinned with water if you wish to have parts of the drawing in greyer, lighter tones.

If you plan to reproduce your drawing, you should only use neat, black ink. Ochre and sepia coloured inks are also available, which are very effective whether used alone or combined with the black ink.

Pens Pens are made of steel. The ordinary dip pen is excellent, as it is very strong. Even when it is worn down, it is very good for producing a firm, thick line.

The pens known as drawing pens produce very fine lines, but they tend to scratch the paper, especially when new. For detailed work, such as lettering, the Gillot nib is the best. Pen work can be combined with brush or wash work, and even with water-colours. Certain artists achieve interesting results by working on damp paper. The ink spreads to produce broader lines. Apart from the special pen for drawing lines, which is essential for frames and lettering, there are also several types of fountain pen which can be used to obtain a wide variety of lines of constant width.

Also available are Japanese pens, made of bamboo with the end cut to shape. Strong lines can be drawn with the end of a paint brush made of soft wood, if you bevel the end. In some works which are intended for reproduction, you can obtain grey tones by scattering droplets of ink with a toothbrush and a pad. (See the chapter on Lithography).

"The Harvesters". (Pen and Indian ink.)

1. Pen holder with ordinary drawing nib.
2. Pen holder with very fine nib.
3. Pen holder with "Sergeant-major" school nib.
4. Pen holder with "Jenner" nib for scratching.
5. Scraping knife.
6. Razor blade.
7. Ink rubber.
8. Piece of untreated bamboo.
9. Piece of cut bamboo.
10. Japanese bamboo pen.
11. Goose quill.
12. Goose quill with feathers removed.
13. Various felt pens.
14. Fountain pen with felt tip.
15. Various bottles of Chinese and Indian ink.

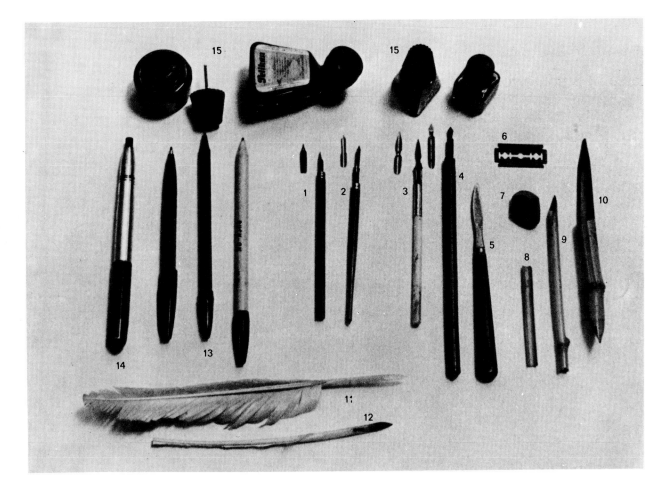

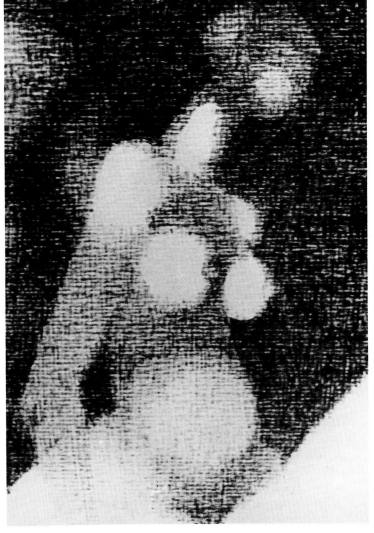

Two quill drawings by Claude Nassiet.

WORKING ON STRETCHED PAPER

Working with paper on a stretcher is very rewarding. Moreover, there is less tendency to scratch the paper, and it is easier to fix.

The technique is simple: the sheet of paper should be placed on a clean table with the drawing surface against the table. The back should be thoroughly dampened with a wet sponge. This should be done first lengthwise, then breadthwise, as quickly as possible. A painting frame should then be placed on the paper, leaving a margin of at least 5 or 6 cm all round. A square of paper should be cut from each corner to prevent wrinkles forming in the paper. The longest sides should be folded back over the frame and fixed with glue, drawing pins or staples. Then the shorter sides should be fixed in the same manner. The frame and paper should be removed from the table and allowed to dry. The paper tightens on its own, like a drum skin. This is easily the best technique.

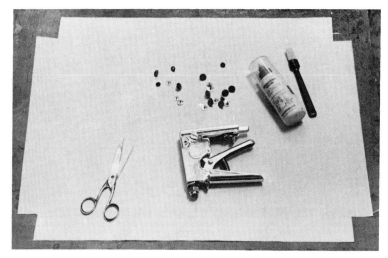

The sheet of paper is cut at the four corners so as to make a square in the shape of the frame. On the paper: drawing pins, glue, scissors and stapler.

The paper is reversed on a clean board and dampened evenly all over.

A frame is laid on the damp paper. The four corners should fit into the four cut corners of the paper. The edges are folded back and fixed with drawing pins, staples or glue. The paper will be wavy at first but will become taut when dry.

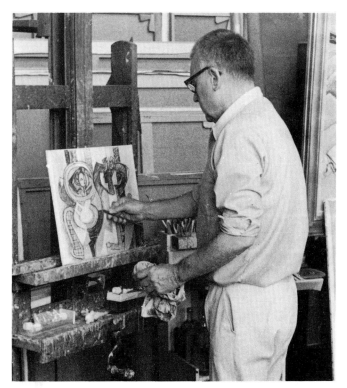

The paper, stretched on a frame, is placed on an easel.

FELT-TIP PENS

Felt-tip pens, both black and coloured, have been available for several years. They contain their own ink, and have tips of different thicknesses made of synthetic textiles, or synthetic felt.

BRUSHES

There are brushes to suit every technique and taste: water-colour brushes, Japanese brushes, wash-brushes, oil-painting brushes, etc.

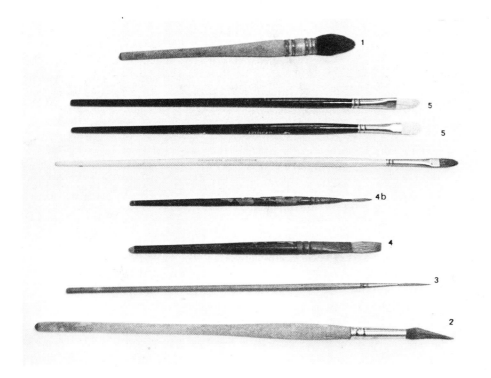

1. Brush for washes.
2. Brush for washes.
3. Brush with very fine hairs.
4. Brush with thicker hairs.
4b. Same brush (side view).
5. Sable brushes (for oil painting).

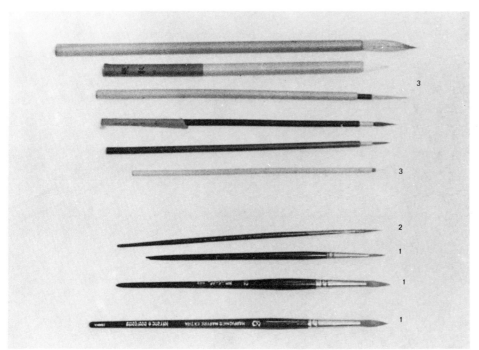

1. Various sizes of sable brushes.
2. Very fine sable brushes mounted on goose quills.
3. Japanese brushes.

Method of outlining with a fibre brush. Sufficient colour should be prepared beforehand. If the quantity on the brush is insufficient, dip the brush in colour and *start again from the beginning*.

Note how the left hand holds the ruler, by pressing on its surface. This can be done also on a vertical or oblique surface (wall, or canvas on an easel).

Method of holding a sable brush for drawing.

Method of holding a Japanese brush for drawing.

PAPER

The name comes from papyrus, a reed of which the Egyptians used the skin.

They rolled it out, creating bands which, when they were interwoven and smoothed with pumice, were made into rolls.

In the ancient world, papyrus replaced clay tablets, wax-covered wooden blocks and lead.

In the Middle Ages, the break in contact with the East meant that papyrus was replaced by parchment and vellum, prepared from sheep, goat and calf skins and carefully smoothed with pumice. The finest quality came from still-born animals.

Paper as we know it was created in China and Korea in the first century A.D. It was introduced to the West by the Arabs in the 11th century.

If you examine paper under a microscope, it looks like a sort of felt made of interwoven fibres. The longer the fibres, the better the quality of the paper.

Linen rags are the basis for the best quality paper. They are reduced to small pieces by boiling, and kneaded to separate the fibres, which form a thick paste.

In the old manufacturing process, the paste is spread on a metal frame and allowed to dry.

The rectangular pieces which result from this process are then placed in piles on felt and strongly pressed. The sheets thus produced are allowed to dry.

However, most of the paper we use is made from wood fibre (or from plants like alfalfa, which is used for luxury book printing), reduced to pulp and processed by efficient, complex machinery.

Chinese and Japanese papers are made from the bark of the mulberry tree, the lime tree, or from bamboo.

Natural paper absorbs liquids (water, spirits, drawing ink and printing ink solvents). Filter paper and blotting paper are natural papers.

To give paper its required characteristics, a certain quantity of glue (gelatine or skin glue) is added to the pulp to make it less absorbent.

Using very little glue, a vellum paper is produced which is suitable for engraving. (1)

Vellum with a larger quantity of glue is used for lithographs.

Different drawing papers contain larger or smaller quantities of glue.

Ingres paper, which is a laid paper, is used for charcoal drawing.

Paper for water-colour and gouache contains a high percentage of glue (2).

These papers usually have a surface with a coarse or fine grain, while the reverse is less rough. According to their grain, these papers are known as Hot press, Not, and Rough. Sometimes you can see the mark of the cloth on which the paper has passed through the machine. The manufacturer's watermark can be seen when the paper is held up to the light.

Bristol board is very smooth and is used only for work with a fine pen.

Layered paper used in printing is covered with a layer of chalk or baryta, and glue. It cannot be used by the artist except as scraper board. (See below.)

Apart from these papers, many great artists have used any sort of paper that came to hand, including newspaper and wrapping paper, but only the papers described above are suitable for retouching, rubbing out, etc.

Paper is generally sold in rolls (usually 1.5m x 10m), or in sheets. When sold in sheet or block form the sizes range from A1 to A7.

A1 paper measures 594 x 841 mm ($23\frac{3}{8}$ x $33\frac{1}{8}$in).
A7 paper measures 74 x 105 mm ($2\frac{7}{8}$ x $4\frac{1}{8}$in).

500 sheets make a ream.
25 sheets make a quire.

The strength of paper is measured in grammes per square metre.

80g to 120g for Ingres drawing paper.
160g to 300g for water-colour and Bristol paper.

Water-colour boards are stronger and more rigid. They have the advantage of not warping and of retaining humidity for a long time when wet.

Good quality papers tend to have a slightly warm tone. Printers have made "bleached" papers very fashionable. Manufacturers also offer a whole range of coloured papers.

Scraper boards are made from thick card covered with a fairly thick layer of chalk or baryta. The artist covers them, either partially or totally, with a layer of black ink. When the ink is dry, it can be removed by scratching with a sharp point. The white beneath then reappears, giving a white drawing on a black background. This looks very similar to a woodcut.

The ink should be applied thinly, otherwise it will penetrate the layer of chalk and scratching will be difficult.

Saint-Paul de Vence. (Charcoal, pen and wash.)

(1) This is not the same as vellum made from calf-skin.
(2) You can test how much glue is in a paper by touching it with the end of your tongue: paper containing glue does not stick to it.

1. Compasses with pencil holder, and a pen for drawing lines.
2. Dividers with pencil holder.
3. Dividers with pen for drawing lines. (Also a pencil holder.)
4. Two pens for drawing lines.
5. Protractor.
6. Set square.
7. Graduated ruler.
8. Rubber.
9. Drawing board.

Original French text by
Robert Cami
Teacher, head of the engraving studio at
the *Ecole Nationale Supérieure des
Beaux-Arts* in Paris.

Reeds

Goose quills

Silver point

THE REED, OR CALAMUS

The reed should be dry and equal in size to a pencil. Bamboo is harder and can also be used. The calamus should be cut and split like the goose quill. This is excellent practice for the difficult art of cutting a pen.

Safety ink bottle

If you are drawing in the open air you run the risk of spilling your ink.

It is wise to use a safety ink bottle. This can be made from a wide-necked bottle with either a screw top or snap top plastic closure. You should use a plastic, reed or bamboo tube of the correct length for the bottle (see illustration), so as to leave a certain amount of ink which will not pass the base of this tube, held forcibly at the other end by the neck of the bottle.

If the system is to work efficiently, it is essential that the ink does not go higher than the base of the tube, so that only the tip of the pen is covered with ink.

With this tube in the bottle, even if you upset the bottle, the ink spreads around the tube and will escape only with great difficulty.

Indian ink should not be used undiluted. Water should be used to soften the black, and by using two or three bottles a wider variety of shades can be achieved:

very diluted ink for pale tones.
less diluted ink for deeper tones.
slightly diluted for the blacks.

The principle is the same with coloured Indian inks. You can also produce varying shades by changing the angle of the pen to the paper.

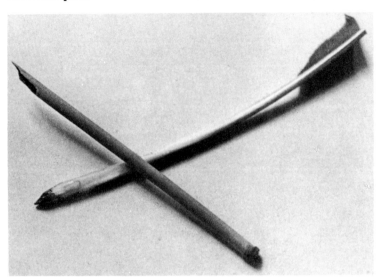

Reed and quill.

GOOSE QUILLS

Why should we return to the old techniques, in particular the goose quill? As this is a natural product it is flexible and can be adjusted to suit individual requirements. So the artist can use it to produce his own style. All our modern instruments have replaced older ones, but without always preserving the special qualities of the latter. The advantage of a goose quill over a metal pen is that it is very supple and glides over the paper, producing a wide variety of strokes, thin or thick. It has been used from time immemorial.

The choice of pen should depend on its firmness when held in the fingers. The best types are the following:

1   Goose quill: this is the most supple and has the greatest proportion of handle.

2   Turkey quill: this lasts longer but has a shorter handle.

3   Crow quill: this is best suited for very fine work.

If you wish to strengthen the handle section of these quills, you only have to dip them in nitric acid for a few minutes. The lateral barbs on the goose quill should not be used, and artists removed them in the old days.

The penknife. Formerly this had a very narrow, sharp blade with a large handle to fit well into the hand. As the classic penknife is no longer available, you should use a penknife with a well sharpened blade and as thick a handle as possible.

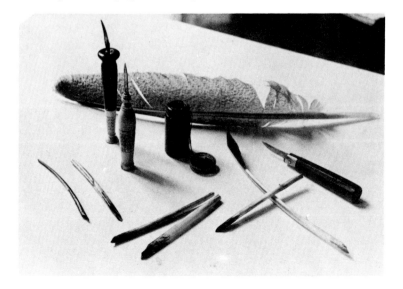

Assorted knives.
Spill-proof ink holder.
Goose quill. Turkey quill. Crow quill.

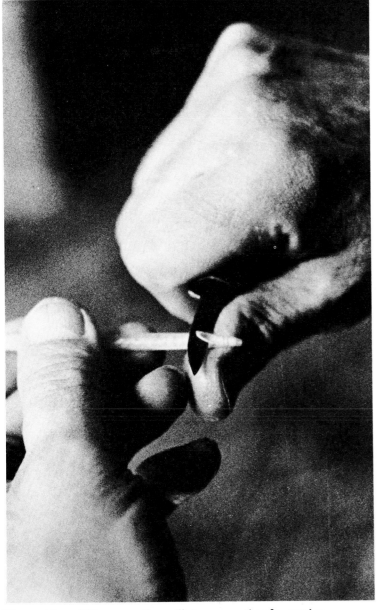

The position of fingers on the quill, in preparation for cutting.

Cutting pens

1   The outside of the quill should be cleaned by scratching with a knife to remove the thin layer of skin.

2   The end should be cut as a bevelled edge.

3   Take a piece of wire, hooked at one end, and push it through the quill tube, while turning it, so that you remove the inside.

4   Prepare to split the quill by making a cut of about 3 mm. The cut will widen due to the thickness of the knife blade.

5   Insert a metal rod (a nail or knitting needle) and, by pushing it upwards, split the tube beyond the cut. The two sides of the tube automatically spring back together again. You can stop the split by placing your thumbnail on the tube.

6   Make a wide notch in the bottom of the tube on the opposite side to the split, which should remain in the centre.

7   The most important and delicate step is to cut the point of the quill so that the left and right sides are identical and the point reaches the same level on both sides.

This operation will control the length of the split, a long split giving a supple quill and a short split a firmer one. The operation is completed with a succession of small adjustments carried out with a sharp knife.

You can judge the length of each point by pressing it gently against your fingernail.

The quill is now ready for use, but it cannot hold much ink and needs to be dipped often into the inkpot.

To remedy this, you can transform your quill into a fountain pen. You will need to cut two small pieces of thin brass, 1 or 2 mm in width, to fit the width of the quill, and 3.5 to 4 cm in length. Make them into the shape shown in the photograph on page 18. Insert this into the tube, so that the most curved end acts as a spring to hold it in the quill tube. The less curved end should reach to about 1 mm from the point. The small space left between the curve of the metal and the sides of the tube allows a small reserve of ink to be retained, which should last for several minutes.

To obtain thick lines with your quill, you should press on the point a little. For thin lines, use the quill very lightly, or use it sideways or backwards.

With frequent use, the point of the quill will need to be resharpened from time to time.

African landscape.
Sketch drawn with goose quill by Cami.

SILVER POINT

Silver point is a technique of drawing which was very much in use from the 13th to the 16th centuries, but then fell out of fashion.

It is a technique which allows great accuracy, and it has a characteristic "lightness".

PREPARATION OF THE PAPER

Cennino Cennini advised burning bones, making them into powder and adding water and gum to make a suitable preparation for the paper.

The simplest technique is to cover a sheet of drawing paper with a fairly thin layer of gouache with a white base. (It can then be coloured as desired). White lead powder, mixed with water and a little gum arabic, is also a good preparation.

The drawing instrument should be a piece of silver wire, the thickness of a pencil lead, which produces a very delicate grey colour. Yellow or red copper gives a more yellowish, less solid result. Gold can also be used.

2 or 3 cm of the silver should be placed in a propelling pencil. The end can be rounded as required on an oiled stone, with emery paper, or a fine file.

Mistakes are difficult to rectify, as an eraser will remove the prepared base. The best solution is to cover over mistakes with the same original preparation.

As the metal point glides easily over the paper, the artist derives great satisfaction from his work and can achieve very subtle effects. Lines can be drawn very precisely, producing a richness and clarity which are the hallmarks of this technique. Because of this, the technique is not suitable for large drawings, but small drawings bring out its best qualities.

Coloured paper gives an added charm to the works of the great masters: Leonardo da Vinci, Raphael, Dürer, etc. Without wishing to copy these great men, we could well follow their example by using coloured bases.

Enlargement of a silver-point work by R. Cami. (Original size 11 x 12 cm.)

Original French text by
Paul Girol
Winner of state travel scholarship.
Ile de France Prize (water-colour).
Francis Smith Prize.
Silver medal: City of Paris.

Colour wash

Let us start by listing the materials you need:

1   A folding palette in enamelled metal.

2   A jar or tube of water-colour paint (peach black, blue-black, sepia, Vandyke brown or burnt sienna).

3   Three wooden-handled badger brushes set in quill — the first very thick and bulbous (about 13 mm at the thickest point), the second medium (about 9-10 mm), the third smaller (about 6-7 mm).

They should all form into a good point after dipping them in water and drying them by lightly shaking to remove the excess water. Obviously, when you work you will choose the one whose size is most suited to the scope of the work in hand.

4   A water jar.

5   A portfolio.

6   A few sheets of paper (Arches or Rives) suitable for colour wash or water-colour. It should be strong but fine-grain, and the same size as the portfolio. A drawing block is also suitable.

7   A folding stool (especially useful for outdoor work).

It is possible to use an easel, but colour wash, like water-colour and gouache, can be worked on the knee, using the portfolio to lean on.

COLOUR WASH TECHNIQUE

Colour wash, or monochrome work, is a method of indicating the tones of the subject portrayed by applying washes of one colour only to a drawing. A brush is loaded with water and a quantity of the chosen colour. The higher proportion of water to colour there is on the brush, the weaker the resulting tone. As we are using only one colour on the palette, we have to gauge the values of the colours of the subject so as to give the correct tones. One important point that you should always bear in mind: the wash must always be sufficiently diluted to retain a certain degree of transparency, contrary to other processes (like gouache or oil painting) which have an opaque quality (called covering).

A preliminary warning: avoid tints in which the colouring matter is too thick for the quantity of water contained in the brush. In colour wash the paper acts as white.

A second warning: never try to go over a wash, either wholly or partially, with another while the first is still wet. You must wait for the first to dry or else you will produce stains, blots and marks.

It is possible to introduce or "run" one tint into another while it is still wet, but only if the second colour is denser than the first.

In this way, you can make accents of deeper tone which will not have hard edges but will blend softly into the first tone.

But do not overwork this process because, even if you could run all the tones successfully, the result produced would be blurred and unpleasant, giving a fuzzy appearance to the wash.

Whenever you go over a tint, whether it is dry or still wet, work carefully, without rubbing the bristles against the paper in case you brush away the first colour.

A third warning: do not let a wash which is still wet come into contact with one to be laid directly next to it. That is, not unless you want it to run in, in which case the second tint must have a greater colour density than the first.

A tint can be shaded when it is being laid by blending the brush strokes that have just been laid on the paper into the next strokes, without waiting for the paper to dry. These successive strokes are laid with the same brush lightly dipped into clean water so as to weaken the tint that it holds. This can be repeated several times, according to the effect of shading you wish to obtain.

When you are beginning or continuing a painting, how are you to judge the extent to which the paper has dried after it has been damped? All you have to do is look at its surface, holding it against the light. If it is not shiny, the water has penetrated right into the paper and you can paint on it without danger of seeing the wash spreading beyond the desired areas.

In colour wash, some of the pigment belonging to the tones laid on the paper as the work progresses penetrates with the water into the grain of the paper. The colour is said to "sink in", and this phenomenon is more or less noticeable depending on the colour being used.

Colour wash by P. Girol.

Village in Provence, P. Girol. (Drawn with a bamboo brush, and highlighted in sepia.)

P. Girol. Fishermen at Nazaré, Portugal. (Coloured ink wash; black, grey, sepia).

INDIAN INK WASH

Indian ink wash is applied in exactly the same way as water-colour wash. Black Indian ink can be used, but to obtain a more extensive range of tones, and give greater warmth and variety of expression, sepia and grey waterproof inks can also be used. Using a grey ink, the grey tones become finer and more delicate than with Indian ink, and offer further possibilities in the range of half-tones.

The contribution of sepia tint to a wash is to give more flexibility and, most of all, more life.

It is interesting to note that indelible inks are better than Indian ink for outdoor work; they are slower drying, and allow a more supple and flowing stroke. This is especially noticeable in the preceding drawing, sketched with a bamboo brush.

COLOURED INKS

Coloured inks can be used with the addition of some water instead of water-colour itself. They are adaptable in use and can be obtained in some delightful colours. Interesting effects can be obtained.

When drying, the tones laid on the paper become paler — more or less so according to how wet the paper has been.

As the technique for colour wash is very much like that of water-colour, you will find it most useful to read the section on Water-colour in this book.

Monochrome is a style of painting in which one single colour other than black is used.

Paul Girol in his studio.

Bottle of black Indian ink.
Bottles of waterproof ink: sepia and grey.
Some brushes.
Palette.
Water-jar and two or three pots in which the half-tones can be prepared in advance.

Ivry-le-Temple. (Wash in grey and sepia inks.)

I-30

Water-colour

Boatman, in front of the Popes' Palace at Avignon. Water-colour by Paul Signac.

Water-colour is a process of synthesis and simplification.

Synthesis implies preliminary analysis with the object of eliminating inessential detail so as to bring out the inherent nature of a subject. Signac was right in saying, "We cannot include everything in a water-colour". So, do not try to say everything; confine yourself to the essential.

You will be concerned, simultaneously, with composition, tones and colours. The first stage is to make a concise, un-complicated drawing to give an underlying structure to your work. This framework is usually drawn lightly in HB pencil. Because of the transparency of the washes you should not press so hard that you make indentations which would show up in the finished work. Some experienced artists do this

drawing with a fine brush dipped in a pale, neutral tone (for example, ultramarine mixed with burnt sienna). You can also express the main areas of shade, using this same pale and neutral tone, laying it with a thicker brush so as to express broadly the immediacy of your first impression. Because of the neutral quality of the wash, it will barely affect the shadow colours of the subject. If you have to use a soft rubber to correct your pencil work, do this with care.

You may wish to do the initial drawing with a pen and Indian ink, or perhaps with a reed pen or a wooden stick. But, in this case, it is advisable to strengthen the colour you subsequently use.

EQUIPMENT

3 sable brushes of different thickness.
1 thick squirrel brush set in quill.
Bulldog clip.
Large and small palette.
Water jar.
Rag.

Now let us lay the washes on the paper, considering ways of applying them to the support. Remember that the greater the dilution of the pigment with water, the weaker will be the resulting tone.

Study in shading. Tone progressively lightened with water.

The essence of water-colour is its transparency.

Do not, therefore, make your dilution too thick. Nor, on the other hand, run the risk of making it too thin and anaemic for the sake of transparency. The water-paint brush is more supple and flexible than the type used in oil painting. Its belly enables it to take up a large amount of tint. This makes it possible to apply generous quantities of tint to the paper, giving great freshness to the work, with its characteristic rich and fluid quality.

Detailed work is carried out with the aid of a fine brush which you will not need to fill with very much water. Just have it sufficiently moist to form a fine point.

Details worked with a fine brush.

A flat wash — the paint is prepared first so that the same quantity of water is used for the whole wash.

I LAYING FLAT OR EVEN-TONE WASHES

When covering a large area of paper with an even (or almost even) wash, you should prepare in advance as much colour as you think you will need. This can be done either in one of the hollow compartments of the palette, or in a jar, and mixed up evenly by stirring it with a fairly wide-bellied brush. Squeeze the brush gently against the edge of the jar or the smooth ridge dividing the palette, so that no drops can fall onto the paper to cause unwanted stains. Lay the wash on the paper with a full brush, both the point and the belly coming into contact with the paper at the same time. Work in a downward direction, with short, vertical, or slightly oblique hatching, overlapping the strokes to blend them together. If you have chosen a sufficiently thick brush to cover the paper in one go, you will not need to take up more tint during this first stage. Note that, at the bottom of each stroke, a small amount of excess colour will appear if the support has been slightly tilted (such as on a desk). Continue in this way until the desired area is covered, and when you have finished, remove the excess tint from the lower part by using the point of the brush, having first partly squeezed it out. We stress 'partly' because if it were completely dry, it would take up too much tint and weaken the tone of the area immediately above.

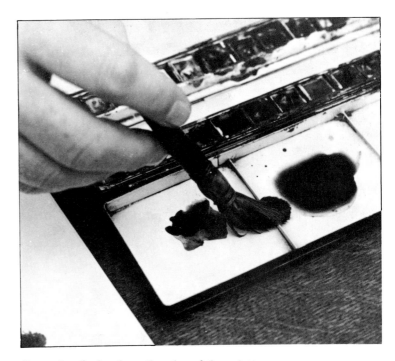

Squeezing the brush on the edge of the palette.

To digress slightly, water-colourists often get into a habit which they later find difficult to break. That is, sucking the bristles of their brush to clean off some of the tint. It is true that it is one of the best ways of adjusting its moistness and reshaping the point. The colours are, no doubt, very watery and dilute and not at all harmful. Nevertheless, we recommend pressing the brush gently against a piece of blotting paper or drying it with a soft rag. You can also dry the bristles by giving the brush a slight flick.

Hatching, especially over large areas, will blend better if you remember to wet the paper in advance by spreading a moderate amount of clean water over the surface to be covered, using quite a thick, clean brush. Before applying the colour, wait until the paper has absorbed the water and is no longer shiny. You can also use a wet sponge to dampen the back of the paper and wait for the water to penetrate.

Flat wash on wet paper.

Wide brush-strokes on dry paper, using a very wet brush.

Insufficient water in the brush.
The strokes do not blend well into each other.

It is vital to work quickly when applying the wash, or else the water in the band of colour just applied will evaporate and the water in the next one laid will penetrate the first, causing stains and rings.

I-36

II BLANK SPACE SURROUNDED BY FLAT WASH

Next, we will try spreading a flat wash over a large area so as to enclose a space.

In the middle of a sheet of paper, draw any motif you like — a flower, say — which will stand out as a white silhouette once the tint is laid. Lay the wash, proceeding in the same way as before. You will have to take great care, as you must not run into the space left for the motif. Work alternately on one side and then the other. If the bands tend to dry out it means that you are probably not working quickly enough.

It is useful, therefore, to have previously wetted the paper, as this delays the absorption and drying of the wash being laid. Do not worry if this is not absolutely even. We are not trying to achieve an architectural finish. It is simply a question of getting your hand in, acquiring skill in using the brush, and learning to work rapidly. Moreover, it is not advisable to prepare a large quantity of tint in advance when working from nature since the colours in a subject are rarely identical, and it is better to try to capture the exact one for each part of the picture. Perfect regularity is not necessary, as light creates a vibration and this dynamic quality, or movement, should be reflected in the overall tonality.

Water-colour (detail).

Leaving intentional blanks on the paper is one of the major difficulties of water-colour.

If you are painting a sky, for example, you must reserve blank space for all the objects which will appear in it, and are of a lighter tone. Also, the yellow ochre of a chimney, for example, will be neutralised by the blue of the sky if the two colours are overlaid. It is therefore important (for this reason and to preserve transparency) that as few colours as possible are overlaid.

III STRENGTHENED AND WEAKENED TINTS

It is possible to increase or diminish, strengthen or weaken, the intensity of the tints laid on the paper. We will start with weakened colour, whereby we obtain transitions of tone commonly observed in nature (in sky, water, etc.). These transitions can be sudden or, alternatively, can present a wide range of nuances, or subtle changes, varying from dark to very light. (A nuance, here, does not mean a change in colour, but rather a change in the tone, or value, of that colour.)

In the first case, proceed in the following manner: having applied a substantial amount of tint to the paper, rinse the brush thoroughly in clean water and then, without squeezing it out, begin working from the lower edge of the tint, taking down with it, in one stroke, the excess colour that has accumulated. For a large area, repeat this process, using the method we have previously suggested to obtain an even tone. The only difference is that, since the colour in the liquid edge formed at the base of the first band of brush strokes is lightened by the clean water contained in the brush, there is a sudden definite weakening of value in the second band.

In the second case, the process involves taking a little clean water onto the brush which has not had the original colour washed out. In this way, the tint that has been laid will be softly and evenly weakened in tone, the transition from dark to light being obtained by just a few brush strokes.

Darkened tone.

When you reach the lower edge of the area to be covered, remove the excess tint with the tip of the brush (moistened only) so as to avoid the liquid edge causing a darker strip to appear as it dries.

The procedure to follow for strengthening, rather than weakening a tint, is the opposite. Increase the amount of colour on the brush, either in one go or gradually — a few rapid, circular movements of the brush against the palette before painting will assist you to obtain an evenly mixed dilution. This is necessary for the colour to dissolve adequately in the water on the brush.

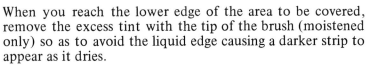

Lightened tone.

IV VARIEGATED WASH

Very often you need to lay a wash which is not just one colour, or tones of one colour, but consists of several different colours blended into one another. This must be applied with a direct and sure hand, in one go and without unnecessary brush strokes. Suppose you want to present a grey background made up of burnt sienna and cobalt, in which sometimes one colour will be dominant and sometimes the other. First, damp the paper with clean water. Next, mix up the two colours by making up a moderate amount of tint in the hollow compartment of the palette. Then, making sure there is no longer any shininess left on the paper, lay some of the mixture, working with the brush half full. This does not require you to proceed in even bands, but what is necessary is to see that the brush always has a moderate supply of tint so that it damps the paper evenly.

Then, blend in other strokes, using increased amounts of each component colour alternately. Sometimes keep the value of the tints the same, sometimes strengthen or weaken it. The effect will be a series of gradations of tone, numerous transitions which vary and enhance the background colours through strokes which are subtly blended together.

It is possible to go back over this work for rebuilding. This is not a contradiction of what we said earlier, as long as the areas to be touched up are still wet and the brush is kept moderately full.

This exercise can not only be carried out with two colours but with three, or even more. In water-colour, you should show by constant transitions the variations of colour and tone to be seen on the object or motif you are painting. Working in this way, you reduce the number of times you touch up or glaze, since you achieve the desired variation in colour in one go.

Variegated wash.

V WET-IN-WET

Taking a recently done painting while it is still wet, choose a section of light tone which still has a slight shine. Take some cobalt or burnt sienna on the brush; it does not matter which colour as long as the proportion of colour is strong. (At this point we are only concerned with demonstrating the technique). Mix in a very little water and apply the tip of the brush to the chosen place. This slight touch of colour will spread gradually, becoming progressively lighter towards the outside. The centre will retain a noticeably deeper tone. This is what is called wet-in-wet. Above all, the density of colour in the tint you are making run must be stronger than that of the colour you are running it into, because if it is not, a pale ring will appear. The wetter the paint receiving it, the more the run-in colour will spread.

Using this technique, you can highlight certain places with accents which blend at the edges into the tone that they strengthen. This process should not be used too freely, or an unattractive lack of definition will result.

As run-in colours automatically become progressively weaker at the edges, they can be successfully used to suggest the roundness of an object and bring it to life. This method can also be used for giving an impression of fluidity and haziness, as in reflected light on water, or distant clouds, etc.

Water-colour (detail). Run-in colours, overpainting and white spaces.

According to the effect you wish to achieve, colours can be run into another shade of the same colour, or into a different colour.

To sum up, remember that wet-in-wet can be used to obtain either a gradual change in tone, or a gradual change in both colour and tone simultaneously. If you wish to restrict the amount the run-in colour spreads into the one receiving it, use a thicker paint when the paper is dryer. If, however, you wish it to spread widely, use a thinner paint and run it quickly into the previous colour whilst this is still very wet.

VI GLAZING

Wet-in-wet is only one technique available to the watercolourist. Transparent water-colour can be used as a series of thin layers of colour overlaid one upon the other. This is known as glazing. It is the traditional way of strengthening tones, and has the advantage of avoiding heaviness and fuzziness — frequent disadvantages in graduated tints.

Once the paper has been covered with tint, you can lay another over it, but only if the first one is perfectly dry and the brush does not scratch it as you paint.

If the second layer of colour is the same as the colour underlying it, the result will be an increase in intensity.

If the colours are different, two things could happen.

(a) Let us start with two transparent colours. These will produce an optical mixture of colour when they are overlaid. The situation remains the same if only the underneath colour is opaque.

(b) However, if the top colour is opaque, whatever colour is beneath will be neutralised by the opacity of the second colour.

This last circumstance is, therefore, to be avoided. However, since opacity decreases as the proportion of water added is increased, it is possible to overpaint with a tint of an opaque colour, as long as it is very watery.

This leads us to reconsider the use of glazing. If this method is used appropriately and not indiscriminately, you can heighten the colour of an underlying tone, or, on the other hand, weaken it with a light tint containing a complementary colour. But again, this should only be applied over completely dry tints. So as not to mix the colour of these, apply the brush lightly, well charged with paint but not over-full.

VII JUXTAPOSED TINTS

In water-colour, you not only overlay tints, you begin by laying them side by side. This is not particularly difficult, though there is just one fundamental warning: do not let the colour you are laying come into contact with the first colour if this is still wet. If you are working on paper that has been thoroughly soaked, it is advisable to leave a very narrow space between the colours so as to prevent one colour unexpectedly running into its neighbour.

According to the dictates of the subject, you can select places to leave tiny droplets of tint. With the help of such deposits of colour, a painting which has long since dried retains a pleasing, watery freshness.

Colours must be given a slightly greater intensity than they have in nature because, as they dry, they become much paler, especially when you work on paper that has been thoroughly wetted. This can be clearly seen if compared with a touch of paint laid on dry paper.

CORRECTIONS

When you are at the beginning of your work, and you consider that you have laid a tint badly, the best thing to do (if it covers a large area) is to wash the paper all over with a very wet sponge. If the area is small, white blotting paper can be used. Once the colour has started to dry, it is impossible to regain the original whiteness of the paper, so wait for it to dry completely before trying to modify the unwanted colour with a glaze. Tints made up of dense colours are easier to remove than those containing fluid colours, as they tend to remain more on the surface of the paper.

When working in water-colour, you should always try to achieve the right colour first time off, and only when you have failed to do this should you resort to glazing.

BRUSHWORK

The brush is held in the same way as a pen. Never scrub the paper with it, but let it guide the colour over the whole area to be covered. When working in one colour, paint progressively from top to bottom and avoid laying your strokes in all directions and too far apart. Whenever possible, work in broad brush strokes. Do not make small, timid dabs if one good, bold stroke will do. When working near an area which is to be left blank, hold the brush in a more upright position so that its belly does not trail over this part.

According to the texture of the object you are painting, vary the pressure on the brush as it moves across the paper. Strive to suggest the fabric of the object and avoid a thin, or mean, touch.

COLOUR LIFTING

Sometimes certain highlights get lost, especially small ones which tend to get covered over by the other tints you lay. To rediscover these, you can use a lifting-off, or removing, technique. For small highlights, first wet the place with the tip of the brush, dipped in clean water. Wait a moment before drying it with white blotting paper. Then, wrapping a piece of clean, finely woven cloth round the end of your index finger, quickly dab the wet colour and so remove it. Like all corrections, this operation must be carried out quickly and without hesitation. If not entirely successful the first time, it can be repeated — but not too often, or the surface of the paper will be rubbed away and will not take new paint. For coarse-grained paper, the only remedy is to use a scraper. The blade should be held at right angles to the paper to avoid cutting into it. With tints that have

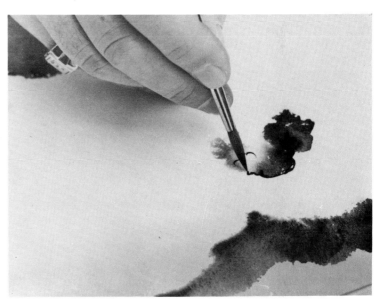

Correct way of holding the brush.

just been laid and are still shiny, brilliant highlights can be obtained by pressing a pellet of bread, which you have kneaded with your fingers (and kept clean in the process), gently over the paper.

Finally, the background too can be given highlights by using the tip of the brush with very little water in it. It must be washed frequently — in fact, almost every time that it has lifted some tint.

At no time in genuine water-colour can you use white gouache to create highlights: it is too opaque. Clearly, if light-toned areas are to stand out against certain other tints, care must be taken to leave blank space. This, as we have said before, is one of the difficulties of water-colour, especially if these spaces are narrow and complicated in shape. With practice, however, you will manage to do this more easily.

If your brush should slip, making the colour run over the edge of the shape you are painting, and you do not have any blotting paper to soak up unwanted smudges, you can work the paint back inside the shape, using a completely dry finger.

PROCEDURE OF WORK

The traditional procedure of work is to lay the luminous tints first, then the half-tones, followed by the shadow, and lastly the details, accents and, if necessary, glazing.

We have already said that, according to the nature of the subject, water-colour can be washed onto paper that has been thoroughly dampened, or directly on to dry paper. You can also use the two processes in conjunction. For example, you brush the back of the paper with water, covering the places where you intend to lay sky and clouds, water, or any distant features, while strong tones and accents are laid on dry paper. In any case, avoid making the paper too wet, or your work will become indistinct and fuzzy.

Let us conclude by reminding you that water-colour is a more spontaneous medium than oil painting. When you are overlaying tints, remember that, if you want to retain transparency, only one or two tones can be overlaid for the background features and two or three in the foreground. A water-colour must be "washed" on, simply and boldly. So focus your attention on essentials. In the foreground of the picture, your work should be almost like a mosaic. In this way, the colours will not be modified as they most certainly would be if you tried to run them together.

Accuracy in the tones that create the effect; exact analysis of colour in search of its essential nature; simplicity attained through deliberate rejection of useless detail: these are the three virtues you should strike to achieve. Work boldly and train yourself to be able to "throw off" a water-colour at one attempt. But, if you go wrong, don't despair. Many an artist has had similar setbacks. You will, at least, be working to perfect the freshness of approach which is part of the appeal of this delightful art.

SOME TECHNICAL TERMS

Wash: paint. The term is used because of the nature of the diluting medium, water. To say that a water-colour is mainly *washed* means that it is painted in broad areas rather than with fine brush strokes.

Working with water: this is to have your brush always sufficiently full, so as to maintain the necessary degree of moisture, which is such an essential characteristic of this medium.

Dryness: a fault in a water-colour, due to insufficient quantity of the diluting vehicle — water. The resulting effect is meagre and lacking in impact.

Running: a term used to describe colour that bleeds, or runs, over desired edges.

Brio: a term used to describe the spirited execution of a water-colour: one is immediately aware of the artist's technical mastery, his speed and assurance in handling the medium.

Singing: a water-colour can be said to *sing* when its colours set each other off or harmonize in a manner pleasing to the eye, just as musical harmony pleases the ear.

Original French text by
A. Hambourg
Officer of the Legion of Honour.
Artist appointed to the *Ministère de la Marine*.
Honorary artist to the *Ministère de la Guerre* (Artist to the Armed Forces of France).
Winner of numerous prizes for drawing and painting.
Grande Médaille de Vermeil: City of Paris.

WATER-COLOUR SKETCHES OR "NOTES"

"This kind of 'note taking' from nature is most successful if the artist is fully conversant with water-colour technique. The work must be executed with speed so that the brush strokes recreate a feeling of spontaneity and convey the idea of synthesis, which is achieved by a rapid grasp of essential elements. Retouching should be avoided, and the work should be carried out with rhythm and energy.

"Once it is felt to be going wrong, it should be torn up and started again. No attempt should be made to correct or make good the error. A great number of drawings, sketches and colour notations will need to be done, and there should be no hesitation in jettisoning many of them.

"A few water-colour touches can be added to a rapid pencil sketch or to one that has been worked with a brush barely moistened with a very light tone. Such sketches are very useful to the artist as he travels, since through them he can recapture at a future time the subjects whose essential rhythms, tones and atmosphere he will have retained in his memory."

"Horses and riders in the ring". Water-colour by A. Hambourg (size 13 x 21).

RECOMMENDED EQUIPMENT

— sable brushes of different thickness (1 or 2 fine ones). The brushes should be new, or nearly new. They should be changed frequently so that they keep their point, their flexibility and, above all, their spring.

— pots of water-colour. Small water-colour boxes can be obtained, containing cakes or pans of water-colour, which are practical and have a small palette (to be cleaned after use).

— several jars (jam jars) for water, to be changed frequently and kept clean.

— clean, soft rags of smooth material (such as old shirts or well-worn sheets) for wiping the brushes.

— easel that can be used outdoors as a table with folding stool or high seat (so as to prevent tiredness while painting).

But a folding table on which one can prop up the portfolio or notebook is even better!

— a portfolio to which you attach the paper with clips, not drawing pins which leave ugly holes (some water-colourists use sketch pads with rigid covers).

— paper. For these water-colour "notes" it is good to use quite a smooth paper, of a fresh whiteness that will set off the niceties of the technique, and on which the brush glides easily. This will assist rapid execution, but any other paper can be used according to preference (textured, heavyweight, tinted).

This equipment can be carried in a satchel or haversack (a fisherman's bag is ideal).

"The port at Cannes". Water-colour by A. Hambourg (size 9 x 12).

Original French text by
Michel Ciry
French National Arts Prize 1945.
Eugène Carrière Prize 1958.
Grand Prix du Conseil Général 1962.
Ile de France Prize 1964.
Grand Prix de Montrouge 1965.
Member of the Academy of Arts in
Florence 1965.
Wildenstein Prize 1968.

Detail of a water-colour by Michel Ciry.

Ciry takes about six sessions of an hour or an hour and a half for the large water-colours.

First, he stretches the sheet of paper on a plywood stretcher (paper: heavyweight Fidelis Arches). When the paper is dry he builds up the drawing with great precision in lead pencil.

Wetting the paper all over once more with a sponge, he sketches in the light tones with a large (squirrel) water-colour brush.

Then, as he works, he dampens the areas to be worked with a flat brush which is passed lightly and swiftly over the paper so as not to lift the tints that have already been laid. He continues painting with sable brushes, progressively building up tone.

Water-colour requires a great degree of concentration since it is at one and the same time a very spontaneous and a very analytical art. The whites must always be expressed as blank space, and the light tones, once they are laid, should be left.

Michel Ciry finishes off the painting with the accents, using the long, fine brushes called *filets*.

Palette used by Michel Ciry:

Naples yellow
Yellow ochre
Lemon cadmium yellow
Cadmium orange
Cadmium red
Alizarin carmine
Venetian red
Emerald green
Cobalt green

Cerulean blue
Cobalt blue
Monastral blue
Ultramarine
Payne's grey
Ivory black
Chinese white (used very little)

"Portrait of a woman". Water-colour by Michel Ciry.

Original French text by
Michel Chaumet

Gouache

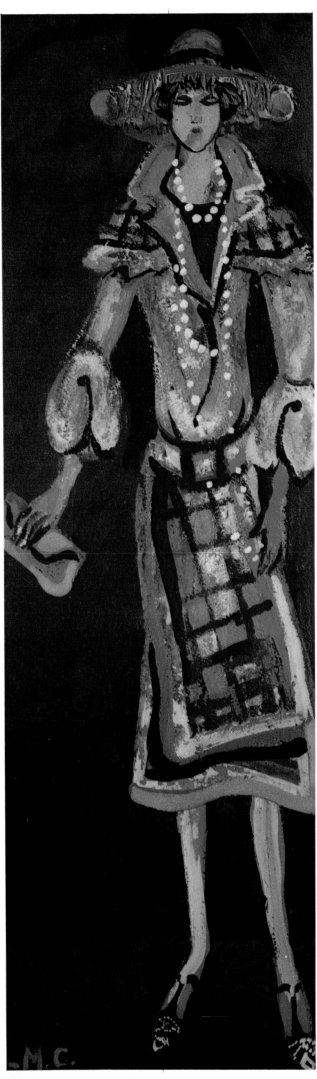

1 COLOUR CHARACTERISTICS

Gouache is characterised by the fact that the colour is diluted with water and worked with a brush dipped into the mixture. The colours are made up of finely ground solid pigment with an additive of size — a kind of glue enabling the colour to adhere to the paper. Size consists of water-soluble gums, such as gum arabic, dextrine and some gelatines. Added to this mixture of pigment and size are substances that give it a slow drying property and flexibility in application.

The colours used in gouache are said to be *covering*, which means that they allow no trace of the surface on which they are laid to show through. For example, you should be able to cover a dark colour with a light one without detriment to the light one. This is achieved when mixing the colour, by introducing a higher proportion of pigment than of size: i.e., by volume, there should be more colouring matter than size.

Gouache, therefore, always resembles a paste, and contains very little water.

Gouache is worked with a wet brush, which makes it more liquid and easier to apply. But, if it is diluted too much, it will not "cover". The water used should be as clean and pure as possible.

Because of the high proportion of pigment to size in good quality paints, gouache produces a matt tone. If the coats of colour are laid too thickly, an unattractive cracking, or crazing, appears when the paint dries.

Ranges of gouache of differing quality are available on the market.

II   EQUIPMENT AND MATERIALS

Essential requirements:

1   A white palette in china, porcelain or plastic.

2   Paper (Arches, or any other make).

3   Tubes or bottles of colour. Tubes are more practical. The correct consistency for gouache is not unlike thick cream, so, if bottles of colour are used, the contents should be stirred every three to four days to prevent hardening. To stop the colours drying out you could even cover them with a thin layer of clean water after using them, especially if you are not going to use them again for some time. Next time, all you need to do is pour off the excess water.

4   Brushes. You should use the kind of brush that suits you best, according to the demands of the work you are doing.

Do not forget to clean them well in water after use, and arrange them to dry in a container, with the bristles uppermost.

5   Water, of course, and plenty of it because it soon gets dirty with gouache and needs to be changed frequently. Do not forget that the colours dry quickly on the palette, so it is preferable not to apply them too liberally, even if this means refilling more frequently. (With a little clean water and a clean brush, carefully wet the colours left on the palette to prevent drying.)

The paper can be placed on a table, pinned onto a board on an easel, or on a wall if the work is for mural design.

Gouache is especially useful for working on designs for wall-papers, fabrics, tapestry, posters, catalogues or other advertising material, as it suits the usual proportions of this type of work. But this does not mean that you cannot paint still life subjects, flowers, landscapes or portraits. Since this is a covering process, we can sometimes use an impasto technique, which will be useful mainly for those areas representing solid objects, or for brilliant lighting effects and strong highlights.

For the sake of variety, smaller or greater amounts of water can be used.

You should bear in mind that gouache becomes lighter when it dries, and adjust the colours you use accordingly. In other words, work in deeper values.

If you need to superimpose colours, you must begin painting with a more liquid substance and, as the layers of paint are increased, the paint on your brush should be thicker. Begin painting by laying the deeper tones and finish with the lighter ones, as these usually have to be impasted to achieve the desired luminosity. Do not let the impasto be too exaggerated, however (at least not on areas of any size), for fear of irreparable cracking when dry.

The consistency of the foundation that you lay should be quite liquid so as to cover the painting surface quickly and achieve the immediate effects of blending, mixing and shading off the colours. This preliminary work will gradually be covered by thicker and more covering brush strokes.

Gouache dries quickly as it contains little water, so you can add to and cover a colour entirely by laying another over it. But take care, as gouache colour runs very easily, and, if the colour being laid is a little too liquid, the previous colour will lift and run into the new one. This can be a problem, but at the same time it offers new possibilities once you are experienced in the use of gouache. Interesting effects can be obtained by allowing the colours to blur and blend into each other.

A consequence of the covering quality of this process is that, as you lay your colours, the guidelines set up in your preliminary drawing will disappear. The more you build up the colour, the more you lose sight of the original drawing. You will need to reinforce this, therefore, with strong outlining strokes before you start painting. This is not necesarily a drawback since your object is to cover this drawing. In any case, as long as you follow the procedure we advise, by using thin and liquid paint at first, your drawing will remain visible for some time.

Your increasing skill and familiarity with gouache will enable you to make use of another possibility opened up by the medium. If you want to lighten a whole area of your painting once it is dry, begin by preparing a light and liquid colour, like milk. Use a large brush and, taking care to work lightly, rapidly apply this thin gouache without lifting the colours already laid. This will cast a kind of transparent veil which will agreeably alter the colours underneath and give you the effect you desire. Several washes can be laid on top of each other, but allow each one to dry first. Accidents can happen: sometimes the underlying colours reappear and form a deposit. But most of these accidents can be saved. The process of laying a thin gouache corresponds to that of glazing in oil painting.

When it is a case, not of glazing over paint, but of entirely covering the still virgin paper, you must first damp this lightly with a large brush charged with clean water. Then dip the brush in the colour solution and paint in wide bands, blending the edges smoothly into each other. One can lighten the wash, of course, by adding water or white gouache.

Original French text by
M. Marko

Pastels

Marko at his work table.

Although, in substance, pastel and paint are much the same, in use and application they are quite distinct. Pastels are small sticks of dry coloured powder ("pigment"), which is mixed into a paste with a little gum, before being moulded into shape. The gum is added for a few reasons: firstly, it ensures that, when applied to paper, the pastels do not crumble to pieces; secondly, the texture of the pigment combined with the gum is ideal for several purposes — from drawing in detail to spreading colour over large areas. (NB. pastels of varying densities are available, ranging from the softest pastels to the harder, grittier ones); and thirdly, when the pastel is applied to the chosen surface (the "support"), the gum acts as a kind of fixative. With this definition in mind, we can deduce a number of things about the art of drawing with pastels.

The technique used will, of course, vary, depending on whether the artist is painting onto a white support or not. The artist may, for example, choose to work on coloured paper, or he may be working on paper that has already been party or entirely coated with a first layer of pastel.

When using pastels, you should remember the following points:

a) Unlike any other medium used in painting, pastel is applied directly, in its more or less original form, to a white, grey, or slightly tinted surface, i.e. as a powdered pigment. Apart from the minimal amount of gum needed to bind the powder, no diluting or adhesive liquid is added prior to use. One of the great advantages of working in pastel is that these coloured powders are chemically sound; that is to say, they neither oxidize on contact with air, nor do they react when exposed to light for long periods of time; they remain as intact as they were when first applied.

b) Because the artist is applying coloured powders, which are opaque, to a surface which may well have already been shaded with other pastels, he can produce velvety textures and colours rather like those seen on a butterfly's wing. The effects that the artist can create by the layering and blending of pastels are exclusive to this particular medium.

c) Another advantage, unique to this medium, is that there is no need to mix colours, because these sticks of coloured powder are manufactured in such a wide range of shades that the artist will always be able to find the precise shade of colour to suit his purpose. Pastels present the artist with a choice of colours that are purer and more vivid than those offered by any other medium used in painting.

d) Because pastels come in the form of small round sticks, they are a simple and practical medium, particularly well tailored to the artist's needs. He can project ideas onto paper with great ease and precision; the artist's energy can be expressed instantly, and more or less vigorously, depending on how the artist handles the pastels, so that no spark of spontaneity is lost.

e) Because preparation of materials is minimal — colours do not have to be mixed in advance — and because of the ease with which colour can be spread onto paper, the immediacy and freshness of the drawing is preserved.

f) When working on a coloured surface, or one that has already been overlaid with a coat of pastel, the following principles should be observed:

i) A principle fundamental to all kinds of painting is that a drawing or painting is not the product of a single visual memory, reproduced more or less accurately, but rather the inspired interpretation of a number of different images, or fragments of images. These fragments are worked into a composition which is at once an expression of simplicity and vitality, accessible to the viewer in terms of both colour and form. The elements of the picture complement or contrast with one another so as to create a visual harmony corresponding exactly to the poetic imagination of the artist.

First stage.

Second stage.

The completed work.

ii) This is, of course, true of all the techniques used in painting, but let us take the case of the pastellist in particular. Even at the conceptual stage, the artist will have to bear in mind that he will be using the pastels to apply colour, either thickly or thinly, and with varying degrees of pressure, to a white, coloured or prepared surface.

In the first case, where the artist is working on a white support, he must apply the colours as evenly and boldly as possible.

In the second case, the artist is working on a tinted support and will need to take into account the fact that he is applying colour to colour. The artist will consider, when selecting colours, the effect of the tinted paper on the colour applied and will also choose colours which are harmonious with the paper since not all of it will necessarily be covered.

In the third and final case, the artist has already applied an undercoat of pastel to the support. This is what we call a *ground*. Here the application of pastels is far more complex than it was in the first two cases, and will require greater concentration and imagination. Each stroke of colour will need to be considered not only in terms of its precise location on the painting, and the colour of this area, but also in terms of the technique used to apply the second layer of colour to the already existing one. This means paying attention to whether the strokes are light or bold, the colour opaque or transparent, and the contrast between the two layers more or less pronounced. It is advisable to apply a fixative to the ground so that the two layers remain quite separate. This will give the artist a greater measure of control in achieving the desired effects. It is, of course, true that fixing the undercoat is a process which need not necessarily be respected; it is not unknown for the blending of two untreated layers of colour to produce particularly subtle, surprising and pleasing effects. You should always remember that the rules governing the techniques of artistic expression are flexible. In Art, there is really only one golden rule: obey your imagination.

As you can see, the techniques discussed above fall neatly into three categories. Pastels that are applied onto

(i) a white surface;

(ii) a tinted/coloured surface; and

(iii) (for a more elaborate finish) a surface to which pastels and a fixative have already been applied.

To sum up, then:

The main factor that distinguishes the use of pastel from any other medium is that the artist "writes" with a solid stick of colour. But, unlike writing, in which the letters are significant in themselves, one stroke of colour is not independent from the next one: in isolation, it has no meaning. The artist must integrate each stroke of colour with those he has already drawn and, where possible, anticipate those he intends to draw.

It is important that, at first glance, the final product looks like a painting, i.e. an interpretation of reality, and not a strict reproduction of reality. The viewer should be able to discern, just by looking at the painting, that it is composed of strokes and layers of different colours and tonal values. Because of its delicate lines and the subtlety of its velvety finish, pastels are an excellent medium for evoking aspects of reality as perceived by us. To avoid lapsing into the use of techniques adopted for "trompe l'oeil", it is a good idea to give full play to all the elements that are characteristic of pastels: fine lines that are, quite clearly, the product of slender sticks of colour, and dashes of coloured powder that are applied with precision and subtlety; these may be juxtaposed or superimposed, but they are always well defined.

Fixing with an aerosol.

Original French text by
Marc Havel
Chemical engineer, I.C.P.

Colour

THE EFFECT OF BINDING AGENTS

	Water-colours	*Gouache*	*Tempera*	*Oils*
Drying time	Very quick.	Very quick.	Very quick.	Slow.
Suitability for blending	Difficult to successfully blend one colour into another.			Ideal.
Suitability for graphic painting	Well suited to detailed drawing, diagrammatic representation, etc. Precise and clear.			Soft, supple brushwork.
How to lighten colours	Water down the colours.	Use white.	Use white.	Use white or apply a glaze.
Suitability for masking one colour with another	Possible in certain cases but not ideal.	Possible but must be done quickly — there is always the risk that the colours will run into one another.	Highly suitable — no risk of colours running into one another.	With oils, this process is lengthy — the undercoat must be left to dry out completely or alternatively be treated with fixing agents.
Finish	Translucent, luminous.	Muted tones rather like pastel shades.		Rich, deep colours.

THE CONSTITUENTS AND PROPERTIES OF PAINT
THE IMPORTANCE OF BINDERS

Every medium used in painting is the result of grinding together two components: firstly, a powder called *pigment* and, secondly, a glutinous substance known as *binder*. Pigment gives every colour its unique tone, and its ability to alter other colours or to mask them totally. The binder, which is used in a liquid form, has three functions. Firstly, because of its consistency, it enables us to manipulate and apply the paint more easily. Secondly, because it solidifies as it dries, it ensures that the colour adheres to the support and remains there. Thirdly, it is of prime importance in determining the visual effect of a painting.

There are a variety of binders and each of these corresponds to a different technique in painting; indeed, the techniques have adopted the name of the binders: gouache, oils, tempera, acrylics, etc. In the case of gouache or industrial paint, where the ratio of binder to pigment is high, the painter need only dilute it as necessary, with water or oil, as he is using it. But with the other techniques, particularly oil painting, the paint is manufactured with a minimal amount of binder. Here, it is up to the artist to modify his paints in accordance with the effects he is trying to achieve. This is done by adding one or more of a variety of solutions which we shall now take a look at.

We rarely stop to think how important binder is in painting. But clearly it is the most significant constituent of paint. As we have already mentioned, paint medium is usually named after the binder it contains, since it is the binder and not the pigment which distinguishes one medium from another. Take the colour yellow ochre for example. Every medium includes yellow ochre in its colour chart; it also forms the base of some of the enamel or gloss paints used in the building trade or manufacturing industry. It does not, as such, account for the differences between mediums.

It is primarily the differences in the nature of the various binders which determine the method of handling the medium and the appearance of the finished work. It would be easy enough to illustrate this by placing two small amounts of the same powder (preferably yellow or white) on a plate of glass and adding diluted gum to one and oil to the other. The results we obtain could be fully monitored by testing each solution on a piece of paper.

We might be tempted to interpret these results simply as a difference in time taken for each medium to dry. We might think, for example, that, with water-colours, the drying time is so short that the artist cannot possibly work at length on his painting as he might do with oils. But this assumption could be misleading; the differences between these two mediums are obviously more complex and we need to take another factor into account. The property of oil is such that it has a tendency to run, so that one colour merges into the next, causing at best a slight oil stain, at worst a loss of clarity in the graphics. Another problem arises with water-colours: the paint tends to cling to the spot to which it has been applied. Whatever the artist's level of expertise, he may well have difficulty in preventing rings from appearing, in spreading paint evenly over the paper, and in blending one colour into a neighbouring colour.

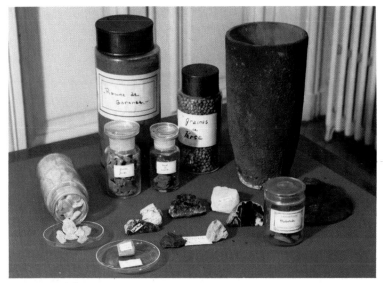
Raw materials.

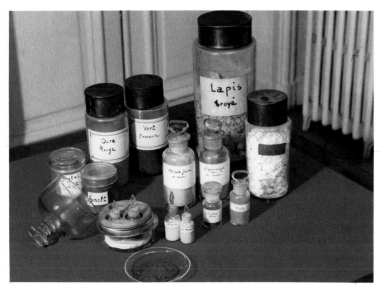
Pigments.

Grinding pigment and binder by hand.

Mixing the pigment and binder.

Grinding pigment and binder by machine, using granite rollers.

The same colour will be more opaque as a water-colour than it will be as an oil paint. Water-colours are not as bold or as clearly defined as oils; neither do they have the same depth of colour. Goauche has a cloudy, opaque finish, and it is only when water-colours are well watered down that they appear transparent. Any medium used in painting is only really of use when it can offer the artist a choice of opaque and transparent colours. Opaque is generally used to mask one colour with another, and transparent paint is important for modifying and highlighting the colour it is laid over.

Once the ground has been applied to the support, the painting is developed with successive layers of paint, super-imposed onto one another. Of course, this is not the whole story: there are also such processes as blending one colour into its neighbouring colour (which can only be done when the paints are fresh and moist).

Conversely, when overlaying one colour with another, you must ensure that the undercoat is quite dry, so that when the next layer of paint is applied, the existing colours do not lift and blend. Water-colours are not easily blended, but some mediums, e.g. tempera, lend themselves to rapid super-impositions of paint. Oil paint, however, is an ideal medium for blending, but it is a very time-consuming process. Each layer of paint must be completely dry before successive layers are applied.

The oil paint that we buy in tubes comes in the form of an extremely thick paste. Its consistency is a great asset to the painter since it is, without any doubt, much easier to thin down paint than to thicken it up.

You will find that, more often than not, it is necessary to add thinner to paint. The type and amount you use will, of course, depend on the effects you wish to achieve in your painting, and this is something you will discover as you go along, by dipping your brush into oil and thinner and testing it out on the palette.

You will soon become accustomed to gauging the type and amount best suited to your purposes: pure oil, neat thinner, or a thinner and oil-based solution.

FLASHE

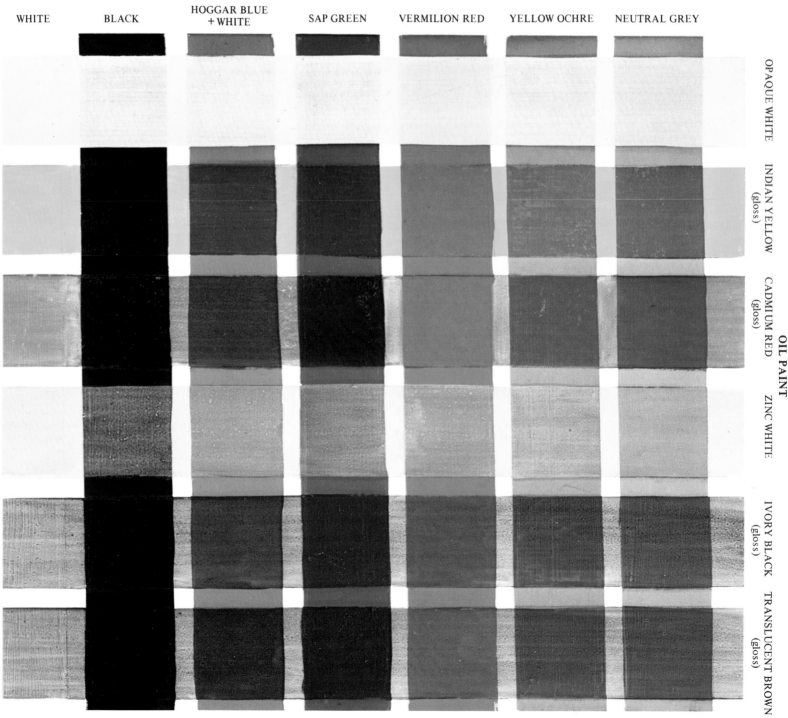

WHITE | BLACK | HOGGAR BLUE + WHITE | SAP GREEN | VERMILION RED | YELLOW OCHRE | NEUTRAL GREY

OPAQUE WHITE

INDIAN YELLOW (gloss)

CADMIUM RED (gloss)

ZINC WHITE

IVORY BLACK (gloss)

TRANSLUCENT BROWN (gloss)

OIL PAINT

I-58

DILUENTS: SOLVENTS AND THINNERS

Thinners and solvents can be mixed with oil paints in any proportion but, unlike oils, they are volatile. When exposed to air they evaporate completely, and, for this reason, must be used with skill and speed if they are to be effective. Thinners and solvents perform exactly the same function in oil painting as water does in gouache. It alters neither the quality of the paint nor the finish, but makes for easy application and fine brushstrokes.

However, the finish may be modified indirectly. You may find that, when applying oil paint that has been diluted by a thinner or solvent, the undercoats of primer and paint will dissolve. And the more porous the canvas, or the less an undercoat has dried, the greater the effect of the solvent will be. Because the oil in the freshly laid paint has been absorbed into the underpainting, the surface layer of paint will become "embued" or sink, appearing dull and matt, losing its richness of colour and, in some cases, its adhesive quality. This is more likely to occur either with a less volatile thinner, which takes longer to dry, or with a particularly powerful solvent.

Solutions like acetone, toluol, trichlorethylene or ester, used by restorers, are not suitable for painting because they are very strong and may cause considerable damage. Some of them also evaporate so quickly that there would not even be enough time to spread the paint over the chosen surface. As for petrol, it dries far too quickly and contains products that are unsuitable for painting, and should therefore be reserved for the car.

The two solutions we have yet to discuss, and which are in fact the most widely used, are rectified turpentine and petroleum distillates.

However, in recent years, the techniques used to refine these materials have greatly improved. A whole range of petroleum derivatives have come onto the market and, of these, the most ideally suited to painting is white spirit, which, like all petroleum spirits which are refined and adapted for use with paints, is characterised by the speed with which it dries.

Although some people are allergic to pure turpentine, it is not a harmful product, and the one great advantage of using turpentine is that it is an excellent agent for drying out oil paints. It is important to remember that its purity is not only a result of the refining process, but also depends on the way in which it is subsequently stored by the user. Even the smallest amount of air will cause oxidisation, increasing its density and resulting in the formation of a sticky deposit — particles of soft, non-volatile resin — which appears round the edge of its container or on the brushes after they have been cleaned with white spirit. For this reason, you should ensure that the white spirit you use has not been exposed to air but has been stored in a hermetically sealed jar which is filled to the top. It is not uncommon for painters who use white spirit that is not correctly stored to complain that their paintings do not dry out properly.

We can test the quality of thinning solutions by pouring a little onto a small plate of glass. If this evaporates without leaving a trace of deposit, then it is suitable for use. Similarly, if we wish to compare the drying times of various solvents — turpentine, petroleum spirit, etc. — we drop a little of each onto a piece of paper and see how long it takes to evaporate. Here again, any solutions that leave a deposit after evaporation should be abandoned. If we were putting oil or varnish to the test, then we would expect a permanent transparent stain to appear on the paper; with a diluent, however, such a stain indicates the presence of deposit.

DRYING OILS

A characteristic common to all oils is that they do not evaporate. Many vegetable oils (e.g. olive or groundnut oil) do not harden at all but retain their liquid consistency indefinitely. For artists, the only usable oils are those that solidify on exposure to air and light to form tough adhesive films which bind the pigments firmly to the support. These are called drying oils, and may be used initially when grinding down colours, or later, when mixing colour on the paint palette.

Even though these oils are known as drying oils, their transformation is caused not by evaporation but by oxidisation, a slow but consistent process. The oil absorbs oxygen from the air and solidifies as it does so, becoming measurably heavier in the process and increasing in bulk. Since it can take years, even centuries, for the paint to oxidise entirely, we do not wait until it is absolutely dry before applying protective varnish, but do so when it has thickened considerably but is still relatively pliable, as we shall see later.

Throughout its execution, therefore, a painting must be constantly exposed to air. Even so, the top coat, which is in direct contact with air, dries much more quickly than the undercoats.

The surface layer will begin to form a skin, and the harder this skin gets, the more effectively the air supply to the undercoats of paint is cut off. The undercoats, therefore, do not dry out, but remain soft. They are "trapped" in their still liquid form and, as a result, the paint will begin to spread of its own accord wherever there is a space for it to do so. This is most likely to happen where the artist has used a porous support because the support will then absorb the binder contained in the paint. Deprived in this way of its cohesive and adhesive qualities, the paint will eventually peel off the canvas. Another problem is that, even if the support is not porous, but is insufficiently dry, then on contact with the oil it may dilute and swell, producing tensions in the material and eventually causing the paint to crack.

The following tips, which we shall remind you of now and again, will help you to avoid some of these problems.

1   After applying each coat of paint, leave the painting to dry for long enough to eliminate the risk of the surface layer of oil paint and the diluents destroying the undercoats. The undercoats should not simply be resistant to the touch; you should be able to lightly draw your fingernails over the surface of the painting without damaging it. There is no standard duration — it depends on the number of layers being applied by the artist, and, of course, the choice of medium. As long as the paint seems to be quite cohesive (you will probably need to leave it for an afternoon, or overnight), then you should be able to apply more paint without causing any noticeable flaws.

2   Make sure you observe the "fat on lean" principle. This means that a superimposed layer of paint should contain more oil than the undercoat. This will make the paint more malleable. The paint you buy in tubes is usually oily enough for an undercoat and you will not generally need to add other oils.

3   It is always a good idea to use a slightly porous support. In particular, this helps the paint to adhere to the surface, but, in order to prevent it from absorbing the oil from the paint, it is advisable to apply a thin layer of oil (or medium) well diluted with thinner before you start painting. You can then go ahead without waiting for this to dry.

4 Certain products, called *siccatives,* which are compounds of metallic salts dissolved in drying oils or resins, can be used to accelerate the drying process. Siccative de Courtrai, known in English as *strong drying oil,* is made of purified linseed oil into which oxides of manganese and lead have been introduced. It must be used very sparingly since all metallic dryers are very dangerous. They can darken the paint and weaken the quality of the film. Choose them carefully, use a small amount and only when it is really called for. Siccative is best used on undercoats. You should make sure that the underpaint is lean and that it has dried out thoroughly before you proceed to the next stage. If you wish to speed up the drying process, so that you can move onto the next stage without too much of a delay, then you should add a few drops of siccative to the thinner before you start painting. Even then, there are certain colours that may take a few weeks to dry out.

Flake White (also known as White Lead, Cremnitz White, Silver White), however, dries very quickly and it would be a mistake to add siccative, particularly in view of the fact that siccative tends to darken colours in time, and this would clearly be a problem when using pale colours.

The make-up of colours — or, more precisely, the make-up of the pigments — is not the only thing determining the time factor (i.e. the time taken for one coat to dry out, and the delay needed between coats of paint, and the permanence of the final finish). More than anything else, it depends on the nature of the oils used when making up the paints and also when mixing them on the palette.

Let us examine the the two most widely used oils: linseed oil and poppy oil.

In most cases, it is linseed oil that is the most efficient and effective drying agent. Unfortunately, the benefits of using linseed oil are due to the presence of a component which makes the colours turn yellow as they dry. Take, for example, the white paint on a front door. In time it will gradually discolour, but this will go unnoticed because the door is simultaneously being bleached by the sun. Even if linseed oil in its liquid form is refined to such an extent that it resembles water in colour, it will still discolour and ultimately tarnish the finish of the painting.

For this reason, poppy oil is preferred for additions made to the palette while painting. As for making up the paint, the manufacturer uses linseed oil for the colours which have a tendency to dry slowly. Fortunately, these are generally the darker colours, like black and dark blue, which do not reveal any discolouration that has taken place. But colours like white and light blue, in which discolouring would show, together with quick-drying colours, are generally mixed with poppy oil. In this way, the manufacturer is able to maintain a good balance between the drying power of any paint and its freshness of colour.

Clearly, one reason for adding oil to the paint in the final stages is the necessity of maintaining the "fat on lean" principle. But, as we will see later, it is not imperative that we use "crude" oils, i.e. those which are used in their natural state when extracted from the seed. There are a number of derivatives known as mediums which can be mixed in with the paints on the palette and are just as effective.

Oils and mediums are not volatile like thinners; once dry, they leave a permanent deposit. It is this that gives a painting its brilliance and boldness of colour. The higher the content of the medium, the more dilution causes the particles of pigment to separate out from one another into a refractive medium. As a result of this, the paint tends to appear tinged with colour and translucent in quality. This allows light to filter through to the undercoats of colour which then show through, blending in with the surface layers of paint.

If you are using "crude" oils, such effects can only be achieved by applying very thin coats of colour. You should make sure that you use only a very small quantity of paint, diluted with thinner. By doing this, you will avoid a number of pitfalls, such as the paint running, thus making precision impossible. And there is also the danger that the surface will discolour, bubble, or "fold" in time.

In addition to these problems, there are the more common disadvantages of working with oil, in particular the need for long intervals between applying coats of paint — which, until certain aids were developed, made oils an unpopular medium for many years. The question of drying time is even more of a stumbling block for the artist working in precise and minute detail, or relying heavily on transparency to express light and shade.

Heating copal varnish (photo Lefranc-Bourgeois).

VARNISHES

Varnishes are used as additions to liquid paint to change their brushing and drying character, as intermediate isolating layers to facilitate the painting process, and as coatings on finished paintings to protect them from dirt and impurities in the atmosphere. Varnishes are made by dissolving solid resin in a cold liquid solvent such as turpentine (in this case the resin used is usually one of the soft resins, such as dammar or mastic), or by melting a resin in hot oil (these resins are usually harder resins, such as one of the copals).

The process of glazing is very similar to that of varnishing. One way of glazing a painting is to use an oil which has been baked, or exposed to air and sunlight. Stand linseed oil, which is used by some painters, is an oil which has been thickened by a long process of heating. Glazes like these are generally used to give a more elaborate finish to the most refined of paint mediums.

With such solutions, the drying time is reduced all the more since not only do you apply oil that is particularly dry, but the texture is such that you need to add a volatile thinner to make the paint sufficiently ductile. This evaporates quickly and so the paint fixes more quickly as well.

An alternative method of varnishing involves partially substituting the oil with a fluid product which combines well with paint and also makes the colours permanently transparent in quality when it dries out. This happens with certain resins when they are mixed with a volatile thinner which dries out the solution when it evaporates. You will also find that the resin plays an important role in the preservation of the painting. It is far less susceptible than oil to the oxidisation which causes endless and ultimately harmful changes in the composition of oil.

However, resin is more likely to crumble and crack. If you are using resin, therefore, you will need to add an appropriate amount of oil to it to reinforce the resin and make it malleable.

In picture varnishes and retouching varnishes, the resin generally acts as a fixing agent i.e. it is a non-volatile substance. In picture varnishes, the ratio of resin to thinner is high, and therefore the varnish is relatively thick. They contain very little oil, and for this reason if you mix them into the paints with undue care, all kinds of problems will arise.

Retouching varnishes contain a lower proportion of resin. Thus, in most cases, the oil contained in the tubes of paint is quite adequate. So long as the varnishes are added little by little, or even diluted with thinner before being added to the paint, they can be of considerable use to the artist.

However, although these varnishes accelerate the fixing process and increase the brilliance of the colours, their fluidity limits their use. One particular disadvantage is, for example, that a desire for transparency – achieved by applying very thin layers of paint – leads automatically to loss of colour.

For this reason, it has been necessary to find an alternative product, containing a higher proportion of fixative, that can be combined with paint, without affecting the quality of the colours. This can be done by simply adding oil to the resin in appropriate quantities while it is being made up. This method has been practised for centuries and numerous solutions have been produced. These vary in terms of the type of oil and resin used, or in terms of the way in which the artist uses them. Copal varnishes, from which the Flemish or Harlem siccatives are derived, were popular during the last century. However, they are highly coloured, and tend to make the painting go yellow in time. These days, when the artist is always on the lookout for different nuances of colour, there are many painting fluids or mediums on the market which are colourless. The artist usually makes his choice according to the speed with which the fixing agents they contain take effect. Remember not to confuse the fixing process with the drying process. The former is due to the evaporation of the thinner and is characterised by paints that, once fixed, are completely resistant to brushstrokes. The latter is due to the chemical transformation of the oil contained in the paint. That is why, if the artist wanted to accelerate the drying process in order to reduce the interval between applications of paint, it would be advisable to add a few drops of Courtrai siccative to a dipperful of the colourless medium.

There are many ways of using these varnishes. If you dilute the varnish to double its quantity right from the start, you will be able to use it directly from the dipper. Using the varnish in this diluted form does not pose any of the usual problems associated with fluidity, since effectively only very little varnish is added to the paint – just enough to produce a sufficiently oily texture and to add a subtle gloss to the colours. However, by adding the medium in advance, you cannot take advantage of the fact that you have at your disposal a product of high density.

For this reason, it is far better to fill one dipper with thinner and another with undiluted oil medium. In this way, you can modify the effect as you go along by adding solution to the paint in varying proportions from one or both of the dippers. This is a simple routine to grasp and the one great advantage of working in this way, rather than using a solution prepared in advance, is that it is so much easier to practise the "fat over lean" principle, which is the prerequisite of successful oil painting.

On the shop floor: manufacturing canvas.

Mounting and gluing the canvas to the stretcher.

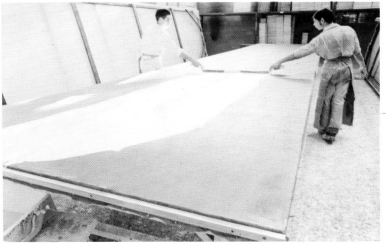

Applying white size.

Smoothing out the canvas and applying the finishing touches.

Photo Lefranc-Bourgeois.

WHY SO MANY DIFFERENT METHODS OF DILUTING COLOUR?

Used by itself, thinner liquifies the paints and, in so doing, it makes them easier to handle. It is indispensable for applying the initial coats of paint, whether this be with a series of adjacent brushstrokes or with thin spreads of colour. When the thinner evaporates, the paints become quite hard, but not to such an extent that they are resistant to brushstrokes. Thinner, then, is ideal for use at the beginning of a painting because it keeps the paint "lean". It makes for a relatively matt, opaque finish.

If we were to proceed along these lines for the entire painting, — something that was frequently practised at the beginning of the century — we would end up with a finish reminiscent of a gouache painting, i.e. displaying an overall clarity with areas of opaque, slightly dull, colour tones. Paintings executed in this way do not age well since the colours tend to fade.

This is where varnish comes in. It is a great asset because it allows you to take the whole process further. But unfortunately no process — not even one involving the use of resin-based solutions — can solve the one problem that has always restricted the use of oils: the task of overlaying one fresh layer of paint with another.

When working with oils, each dab of colour which is applied to the canvas remains fluid for quite some time and can therefore be easily mixed with the paint adjacent to it. This is one of the properties of oil that makes it so suitable for blending. But this becomes a problem the moment you wish to overlay one colour with another (without waiting for the first layer to dry) and still retain the purity of each colour. This can only be done by either dabbing the paint thickly onto the canvas with heavy brushstrokes, or by waiting the requisite number of drying hours between applications of paint. It is easy to see why oil painting is generally regarded as a slow and laborious process.

Interestingly enough, we have written proof that certain paintings dating back to the 16th and 17th centuries, and which have survived the test of time remarkably well, were completed surprisingly quickly. The artists used the technique of glazing, which consists of superimposing transparent layers of paint to achieve depth of colour. The quality of painting achieved with this technique inspired Renoir, Cézanne and, later, Dufy to paint like Rubens and the Venetians. The disappearance from the art world of this technique in the 18th century was referred to as "the lost key".

Saint Luke, by Maerten Van Heemskerck (1498-1574). (Musée des Beaux-Arts de Rennes).

Detail (the transparent jelly you can see in the middle of the picture is medium).

MEDIUMS

Some years ago, after studying manuscripts and carrying out experiments, the techniques used in old paintings were resurrected and the materials reconstituted. The solutions known as mediums were not liquid in form, but were transparent jellies of roughly the same consistency as the oil colours we buy in tubes. Names like Venetian and Flemish medium, etc., are a reminder of their origins and the effects that can be achieved with them.

It is certainly not the case, though, that these mediums are only suited to the techniques used by the old masters. Because they make oils easier to work with and enable the artist to vary the effects achieved with oils, they lend themselves to contemporary styles and techniques and, as Dufy discovered, they are often well suited to the most innovative and most daring of artistic modes. They are also a useful aid for the amateur, student or beginner, enabling them, through experimentation, to make the most surprising discoveries and develop the most unexpected effects.

Without wishing to dwell any longer on the composition of these mediums, we will add just one or two more points in

their favour. They give oil paint a durable quality which enables the artist to use a fairly heavy hand when applying paint, even for large scale transparencies. When mixed with oil colours, these mediums produce a texture that is devoid of the glutinous character which a thick varnish would generate: the oil paint becomes smoother and much easier to apply. And they can, of course, be diluted with thinner if the artist so wishes.

A few minutes after the medium has been applied, it will gel, and you will then be able to paint lightly over the original layer without the two layers of colours mixing.

Medium, then, enables us to work with wet paint, whether we wish to blend the colours into one another or prevent them from blending.

There is no need to add siccative, since the mediums tend to accelerate the drying process, and it is quite possible to start work on the painting again the following day. Medium also reduces the risk of flaws appearing on the surface of the painting, and they improve the longevity of the painting better than oil alone could.

PAINTING A PICTURE: THE FIRST STAGES

Firstly, you should transfer a few colours onto your palette. Then, pour a small quantity of medium into a cup and place it somewhere on your palette so that it is easily accessible. The dipper should contain either petroleum spirit or turpentine.

Dip the tip of your brush in the medium and mix it into an oil colour on the palette, in exactly the same way as you would if you were mixing one colour into another in order to alter the tone. This can be done as you go along. To make the paint more fluid, dip the brush — more freely this time — into the thinner, and add that to the paint.

Start with a little medium (just enough to accelerate the drying process) and then add a considerable amount of thinner. Apply the paint with fine brushstrokes and thin spreads of colour. You can gradually reduce or even eliminate the thinner altogether, but you should always add medium because it is this that regulates the quality of the paint: the more you add, the more opaque the paint will be; the less you add, the more transparent it will be.

What are the advantages of using transparent paints?

1　If an oil colour is transparent, it will appear to be further away than it actually is. Any dash of colour that looks as though it is closer than you had intended it to be can be distanced from the eye by the addition of medium.

2　If two colours are painted in juxtaposition, the more opaque will always appear to be closer to the eye. Shade is partial or relative darkness: in effect, depth of colour. It absorbs light and is therefore translucent. Conversely, opaque surfaces deflect light and therefore define extremely light areas.

3　If you overlay an opaque colour with a translucent colour, and if they are similar in tone, (for example, madder and red vermilion), this will result in bolder and purer — that is, less white — colour.

If, however, the colour tones are dissimilar (yellow on blue or red on white, for example), then the effect will obviously differ considerably from the effect obtained if the two colours were to be mixed.

4　If, on completion of your painting, you glaze it lightly with a pale and highly translucent colour, you will find that this will give it more depth and unity. It will also reproduce the distinctive quality peculiar to certain kinds of natural or artificial light. For example, a perfect shade of Indian yellow will promote the same warm atmosphere as that generated by rays of sunlight.

5　Conversely, if you dilute a light colour (light colours are always more opaque), it will, when applied in thin layers, appear translucent. It will lighten a dark colour, making it seem bluer in tone. This is how the mist in valleys is often represented in paintings. It is, in fact, an excellent way of painting both distant landscapes and, for example, the texture of skin in a portrait.

SETTING TO WORK

How should you choose your medium? This depends very much on the technique you decide to adopt for your painting. In general, the Flemish medium is ideal for use on a painting which comprises only a thin layer (or layers) of quite fluid paint with much reflected light. This particular medium fully enhances the transparency of paint. Venetian medium is more suited to working with thick paint since it lends itself to more immediate use.

It is important, as always in painting, to make sure that the supports you use are of good quality. All sorts of materials can be used for the support: canvas, wood, various types of paper and board. This is, of course, a question of personal preference, but it is important to know something about the surface which you have chosen to work on: viz. what the support (which is in most cases white) is made of, how it is prepared, etc. It is the quality of the support that is in part responsible for the ease and success with which an artist carries out his work. A careful choice of support will minimise deterioration such as paint cracking, sinking, peeling, or colours fading.

Remembering the "fat over lean" principle, we will avoid starting off on an oily ground. Oily paint can always be recognised by its sheen. However, if you do have to work on such a support, you must make absolutely sure that the surface is bone dry. Remember that such a surface will be resistant to thinner and that the commonly accepted method of removing excess oil from an undercoat (i.e. by "rubbing" the canvas with thinner) is almost ineffectual. The best thing to do in this case is to reduce its sheen by "scouring" it with a slightly abrasive cloth and a little water. Then rinse it carefully with a clean, damp sponge and leave it to dry.

Alternatively, you may choose to use one of a number of matt solutions. These can be bought or you can make them up yourself. The casein-based solutions, which are quite cheap, should only be used for rough work, but there are oil-based solutions on the market which are suitable for priming. Acrylic-based solutions are also quite reliable and are widely-used these days. It is easy enough when using these acrylic-based solutions to correct errors but it must be done at the time of application. Because of the highly porous nature of these solutions, it is difficult to spread even the most fluid of paints over them. Rather like ink on blotting paper, the paint dries almost as soon as it has been applied. A poorly corrected error is not only difficult to hide, but may also jeopardize the longevity of the painting. Exactly the same happens with plaster.

This is a simple and practical precaution reminiscent of the advice generally given to the artist working without medium, i.e. to moisten the support with a mixture of oil and thinner.

If you wish to sketch out your drawing first, do so with a soft pencil, regardless of the material you have chosen for your support. If not, you can carry on with the next stage: applying the ground. Bearing in mind that you will be using the same medium throughout, spread a mixture of your chosen medium and thinner over the support. There is not a fixed amount of thinner that should be used; it will depend on how absorbent the support is. However, enough thinner should be added so that the solution can be freely applied with a brush or soft cloth. In other words, it should be "pouring" consistency so that it spreads smoothly onto the surface and seeps into the support or underpriming, thus making it less porous. Don't wait for it to dry, but carry on in exactly the same way with another layer. By applying this fresh solution, you will find that the subsequent layers of paint will spread easily and will blend well. The solution is too weak to make the paints oily, but it contains enough "fat" to ensure that they adhere well.

RESTORING DULL SPOTS

Under this title we will to some extent be echoing what we discussed in the previous section.

After a certain length of time — and this will be different for each painting — certain areas of colour may become dull and matt. For both the finished and unfinished painting, this loss of brilliance can present quite a serious problem for the artist since the harmony and often the overall balance of the painting is in jeopardy. As we have already seen, this could be due to absorption: the undercoats have soaked up some of the binder contained in the colour, or perhaps the paint used in the dull areas contained less binding oil.

"Mercury and Argus", by Rubens. Painting on wood (30 x 40). Musées Royaux des Beaux-Arts, Belgium.

"Inn interior", by David Teniers.

David Teniers.
"Inn interior" (detail).
Notice the interplay of opaque and gloss highlights.

Retouch varnish, a quick drying varnish, is used to restore the original richness of the colour. If this retouch varnish also dries dull, additional coats of varnish should be applied until the matt surface disappears and the colour regains its original quality. But it should not be used to excess, as a heavy coating of varnish is not a good ground to paint on; it may create a glassy surface on which subsequent layers of paint will not hold well and may crack. Retouch varnish should not dry upon the surface as a continuous film but, rather, it should be absorbed into the dry paint just sufficiently to bring back its colour.

If one were to paint over these dead spots without applying retouch varnish, the dull area would absorb binding medium from the new paint, causing the overpainting in turn to sink in and become dull. Retouch varnish can be applied with a clean brush, or a spray can be used.

OTHER MEDIUMS, OTHER TECHNIQUES

There are so many mediums that are of value to the artist that it would be impossible to discuss them all fully here. However, we shall briefly touch on a few of the mediums designed as aids for particular techniques. Generally speaking, these are used by the artist who, having once familiarised himself with the products in common use and, having once acquired a sound knowledge and experience of the more widely used techniques, decides to move into specialist fields. This really is the best way to progress, but there is no harm at this stage in learning a little bit about these specialist products.

The most remarkable solution on the market is one that enables the artist to mix water with oil paint. This would seem an impossible task given that we are dealing with two totally incompatible solutions. It may be easier to understand if we compare this with a solution that is closer to home: mayonnaise. Mayonnaise is an oil-based dressing, but it combines perfectly well with vinegar or water. The essential ingredient here is egg, which binds the two together. A variety of binders are available, casein or "milk glue" to name just one of them.

This will explain why a number of mediums, temperas for example, which are often based on recipes that are centuries old, contain both aqueous and oleaginous constituents.

The unctuosity and plasticity of these paste mediums when mixed with powdered colour is similar to that of fresh butter or cream, both of which contain a natural ingredient of water.

The advantage of using this is that it facilitates finely-worked modelling where the overall design can be maintained with skilful brushwork. It also makes wet-in-wet painting possible.

If you look through the work of Xavier de Langlais, a well-respected authority in the art world, you will find a considerable amount of documentation on the use of egg as a medium. Egg does make for fine brushwork, but must be applied in very thin coats. To reduce time spent on producing an elaborate painting, you may find a thickening medium useful. This can be mixed with diluent if required.

There is another way of mixing water with oil paints. The precedent for this was set by famous painters like Tintoretto and Veronese. The technique used by these artists is noted for the speed with which the painting can be completed, the special effects achieved, and the resultant longevity of the painting.

It involves applying a final coat of transparent oil paint to an undercoat of a light and opaque water-based solution.

Although gouache automatically comes to mind, it is inadvisable to use gouache since this is highly sensitive to humidity, which will in time be generated by the porous support. It is best to use paints which are water-based, but which also become insoluble as they dry. This is characteristic of emulsion paints. Those made with vinyl resins — a relatively new product — have improved the potential of this technique.

Many artists today use Flashe colours for the ground of their painting. Opaque and matt in finish, these prepare the ground well for the final coat of oil paint. Furthermore, the ease and speed with which these paints can be layered is naturally of great value to the artist researching his painting, implementing his design and modifying colour tones. The undercoats of paint are clear, light, and sharply defined, and it may even be possible to superimpose another layer of oil paint the same day. By using medium and ensuring that the coats of paint are not too thick, you will be able to profit from the soft, subtle modelling and the interplay of layered colour to which oil paints lend themselves. (Turn to the chart on page I-58 for a guide to layering colour.)

Tintoretto. Scuola San Rocco, Venice (1565).

Like all techniques that involve mixing two different products, this is only really suitable for work done in the studio. You should also remember that certain types of support are not ideal for painting involving the use of water. In particular, make sure you choose a support with an oily surface. It is best to size this with an emulsion that is compatible with the paint you use for the subsequent coats.

Flashe canvas would be ideal or, alternatively, any type of board which has been suitably primed. You could, in fact, prepare it yourself with an acrylic size. You should not encounter any problems; as long as you are familiar with the various mediums at your disposal and you know how to combine them, you will be able to exploit the potential of these mediums to the full.

VARNISHING

Protective varnish, or final picture varnish, is always a spirit varnish. Cooked-oil varnishes are unsuitable because, when they darken, it is very difficult to remove them from the picture, whereas a varnish made from a soft resin can be removed easily with a mild solvent and replaced with a fresh coat.

Some writers and manufacturers recommend that a picture is allowed to carry on its drying processes for at least a year before a protective varnish is applied, to avoid the risk of cracking. But since in modern cities there is also danger from dirt and grime, others recommend six months. There is, of course, no hard and fast rule, and the length of the drying-out period will depend on both the paint used and the thickness of the coats applied.

It is possible, for example, to have a painting ready for exhibition without waiting as long as six months. Although you may abandon some of the finishing touches, it is imperative that you correct any deterioration in the final coat of paint, e.g. loss of colour, so as to maintain the balance of the painting and to give it a slight gloss. For this, you will only need to apply a very small amount of resin. Retouch varnish is therefore indispensable. You should apply it with a brush or spray it in thin layers so that it does not prevent the paint from drying underneath it.

Once a suitable period of time has elapsed, you can then apply a layer of picture varnish. The object of this is not to add another coat of gloss, which, incidentally, will not enhance the depth of colour, but rather to give the painting a protective film. On this occasion, you should apply a relatively thick and even coat of varnish which will protect the painting from dirty marks and scratches without altering its visual effect. In time, however, the varnish will pick up scratches and spots of dirt, and it is advisable to replace the original coat of varnish with a fresh coat at some stage. It is for this reason that picture varnishes are made up of soft resins which, even when thoroughly dry, can be dissolved with petroleum spirit and subsequently removed with cotton wool. It is possible to strip the painting of its picture varnish without damaging the surface layer of paint since the oil in the paint, once hardened, is resistant to thinner.

One of the great advantages of the soft varnishes (i.e. those which contain turpentine as the solvent) which are readily available in the shops today is that they can be easily removed. It is important that you are able at a later stage to either replace the picture varnish or, alternatively, revive a deteriorating varnish by rubbing it with a cloth soaked in turpentine. Although you do not have to be a specialist in this area, you should train yourself to recognise a painting in need of restoring.

A painting may become soiled during the drying out period. For this reason, it should be cleaned before the varnish is applied. Use a soft brush or cloth (making sure that it is not "fluffy"). Firstly, cleanse the painting with soap and water and then rinse off all the soap with clean water, making sure that the underside of the painting remains dry. Sponge the painting thoroughly and leave it to dry out; humidity is extremely harmful to soft varnishes. The best tool for this purpose is a flat brush. Since the key to a good finish lies in applying the varnish evenly, you should concentrate on working it well into the painting so as to prevent the varnish from clotting or running.

It is also important to ensure that the varnish is fluid enough to be applied without leaving brushstrokes.

In order to spread the varnish evenly, apply it with a criss-cross motion, so that every brushstroke is at right angles to the previous one. You might, for example, work the varnish alternately from the top to the bottom of the painting and then from the right to the left. Do not overwork the varnish. As soon as the varnish shows signs of streaking you should stop, otherwise it will impair the finish.

To achieve all of this, you must work with a fluid varnish that spreads well and allows the brush to travel across the painting with ease. It is sometimes advisable, therefore, to add a little diluent to the varnish beforehand. The varnish will then spread thinly and will not leave a high-gloss skin.

Oil paintings should ideally have a glossy finish. But if you want to use a soft varnish, make sure that the oil paint is not at all absorbent, i.e. that it does not contain emulsion or matt particles. Any emulsion content in the oil paint will absorb the binder in the soft varnish and will then appear as a white film over the paint. In order to avoid this problem, you will need either to use a very glossy oil paint, or to apply a coat of a transparent waterproof solution to act as sizing between the coat of oil paint and the coat of varnish. An isolating varnish which will not combine with the solvent in the soft varnish is ideal for this purpose.

The main advantage of applying a double coat of varnish is the ease with which the painting can be restored at a later date. If you want a matt finish, which is necessary if you produce a very large painting, it is easier to use matt paints from the start. Attempting to force oil paints into an effect which is contrary to their nature would destroy all the rich and distinctive features of one of our most beautiful modes of artistic expression.

Oil painting

This chart sets out the sizes of canvasses or supports under the headings Figure (F), Landscape (P), or Marine (M). The size of a painting which measures 81 x 60 would be referred to as 25P. The sizes of some of the works reproduced in the following pages are given in this way.
(N.B. This is a French system of measurement, and does not apply in England.)

Nos.	FIGURE (F)			LANDSCAPE (P)			MARINE (M)		
0	18	x	14	18	x	12	18	x	10
1	22	x	16	22	x	14	22	x	12
2	24	x	19	24	x	16	24	x	14
3	27	x	22	27	x	19	27	x	16
4	33	x	24	33	x	22	33	x	19
5	35	x	27	35	x	24	35	x	22
6	41	x	33	41	x	27	41	x	24
8	46	x	38	46	x	33	46	x	27
10	55	x	46	55	x	38	55	x	33
12	61	x	50	61	x	46	61	x	38
15	65	x	54	65	x	50	65	x	46
20	73	x	60	73	x	54	73	x	50
25	81	x	65	81	x	60	81	x	54
30	92	x	73	92	x	65	92	x	60
40	100	x	81	100	x	73	100	x	65
50	116	x	89	116	x	81	116	x	73
60	130	x	97	130	x	89	130	x	81
80	146	x	114	146	x	97	146	x	89
100	162	x	130	162	x	114	162	x	97
120	195	x	130	195	x	114	195	x	97

MATERIALS

1 Easel.

2 Palette. Rather than holding the palette, you will find it easier to place it on a stool or a 2-tiered trolley where all the working materials can be kept.

Palette maintenance. First scrape the palette with the flat side of a palette knife. This will remove most of the traces left by the paintbrushes. Wipe the palette with a rag soaked in turpentine. Scrape the palette again and finally wipe clean with a dry cloth.

3 A set of flat and round hog brushes ranging from sizes 4 − 12. Select good-quality paintbrushes and include a couple of springy and pointed sable or badger-hair brushes. Springy, long-haired ox-ear brushes are particularly suitable for drawing lines. These must only be used with a paint strongly diluted in turpentine.

Brush maintenance. Place the brushes in a glass in a dust-free environment, with the bristles pointing upwards. Brushes used for painting in oils must be meticulously cleaned whenever they are used. Get rid of excess paint by squeezing the bristles into a rag or a bit of paper, and then dip into turpentine. Rub the moist tips on a bar of house-hold soap and then scrub them into the palm of your hand under running water. Repeat this progress several times and then rinse the brushes thoroughly in water. A detergent may also be used, but make sure the brushes are rinsed well.

4 Palette knife for scraping and cleaning palette. Painting knife.

5 Pots for diluents, mediums, siccatives, and varnishes for diluting the paint. A siccative speeds up the drying process.

6 A series of paint tubes: flake white or zinc white (large tube No. 40), and the following colours in No. 14: cobalt blue − deep ultramarine blue − cerulean blue − vermilion − pale cadmium red − yellow ochre − cadmium yellow − pale cadmium yellow − pale cobalt green − viridian − pale cobalt violet − burnt sienna − peach black or ivory black − raw umber − burnt umber − madder lake.

Paint maintenance. Before cleaning the palette, if there is any leftover paint which is almost clean, do not throw it away. You will be able to use it again if you submerge it in a dish of water. The paint will then remain fresh. The tube caps can get clogged, so wipe them before screwing them back on. If you have difficulty in unscrewing them, heat them gently first.

Vehicles. A bottle each of linseed oil, turpentine, siccative, retouching varnish, and a couple of other varnishes including picture varnish, and a wide, flat varnish brush.

7 Canvasses and painting surfaces (wood, cardboard, paper, etc.)
There are several kinds of canvasses ranging from very smooth to very coarse (jute). These canvasses can be bought ready prepared, but you can also prepare them yourself. There are two kinds of frames: glued or jointed, the latter using either keys or tenon joints placed in the corners, thereby allowing the canvas to be gently stretched. These are notably more expensive.

Fish-glue in crystal form. This is used as a base for each preparation.

Mix the glue with warm water (approx. 2/10 to 1/10). Melt the mixture in a double-boiler or over a gentle flame.

Spread the glue onto the canvas — it will act as an undercoat.

FIRST STEP: SIZING THE CANVAS

by **Yvette Cauquil-Prince**

The following preparations must all be carried out on stretched canvas, on the ground.

Melt some fish glue in a double-boiler. The correct consistency is reached when it sticks when held between the thumb and forefinger. Spread the glue onto the dry canvas with the varnish knife.

How to prepare a ground suitable for rapid glazing.

— Take some slightly liquid fish glue.

— Add plaster of Paris. (A large glass of plaster of Paris per litre of glue). Mix the two.

— Put the stretched and sized canvas on the floor. Pour some of the mixture onto the canvas and spread from the middle outwards, using a large house-painter's knife. Repeat until the canvas is completely covered. The canvas will appear to slacken but will stretch when drying.

— Leave the canvas to dry for 24 hours.

— Prepare a mixture of equal amounts of linseed oil and turpentine, and thin it down with some zinc white until a light creamy consistency is reached.

— Spread this mixture generously over the canvas with a varnish brush.

— When this coat is almost dry (neither too sticky, nor completely dry), work over it with the palm of your hand. This will immediately give a glazed effect.

— Let the canvas dry for several days.

— Add to this 'traditionally-prepared' canvas some purified linseed oil or a mixture of linseed oil and turpentine. (2 decilitres of turpentine to one litre of linseed oil.)

This preparation is recommended if a glaze is desired. Reduce the amount of turpentine at each successive glaze, and for the final coat add 1/3 picture varnish to 2/3 oil.

How to obtain an absorbent ground.

— Spread a layer of fillion white onto the canvas. Thin it down with water as shown on the instructions.

When this coat is dry, dilute 1 dl of linseed oil in 1 litre of turpentine and add some zinc white until the consistency of milk is reached.

— Spread this mixture onto the canvas, allow to dry, and repeat the process.

— Spread on a mixture of 1 litre of turpentine per 1 dl of linseed oil. (i.e. the same as previous mixture but in inverted proportions.)

— Painting medium may be used as a final coat.

This preparation will ensure a matt effect rather than a glazed one.

How to obtain a coarse-grained ground.

— Spread sawdust onto the sized canvas. (Make sure the glue is still warm when sizing.) Avoid sand or ashes, and use a sawdust that is chemically unreactive.

— When the canvas starts to dry, hold it up vertically and tap the back to get rid of any excess sawdust.

— Prepare the fillion white as in the previous preparation.

A tough and coarse-grained ground will be obtained. When touching up with a knife, the paint adheres well, and has an attractive texture.

Now for a simple preparation which is 'neutral' as it does not really result in any of the glazed, matt, or coarse-grained textures of the previous preparations.

— Spread a layer of zinc white, and equal amounts of linseed oil and turpentine onto the sized canvas.

Never add siccative to the above preparations in the hope of speeding up the drying process. Give the prepared canvasses enough time to dry. (Always prepare several at a time so that you are never without.)

Only thorough groundwork ensures long life for a canvas.

Absolutely unbreakable rule for painting in oils.
"Start lean and finish fat."

In the preparations, as well as during the actual work, start with thin coats which get progressively thicker. The opposite will result in *craquelures* (fine cracks), causing the rapid deterioration of the canvas. (Example: in the preparation for rapid glazing, the glue and the plaster are thin in consistency, while the mixture of oil, turpentine and zinc white are of a thicker consistency: fat on lean.)

When working, it is advisable to start with a mixture of linseed oil and turpentine which will act as a semi-fat diluent. As the work proceeds, gradually decrease the amount of turpentine until you are left with pure oil. In the final coat, add 2/3 of oil to 1/3 picture varnish, and this will act as a fat diluent.

Plaster is added to melted glue.

Plaster and glue are spread over the canvas with a knife.

1 or 2 spoonfuls of oil per litre of turpentine and zinc white.

Zinc white is thoroughly mixed with turpentine.

The mixture must be spread in all directions from the centre outwards.

Zinc white, oil and turpentine are added to the coat of glue and plaster, and worked over with the palm of hand, depending on the desired effect.

Plaster and glue are smoothed over.

Zinc white is removed from the knife.

Diluted zinc white is spread on with large varnish brush.

FIXING THE CANVAS TO A WOODEN FRAME

a) Cut out a piece of linen canvas, making sure that the sides are at least 4 cm longer than those of the frame.

b) Place the canvas on the floor or table, and put the chamfered side of the frame in the middle.

c) Fold one of the protruding edges of the canvas over one side of the frame, and tack a couple of carpet nails into the widest part.

d) Repeat the process for the remaining sides.

e) Pull the canvas tight over the frame (but do not let it crease), using special stretching pliers. Take the nails out of the place where the pliers are being used, re-insert them and hammer them in. Start this process in the middle of each of the frame's sides.

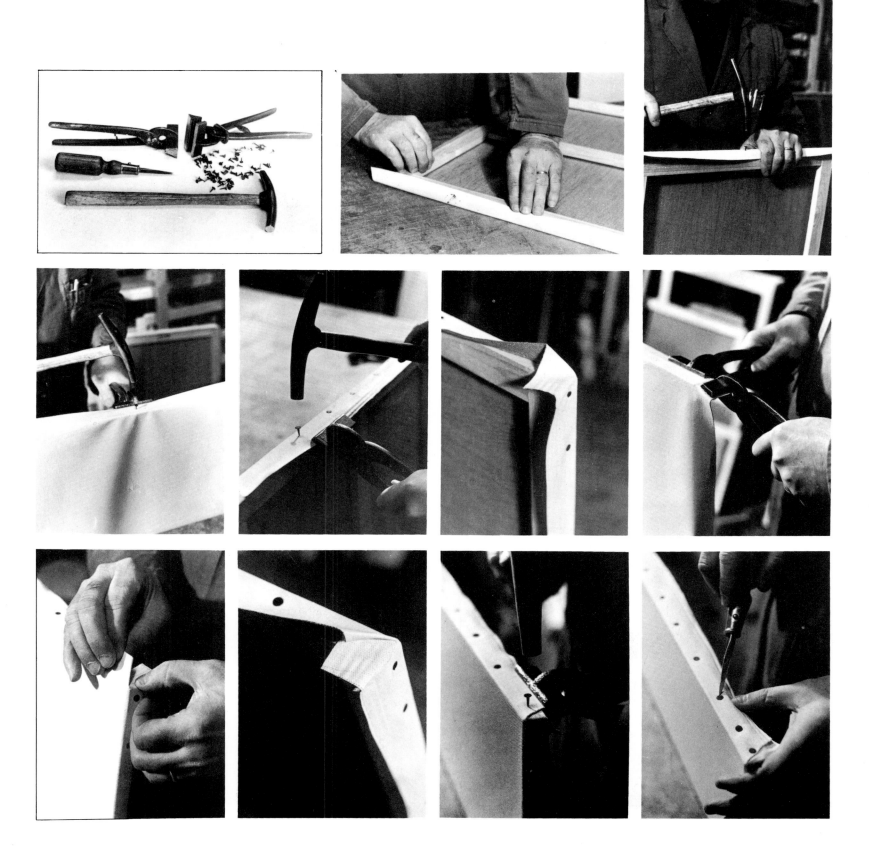

SOME PROFESSIONAL TERMS

Support: the canvas, cardboard or paper on which one works. Generally, brushes with hog or horse-hair bristles are used, but sable or badger are also popular.

Pochade: a generally small painting done at one sitting. A *study* is a more elaborate work in which the subject is studied in closer detail. A study can consist of only one section or detail of the composition.

Sketch: work in which a rough draft of the whole is made. This can also be known as the *cover* as it covers the whole support.

Painting: the final result ensuing from the artist's personal selection and depiction of the subject matter from his pochades and studies. In other words, the finished work.

Chiaroscuro: the balance of light and shadow in a painting. (It corresponds to the harmony, the distribution of light and shadow, and by extension, to the effect created by the contrast between the two.)

Craquelures: these are caused by the movement of the ground and dried paint.

Brushwork: can have two meanings —

a) how the artist uses his brush in a particular way to express the subject.

b) the final use of the brush to outline and accentuate the subject.

Dull spots: the dullness which can occur here and there when the canvas is drying. The dull spots can frequently occur when the ground is absorbent, and to a certain extent soaks up the oil from the paint. The tones become matt, and the values (tonal gradations) lose much of their brightness. This can be a setback when tackling the canvas again. The dull spots only affect certain areas of the painting, and this upsets the balance of values. You can remedy this by coating the canvas with retouching varnish, using a springy brush. This will restore the painting to its original lustre. (Make sure the entire canvas is dry before starting work.)

Blending: the process whereby the colours gradually merge together when the paint is fresh.

Glaze: a layer of almost transparent colour painted over an opaque colour so that the colour of the latter is modified.

The glaze is obtained by thinning paint with oil or glazing medium.

Scumbling: a scumble is related to a glaze in that it is a thin film of colour laid over another paint surface so that it modifies the original colour but does not completely conceal it. Unlike a glaze, the scumble is usually a lighter colour placed over a darker one. It does not necessarily completely cover the underlaying colour. This effect is often used for skies.

Outline: similar to a drawing, but also implies a certain handling. One says "a steady/tight/heavy outline". It also refers to the tackling of certain details or elements of the painting.

Mass: unbroken expanse of light and colour without secondary details.

Body or *paint:* a coloured paste formed by the pigment added to its diluent. The paint may be applied in one go or in several layers.

Fatten: painting by fattening the paint and using it thickly. Conversely, thin paint is well diluted and sparingly applied.

Patina: the particular appearance a painting assumes in time. Patina is a result of:

1) a certain change in tone when exposed to the sun,
2) the yellowing of the coating varnishes,
3) the transformation of oil into a hard and more transparent resin.

Balance (of colours and values): the pleasing or unsatisfactory visual effect provoked by the juxtaposition of various tones on the canvas.

Sacrifices: the omission of secondary details in order to be able to focus on a chosen point. It implies the selection of the most essential or expressive elements and thereby provides the artist with the opportunity of making a work personal to him.

Touch: the way in which the brush is handled, applying greater or lesser thicknesses of paint. Touch can also refer to the actual deposit of paint on the canvas.

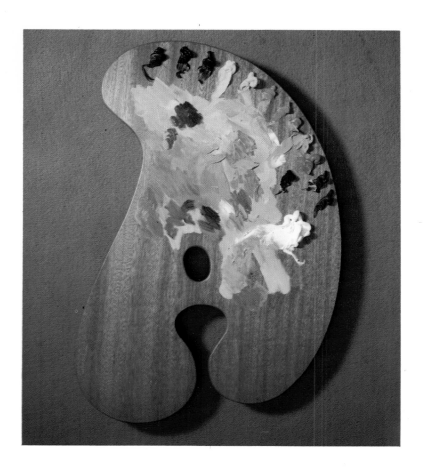

PURE AND ALMOST PURE PAINTS

Pure paints are made up of a compound of pure pigment and its vehicle. Cobalt blue, for instance, is a compound of pure cobalt blue and its medium of water, gouache or oil. Pure paints offer all sorts of possibilities if the artist is aware of their properties.

Almost pure paints are also carefully made up, but the pure colour can often be replaced by a cheaper one: carmine, vermilion, imitation cobalt yellow, for instance. These colours are perfect for studies as they are cheaper than the pure colours.

THE COLOURS

Always set out your palette in the following way: peach black (and siccative), raw umber, burnt umber, yellow ochre, red ochre, ultramarine blue, Prussian blue, sap green, lemon yellow, golden yellow (deep chrome yellow), vermilion, cadmium red, purple red, flake white. Set your paints out from left to right following the colour spectrum. A second, inner row consists of the earth colours and the 'couleurs rabattues' (prepared mixed colours), with black and white in the middle. At the end of the day, put the colours on a glass strip and soak in water. Set the paints out on the very edge of your palette, so as to leave room in the middle for experimenting with different colour mixtures.

Origins and compounds of paints:

Artists' colours (pigments) can be classified according to their origin.
Animal: carmine, sepia and ivory black.
Plant: sap green, madder, vine black and peach black.
Mineral: yellow ochre, sienna, umber. (When heated on a stove, some of these pigments can produce red ochre, burnt sienna, and burnt umber.)

Apart from these colours directly derived from natural sources, there are a great many colours produced by chemical processes:
Blues: ultramarine, cobalt, cerulean.
Reds: vermilion, cadmium.
Yellows: chrome, cadmium.
Greens: viridian, cobalt.
Whites.

Mixing paints can bring about undesirable changes. Avoid this by following some basic rules.

Flake white tends to darken when added to sulphate paints such as vermilion, ultramarine, and cadmium yellow. Do not let this worry you too much, as it has an excellent covering power and dries faster than zinc white and titanium white.

Cadmium red and cadmium yellow are less permanent in their lighter shades (pale cadmium yellow).

Vermilion tends to darken in time, so choose the best quality.

Dark madder lake is an impermanent colour and should only be used in small quantities when being mixed with other colours.

On the other hand, ochres, earth colours, cobalt, ultramarine, cerulean blue, and blacks, are easy to handle when mixing as they are permanent and stable.

However, do not use the following in thick 'impasto' as they tend to crack like varnish: ultramarine blue, burnt sienna, viridian, green madder, and combinations of these colours.

Emerald green, which is invaluable when painting in watercolours, and is considered by some as indispensable to painting as a whole, is not very permanent in its pure form, and undergoes a change when added to almost every other colour.

"The mistral rages over the mountain." Oil painting by J. Chambrin (40 M).

ABSOLUTELY UNBREAKABLE RULES WHEN PAINTING

1   "Start lean and finish fat." The first layers of paint should be less fat than the final layers.

2   Avoid painting a quick-drying colour onto a slow-drying colour. Light colours (containing white) take less time to dry than dark colours.

Oil paints have a good covering power, which is primarily due to the addition of white to the colours used. As a result, the canvas does not show through.

3   Charcoal drawing must be fixed with a spray or re-touched with a paintbrush lightly dipped in paint.
A flat brush should be used to spread the dark tonal values on this preliminary drawing.

4   A thin layer of paint is applied to the support. This can be called the "cover". This rough draft acts as a kind of mattress for the next applications. Restrict yourself to depicting the local colour of the subject as seen in varying lights. Atmospheric values may be painted darker than they are actually perceived. Further treatment of tonal grada-tions and details will come later.

The sketch can be seen as the fundamental representation of the subject in its form and colour. You should enrich it with further layers of paint. Spread the paint generously over the light areas; you will have to add oil to the colours in order to accentuate their brightness. The darker areas require less oil.

Start with the deeper tones and end with the lighter ones. Do not forget to paint "fat on lean" as dark tones require less thickness of paint than light tones. It is therefore logical to end with the latter.

THE KNIFE

Using a painting knife has the advantage of allowing one to apply the paint in a rich and thick coat — and all in one go. The knife looks like a trowel, but the blade is finer and more pliable. Use the back of the knife to remove the paint from the palette. If you want a smooth mixture of several colours, place them in one spot on the palette, and blend them in by turning the back of the knife in a circular motion. Using the blade to transfer the paste to the support, fill in the forms by dragging the blade along, starting at the edge. You will need to repeat this process many times. The original outlines may be somewhat blurred, so re-define them with a brush.

Make sure your knife is perfectly clean when using a new colour.

The most difficult part — and a sign of mastering this technique — is to avoid ending up with "choked" colours. This always happens when superimposing many layers of paint during the experimenting stage. You can eliminate this problem by doing more preparatory studies — unless, that is, you feel capable of making on-the-spot decisions.

Detail of an oil painting by J. Chambrin. Brush and knife used.

OIL PAINTING ON PAPER

Georges Dayez
Artist, member of the *Comité du Salon de Mai*.
Teacher, head of the lithography studio at
the *Ecole Nationale Supérieure des Beaux-Arts*
in Paris.

Many artists paint in oils on paper. There were even times when they stuck sheets of paper onto the canvas by way of preparation. It is useful to know this technique as it offers another means of expression and it does not involve great expense or trouble.

Use any kind of paper, provided the oil does not "sink" through. Tracing paper and brown wrapping paper are ideal. For advanced works, water-colour papers such as Arches or Rives are recommended. Use the back of the paper as it is smoother.

Very attractive effects can be achieved by levelling the paints with some absorbent cotton wool.

The work can be sketched in water-colours or gouache, but these can cause the paper to crinkle. Better still, use oil paints strongly diluted in turpentine.

Do not worry about thickening the paint, or applying the colours with a knife or trowel. An attractive outline may be simply achieved by diluting your charcoal drawing with a paintbrush dipped in oil (mixed with a bit of white if desired).

Stick the finished work onto a thick piece of plywood, or have it stuck to canvas (this should be done professionally).

A matt varnish may be used to produce an effect reminiscent of ancient paintings.

Cadiou
Founder of the *Peintres de la Realité*
school.
General secretary of the *Salon du Dessin
et de la Peinture à l'Eau.*
Vice-President of the *Salon Comparaisons.*
Member of the *Comité du Salon des
Indépendants.*
Honorary member of the *Syndicat National
des Peintres-Illustrateurs.*

Rodolphe Caillaux
Painter, President of the *Salon
Comparaisons.*
Member of the *Comité aux Affaires
Culturelles.*

Jack Chambrin
Winner of travel scholarship from the
state and the Maison Descartes of
Amsterdam.
Fénéon Prize.
Abd el Tif Prize.
Descartes Prize.
Prix de la Signature cachée.
Painter, engraver, mural artist.
Teacher at the Academy Frochot.

Lucien Fontanarosa

Claude Schurr
Member of the *Salon d'Automne.*
Robert Antral Prize.
French National Arts Prize.
Former member of the *Jurys du Prix de
Rome.*
Former teacher at the *École des Métiers
d'Art.*
Artistic director of the *Académie de Port-
Royal.*
Chevalier de l'Ordre des Arts et Lettres.
Chevalier of the Order of Merit of the
Italian Republic.

Vieira da Silva

Zao Wouki

Some artists' techniques

"Strawberries" 16 by 12 cm (blown up by 25%).

CADIOU

He pays scrupulous attention to detail, which results in a photographic depiction of reality. He carefully depicts texture, sparkle, reflection, the "skin" of an object, and the contrast between the various objects.

Apart from the artistic skill vital to a successful work, this "truer than life" reproduction demands the virtues of patience and stamina. (50 − 200 hours for a medium-sized canvas.)

Cadiou draws the model (and a model is absolutely essential) rapidly on a piece of paper in order to find the best setting for it. This will influence the size of the canvas, and will help him to work out the backgrounds and empty spaces. He now interchanges the objects until he finds a satisfactory combination. He sizes the very fine canvas with polyvinyl and titanium white. He then rubs it using a pumice stone (hardness 3 x 0), a procedure known as *pouncing*. Once he has chosen the shape and size of the canvas, he draws in the outlines in charcoal, using simple Cubist shapes.

Using hard paintbrushes, he quickly sketches the essential tonal gradations onto the canvas (diluent: turpentine and some medium). At this point, the sketch resembles a Modern Art painting, except that the varying thicknesses of paint are levelled with a large and soft brush. Successive coats will cover and complete this rough draft. From now on, the artist uses sable brushes, and squirrel brushes for the final touches. The excess paint is scraped off with a knife in order to leave the smoothest surface possible.

Retouches are done on the dry canvas, and the diluent is gradually thickened with oil. A coat of retouching varnish must be used on the dry canvas before retouching it. One may also have to retouch the background here and there in order to cause a blending of outlines.

Recommended beginner's palette: peach black and siccative, raw umber, burnt umber, yellow ochre, red ochre, ultramarine blue, Prussian blue, sap green, lemon yellow, golden yellow (deep chrome yellow), vermilion, cadmium red, purple red, flake white.

Set your paints out from left to right following the colour spectrum. A second, inner row consists of the earth colours and the "couleurs rabattues" (prepared mixed colours), with black and white in the middle.

Cadiou uses dark values and dark "couleurs rabattues" for his sketch. The painting gets lighter as it develops, and the contrasts and vividness are fully realised. Although the realist painters follow strict rules as regards form, they are more flexible when it comes to choosing tonal gradations. Harmony must always remain the supreme judge.

Cadiou uses a watchmaker's eyeglass and a maulstick for the final touches, which demand great precision and delicacy of touch.

Cadiou recommends progressing from dark to light shades (as in all painting). Start with that which is farthest away, and work your way forward. The very subtle differences between one shade and another, caused by superimposing successive layers of paint, add to the impression of relief.

Having previously prepared his own paints and canvasses, Cadiou finds commercially prepared materials more reliable and time-saving. He trusts the manufacturers' guarantee of their organic products' permanence.

He uses pure poppy oil for the final touches, and Dammar varnish after the canvas has been left to dry for a year. Mediums prevent dull spots, but you can use retouching varnish instead. Realistic paintings require the shiny effect provided by a varnish.

Even though this technique requires an almost calligraphic approach so as not to smudge the rest of the work, method must not stifle creativity. Too much concentration will spoil inspiration. The latter will be less stifled if one moves round from one detail to another at random until the visual effect is totally satisfactory.

The artist in his studio.

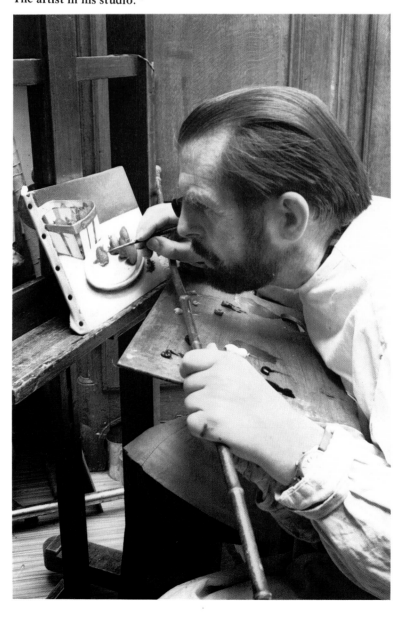

Rodolphe Caillaux in his studio.

Rodolphe CAILLAUX

"I have never wished to use any other canvas preparation than the one I have been using for years. This is how I proceed: I choose a sunny day and pin my canvas to the frame without stretching it. I/then coat both sides with a light mixture of a special glue (Totin) and glycerine.

"I leave it to dry, and then add a second coat — this time a stronger mixture of glue, a small amount of glycerine, and some Meudon white or zinc white in powder form, depending on whether I want a canvas with a greater or lesser degree of absorbency.

"When it is dry, I stretch the canvas gently and add a further coat of the same mixture. I might rub the canvas with a pumice stone or I might leave it, depending on whether I intend to use thin or thick coats of paint.

"Having discovered that each layer may be different, I use retouching varnish for the superimposed layers of paint, the retouches and glazes, and as a diluent.

"I use the following colours: titanium white and filling white, ivory black, burnt sienna, burnt umber, yellow ochre, pale and dark cadmium red, ruby red, crimson lake, lemon cadmium yellow, delta yellow, chrome green, viridian, baryte green, ultramarine blue, cerulean blue, Prussian blue, and cobalt violet.

"Whatever the actual importance of the intended painting, I never do a preliminary drawing. I start off with lean coats of paint, and progressively thicken them until I have found a texture which appeals to me. Once dry, I varnish the canvas in order to intensify or distance the paint thicknesses.

"I use a very fine paintbrush to draw in the outlines as the work proceeds.

"In order to vary the texture, I use brushes, knives, razor blades, painting knives and so on.

"I only varnish the canvas when it is completely dry. If the colour starts to fade in the meantime, a little retouching varnish will restore its original lustre.

"As the layers of paint continue to take effect, you must wait a long time before applying the final protective varnish."

Oil painting by
Rodolphe Caillaux
"The two pheasants" (30 F).

"Bouquet". Detail.

Rodolphe
Caillaux's
palette.

Jack CHAMBRIN

Jack CHAMBRIN is one of that rare breed of contemporary painters who grind their own paints. He maintains that, although this procedure is more time-consuming than merely squeezing paint out of a tube, it has three distinct advantages:

1) A ground paste has the exact consistency required, and, amongst other things, it can provide a certain "body" without undue thickness.

2) An intensity of colour is obtained with a minimum of binder.

3) It is a great deal less expensive: the price of powders is no higher than that of linseed oil.

Jack Chambrin asserts that grinding his powders adds to his feeling of craftsmanship, and provides him with the time to ponder, the time to take a step back from the canvas. It provides him with the opportunity to take a profitable respite from work.

1) He prepares enough colour to last him a week. As the paints tend to dry very quickly, it would not be sensible to prepare more.

2) Two ingredients are needed for the preparation of colours.
Powder: this is sold as powder to be ground with oil, and should preferably be made by a paint manufacturer. Make sure the exact compound is indicated.

Jack Chambrin in his studio.

Pure cold-pressed linseed oil: add only a very small amount of oil to the pigment powder, and let it soak in. Then mix the two briskly together; the longer you grind this paste, the smoother it becomes. Keep on adding powder until the desired consistency is reached.

3) Chambrin uses petrol as a diluent, and Venetian medium as a means of making the colour go further without weakening its consistency.

4) Retouches for the transparent coats are done using Flemish medium.

5) Jack Chambrin uses two large pieces of white opaline as palettes — one for the warm colours, and the other for the cold. The palettes are always kept perfectly clean, and they also act as a surface for preparing the colours.

Jack Chambrin's palette:

HOME-GROUND PAINTS

— peach black
— lemon cadmium yellow
— cadmium yellow
— deep cadmium red
— pale cadmium red
— cadmium scarlet
— deep cobalt blue
— cerulean blue
— cobalt violet

TUBE PAINTS

— zinc white
— ultramarine blue
— deep Japanese green
— mars orange.

How to hold the paintbrush.

How to hold the knife.

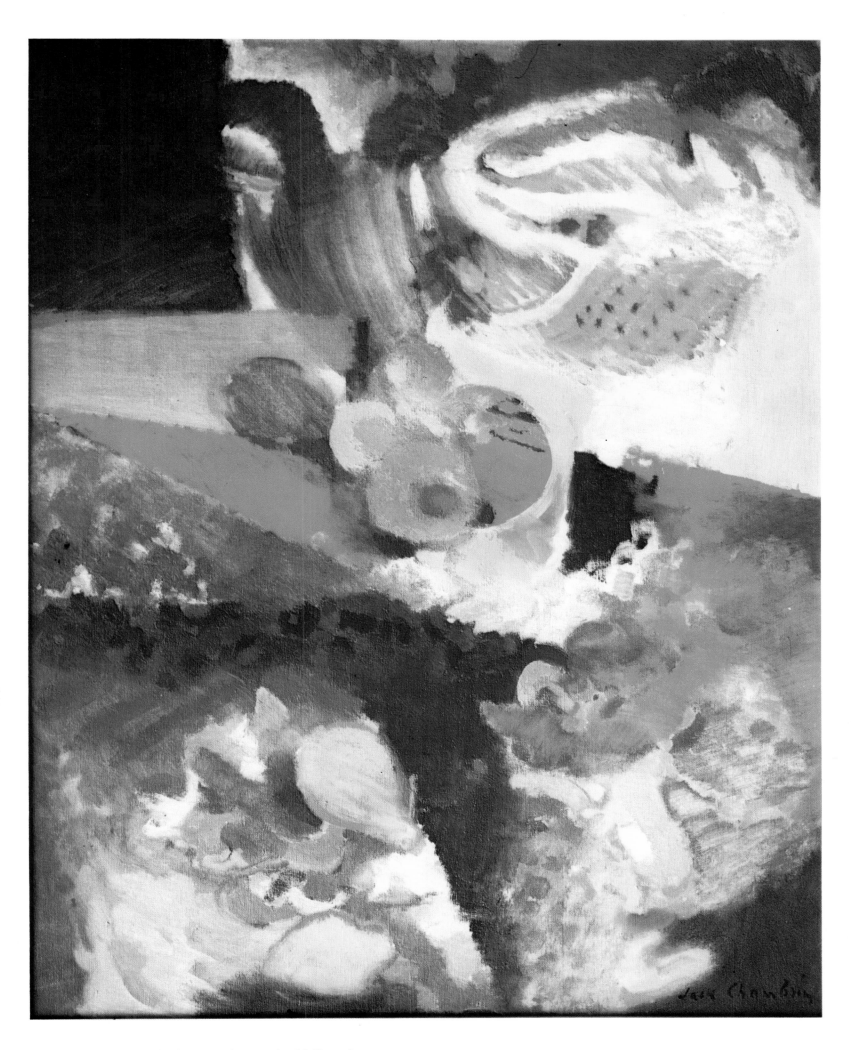

"Fruit plein air", by Jack Chambrin. (Canvas size 30 Figure.)

The artist in his studio.

Lucien Fontanarosa's palette.

FONTANAROSA

The painter, Lucien FONTANAROSA, has complete faith in tube paints. "Unreliable paints carry a warning. One should be able to achieve any combination with 'safe' paints."

Recommended beginner's palette:

— lemon yellow
— yellow ochre
— cadmium red
— burnt sienna
— ultramarine blue
— viridian

Diluent: pure petrol for the first rough draft and then a thicker mixture of petrol and a painting medium for the actual work. Often he uses Flashe paints on Flashe prepared canvasses, but advises you not to use this paint thickly as it hardens like stone, and will make further work very hard!

Final picture varnish: always wait twelve months before using the picture varnish. Put it on in warm weather to avoid "cold spots".

Tools: always clean well. They must be ready to use the next day. "Tools are like good friends waiting to play a game of cards." He uses knives, various-sized brushes, sometimes a rag and sometimes his fingers: "The tools must not lead the artist: they must be lead."

PAINTING PROCEDURE

Use charcoal or a brush for the preliminary drawing, and set the mood as soon as possible so that you know your objective.

"I distribute the tonal values in such a way that each group of similar values is handled in the same manner.

"I distribute the warm and cold tones with the same lean body of paint that I started with, thereby giving the canvas a somewhat uniform appearance. I make my colours go a long way together, and then I let them play out their individual rôles. I then fatten the paint with some medium, and lead them gently to their correct intensities.

"I never glaze my canvasses systematically, and I use the same medium for those areas which require glazing."

"Venice". Oil painting by Lucien Fontanarosa.

CLAUDE SCHURR

Claude SCHURR uses tube paints but hardly touches diluent; if absolutely essential, he uses a small amount of turpentine on its own.

"Red low tide at Plougrescant" (50 F).

He says that when he uses a commercially prepared canvas, he sometimes adds a very light coat of off-white, and works it over carefully with a knife. He thus obtains a supplementary preparation on which he enjoys working.

He never uses varnish or retouching varnish.

When he wants to touch up the canvas, he scrapes away the offending piece, and after a few years this forms the astonishing 'palette mistakes' as he calls them (see photo). He claims that "these teach him how to remain modest".

Claude Schurr's palette:

Black and white.

Blue   — pale cobalt,
             — pale ultramarine.
Yellow — lemon,
             — ochre.
Red   — madder,
             — Venetian.
Light cobalt violet.

The artist in his studio.

Claude Schurr's palette.

VIEIRA DA SILVA

"I invent according to my needs.

I don't like any restrictions when facing my canvas.

I need a flexible technique, one which requires little thought.

I aim to obtain, not a body, but a certain thickness.

I often need a lot of time to adjust and balance the small elements which make up my canvas.

Time means more to me than any technical complication whatsoever."

He uses tube paints, paper palettes which can be thrown away when "limp", and very little diluent.

He does his rough draft with turpentine, and sometimes charcoal.

He uses pure paints, and a medium called "Dilutine" (Watteau), which enables the artist to touch up a dry area easily.

He sometimes applies pure paint with a knife, and then scrapes off the excess paint, leaving only a smooth covering of colour behind.

He does not treat the canvas in a uniform way — some parts are well-worked, and others are less so and allow the texture of the canvas to show through.

He never uses varnish.

"The Library", by Vieira da Silva.

"Triptych" (size: 195 by 358 cm), by Zao Wouki.

Zao Wouki uses tube oil paints, and works on commercially prepared canvasses. He prepares these canvasses simply by wiping them down with some turpentine.

a) His diluent is made up of 1/3 linseed oil and 2/3 turpentine.

b) He uses many different-sized paintbrushes, including the very large ones used by decorators.

c) When he wants a thick paste, he uses coarse-ground colours, and the opposite for a thin paste.

d) If dull spots appear, he uses retouching varnish.

e) He rarely varnishes his canvasses, and only does so after two years, if necessary.

f) He never uses black on wet colours as it can cause craquelures to form.

Original French text by
Camille Berg
Florence Blumenthal Prize.
Teacher of technical education.

Painting with eggs

Painting with eggs can be done using the egg in three ways:

— White and yolk mixed together.
— Yolk only.
— White only.

With the first two methods, the results can darken when dry.

Detail.

Painting in egg, by C. Berg.

Using egg-white only as a medium.

Beat the egg-white with a whisk or fork, but do not allow it to get too thick. Let it settle, preferably in a fridge, for several hours.

Grind some fine powder colours (as with frescoes), preferably with a pestle and mortar, or on some marble, or using a spatula or a spoon on a plate and gradually add the egg-white. When a smooth consistency is reached, place each colour in a jar rather than a metallic container. To prevent the colours from fermenting, add two drops of formol or vinegar. Keep the air-tight pots in a cool place. You can mix the powders before adding the egg if you want a specific colour.

Always mix the paint well before use. Add some water or some emulsified egg if there is the slightest chance of evaporation taking place. Keep some of this white in a jar, so that you can dip your brush into it when you want a more liquid paint or a glaze.

The colours do not alter when drying.

You can use the powder colours in a thick paste so that you can apply them with a knife on canvas, wood or hardboard (prepared without oil). Never use them on commercially prepared canvasses. You can also use them on paper, diluted to be as fluid as water-colours.

You can prepare wood or canvas with a mixture of size and Meudon white, or with a cellulose white (without oil), in several coats (the first ones being heavily diluted with water).

I-99

Palette.

Only set out the amount of paint you need immediately.
— White: in the middle of the palette.
— Cold colours on one side.
— Lightest colours next to the white ranging in order of values, darkest values on the outside.
— Warm colours the other side of the white.
(The browns are always the firmest colours.)

Absolutely unbreakable rule when painting with eggs, as in painting in oils.

One can paint "fat on lean" (on an absorbent or non-absorbent ground), but never vice versa.

Egg paints are insoluble. Use emulsified egg white as a varnish, and spread it over once lightly.
Rubbing with a clove of garlic will also provide a glaze, unless you prefer a matt effect. Egg paints have the richness of oils, but are more transparent.

Original French text by
Georges Dayez
Artist, member of the *Comité du Salon de Mai*.
Teacher, head of the lithography studio at the *École Nationale Supérieure des Beaux-Arts* in Paris.

Lithography

The printing of a drawing or text inscribed on limestone (or on a grained zinc plate).

A lithograph: sheet, print obtained by the above process.

Dayez. "Picking violets" (Vision Nouvelle. Edit. Paris).

The process was discovered in 1797 by Senefelder in Munich, and very quickly reached perfection, superseding the more costly engraving on copper or wood.

The first artists to become famous for their use of lithography were Charlet and Raffet, followed by Davéria and Gavarni. Delacroix, Géricault, Goya and Daumier produced its masterpieces.

At the end of the century, stone, which was often heavy and difficult to handle, was replaced by zinc plates. This period is particularly associated with the work of Toulouse-Lautrec, then Manet, Bonnard and many others. Picasso also produced many magnificent works.

Of all printmaking processes, lithography is the one which gives the artist the feeling that he is expressing himself in the most direct and free manner. Whereas colour printing requires a certain degree of experience, black lithography provides great satisfaction from the very start.

Nevertheless, the artist cannot print for himself without a press, stones, and a complete range of bulky accessories. Moreover, it would be risky to start without first learning from a competent printer.

Most of the time, the amateur will have to carry out his work assisted by a master craftsman or a qualified person who owns a press and can provide him with stones or zinc plates as well as valuable advice.

MATERIALS

1 *The press.* Lithographs are printed by the pressure of a knife edge or scraper, a piece of wood lined with leather, which squeezes the stone and paper together as it slides over the top. Friction is overcome by interposing a sheet of zinc or cardboard coated with tallow. With mechanical presses, the pressure is exerted by a cylinder.

2 *Support.* The calcium carbonate stone is very hard and contains fine pores; it usually comes from a quarry at Solenhofen in Bavaria.

Graining. Before any operation can be started, the previous work already on the stone must be removed. For this purpose, the stone is covered with graining sand or carborundum powder, to which a little water is added. Place another stone of the same size on top and rub together with a figure of eight motion. As soon as the previous work has disappeared, rinse the surface carefully and sprinkle on another handful of graining sand (grain size depends on the type of work to be performed). Repeat until a satisfactory grain is obtained.

The stone can be replaced by sheets of zinc (approximately 5/10 mm thick), grained from 0 to 5, in which case graining can only be done by an expert (of the firm which sells the zinc).

No. 1 is suitable for fine pencil.
No. 2 is more suited to coarser work.

The artist can draw his work at home on transparent or opaque "lithographic" transfer paper.

This work is then entrusted to a printer who transfers the drawing onto a stone for printing.

TOOLS

1 The best drawing ink is bought in sticks, the ink being made by rubbing the stick on a saucer, adding a few drops of water and stirring with the finger. The ink is then transferred to an inkwell (for work with a pen) or diluted to various strengths in several saucers for wash work using a brush.

2 Ink supplied in tins is diluted with water and is applied with a large or fine brush.

Greys can also be obtained by rubbing a toothbrush impregnated with ink against a knife blade or a grid. This is known as brush work (stippling).

3 The pencil is inserted into a holder and used in the same way as an ordinary pencil. Pencils are also available with the lead surrounded by a spiral of paper which is progressively unwound.

The work thus obtained can be altered by scratching it with a razor blade or special scrapers (lozenge or flat) which are carefully sharpened. Part of the work can also be softened or erased with special stones or powdered pumice.

Erasure is further possible by wiping the defective area with turpentine or petrol, although this often leaves a halo or cloudy effect.

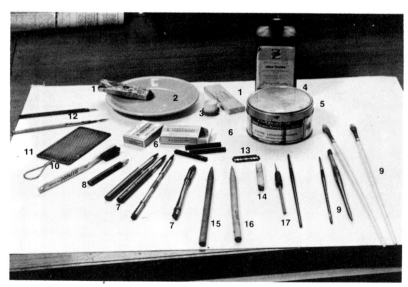

Fig. 1

1. Lithographic ink in sticks.
2. Saucer for preparing the ink.
3. Ink well.
4. Lithographic ink, ready for use, in tins.
5. Lithographic ink in a box for wash tints and large flat tints.
6. Lithographic pencils.
   No. 1 is the hardest and No. 6 the softest.
7. The same pencils, used in a charcoal holder.
8. "Korn" lithographic pencil surrounded by a spiral of paper.
9. Fine and thick brushes.
10. Toothbrush for brushwork (stippling).
11. Grid for brushwork (stippling).
12. Pen holder complete with: a) standard pen, b) drawing pen.
13. Razor blade for sharpening pencils.
14. Erasing stone (soft or hard).
15. Lozenge scraper.
16. Flat scraper.
17. Dry point graver.

Fig. 2 Graining the stone.
Two stones of similar size are rubbed together with scouring sand and a little water in between.
The stone on top is moved in a regular figure of eight motion.
Coarse No. 80 scouring sand is used first to erase the previous work and, after rinsing, the selected grain is obtained by using No. 100, 120 or 150 sand.
After careful rinsing and drying, the stones are ready to receive new work.

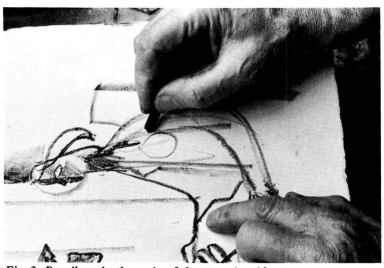

Fig. 3   Pencil work; the grain of the stone is evident.

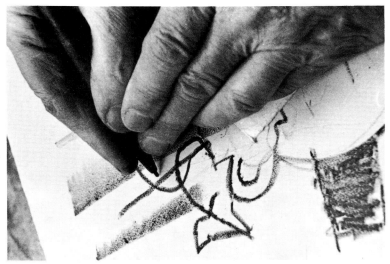

Fig. 4   The drawing is touched up with the scraper....

Fig. 5 ... and finished with the pen (the scraping traces can be seen). The hand is resting on an arched piece of wood (a barrel stave) to prevent contact with the stone.

Fig. 6   The edges of the flats are finished off with the firmly guided scraper. Notice the position of the two hands.

Lithography in eight colours.

Dayez. "The Chianti bottle" (Lublin Inc., Edit., New York).

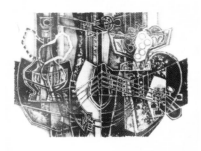

Print (in black) of the dark grey.

Final print.

Beige – grey – sepia – black.

Dayez. "Trio of instruments". Lithography in nine colours.

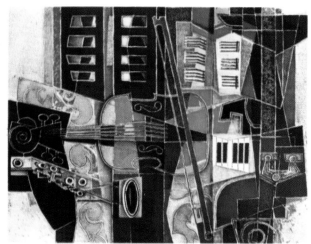

Final print.

Beige – grey – sepia – black.

Dayez. "TOLEDO — The Degollada ravine" (Galanis Edit., Paris).

Detail.

Dayez. "Fishermen's wives at Nazaré" (Cailler Edit., Lausanne).

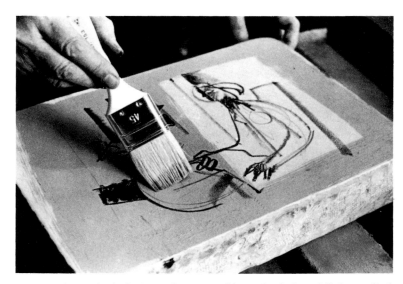

Fig. 7 The etch (solution of gum arabic and nitric acid) is applied after lightly rubbing the work with talc or resin powder.

This preparation is left for at least 12 hours.

Fig. 8

1. The etch is removed with clean water. (Some plates may require a further etch.)
2. It is replaced with a light coat of pure gum arabic solution and dried.
3. The artist's work (pencil or ink) is gently removed with turpentine and rag (see above).
4. The gum is removed with clean water.
5. The stone is gradually inked with printing ink.

Fig. 9 The stone is then placed on the press.

The pressure is adjusted with the screw (3).

The stone is kept moist (notice the sponge and the bowls of water).

The scraper, a piece of pear wood of which the tapered edge is covered with a strip of leather, is held in the scraper box (1 and 2). The scraper is raised in our picture.

PROCESSING THE STONE

When the artist has completed his work on the stone and dusted it with resin and French chalk (talc), the processing stage is reached.

The basic principle of the lithographic process is the natural antipathy of grease and water. Thus, once the stone has been drawn on with a grease-based material (such as a greasy ink or chalk) the surface is treated chemically by means of an etch (gum arabic with a small nitric acid content), which makes the undrawn areas more resistant to grease and sympathetic to water.

Spread this mixture with a wide varnish brush and allow to dry. It must be left to act for at least twelve hours.

Fig. 10   The roller covered with leather, rubber or plastic is regularly coated with printing ink (either black or the chosen colour).

The drawing, which only appeared as an outline, re-emerges.

PRINTING

The etch is carefully removed with a wet sponge. Recoat with fresh gum arabic without acid and allow to dry. At this point, the ink and pencil of the original work are removed with a soft rag soaked in turpentine. Wash with clean water. Ink again with a roller coated with black printing ink.

If the original work reappears, the stone has to be processed again and the above steps repeated with a stronger mixture which must only be left for a few minutes.

If work is to be added, the stone can be made receptive to grease again with a mixture of 3 parts water to 1 part acetic acid. Rinse well, dry and add the work, then process the stone again. The stone is now positioned on the press, the scraper pressure set, and the appropriate ink (or colour) applied.

The sheet of paper is placed on the inked stone, covered with intermediate sheets and finally greased cardboard or zinc to facilitate the sliding motion of the scraper. The scraper box is then locked and the printer subjects the stone to pressure by turning the spider wheel. The travelling bed is returned to its point of origin by a counterweight. The print is removed by carefully peeling it off.

PAPER

The paper most widely used is wove paper strengthened with size, but high-quality prints are also printed on Japanese and Chinese papers. For black and white prints, the paper can be dampened, but this is unfortunately not possible for colour prints since wet paper stretches and the register holes tear.

Printing inks consist of a base of boiled linseed oil (polymerised) to which coloured powders (pigments) are added. Ink manufacturers make a neutral transparent base that may be added to the colour; the amount used determines transparency and may be used to take the colour down to the lightest tint.

Fig. 11   The scraper box (2) equipped with the scraper (1) is lowered and locked. (The screw for adjusting the pressure (3) can be seen.)

The sheet of paper is placed on the stone, followed by a sheet of smooth cardboard or of zinc greased with tallow to facilitate movement of the scraper.

The pressure produced is tremendous.

The press bed on which the stone is placed is moved underneath the knife edge by means of the spider wheel.

Fig. 12   The print is carefully peeled off and the stone is immediately inked again.

Colours

You need to make as many plates (i.e. stones or zinc sheets) as there are colours.

False transfers

To ensure correct register, as many prints are pulled from the principal stone as there are colours. These prints, sprinkled with red ochre, are transferred onto as many new stones.

The artist can then easily locate each colour: a register mark at the two ends of the principal stone is reproduced at the same time as the transfer (the so-called false transfer).

A small hole is made in the stone at the time of printing. The print is also pierced with a pin, thus ensuring the precise register of every colour.

In general, a preliminary run is made of a few prints, known as the *proofs*. Retouching can then be done, whereupon the printing release is signed and the printer starts the final printing run. The artist now has to sign and number the prints.

Numbering

It is customary to use two figures separated by an oblique stroke:

1) the serial number,
2) the total number off, e.g. 45/50.

In addition to the printing run, a small number of prints are usually pulled as well, these being the artist's proofs.

The number of prints which can be pulled from a stone mainly depends on the type of work: colour wash is the most fragile and subject to variations. Brushwork and flat tints allow for a considerable number of prints (1000 or more); such runs obviously call for mechanical presses.

Dayez. "The valley of Varengeville" (Galanis Edit., Paris).

Even pencil.

Even pencil.

Pen and flat tint.

Wash tint with diluted ink.

Wash tint (frog skin) obtained with diluted ink.

Shaded pencil and scratchings.

Pencil rubbed on its edge.

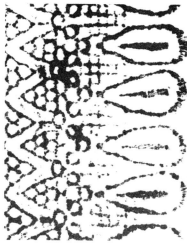

Tracing of an object (embroidery).

Pencil shading.

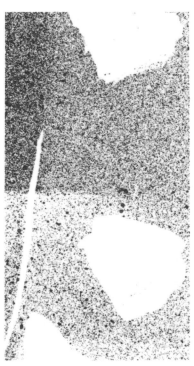

Brushwork (stippling with clear areas prepared with gum solution). Important: in this case the ink should be diluted with petrol instead of water.

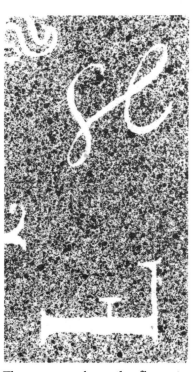

The same work as the figure to the left.
Coarser brushwork.

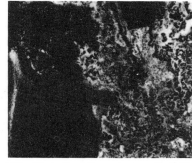

Ink diluted with water applied to a stone liberally coated with turpentine.

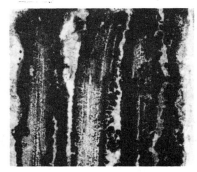

Ink diluted with water applied to a stone liberally coated with paraffin.

I-111

Original French text by
Pierre-Eugène Clairin
Painter-engraver.
Member of the Institute.

Wood engraving

Two processes are used:

1) The older, plank or in the side grain of the wood,

2) From the 18th century, in the end grain of the wood.

I THE WOODCUT

The board to be engraved is taken in the direction of the grain of the wood, i.e. sawn along the length of the tree, and is called *side grain* or *plank grain*.

The artist can engrave with the grain direction facing upwards, across or even at an angle. Since many grained woods exhibit particular patterns these can be used to good effect — indeed an interesting grain often provides the initial inspiration for a print.

The pattern of the wood grain can be emphasized with the aid of a narrow burin cutting exactly along the grain.

Recommended woods: cherry, apple, service and pear, whose grain is very tight and which do not split when drying. However, any wood can be used.

The disadvantage of side grain is that the tool may sometimes lift the grain and cause a break-up of the surface which is difficult to make good. Yet this very difficulty obliges the engraver to work to a design which brings out the best qualities of the wood.

EQUIPMENT AND MATERIALS

— A table, or preferably a bench, slightly higher than the standard height to prevent fatigue caused by the position of the body;

— a magnifying glass;

— a European or Japanese-type knife for contouring, or even a penknife;

— gouges and chisels for hollowing out;

— a small piece of wood, about 8 cm x 5 cm and 3 to 5 mm thick, to prevent crushing the cuts under the hand;

— a piece of glass to display the colours and for mixing them;

— a small leather or rubber roller to spread the colour on the wood;

— a polisher or burnisher, or Japanese baren;

— printing paper cut to the required size;

— the board to be engraved, of the required dimension.

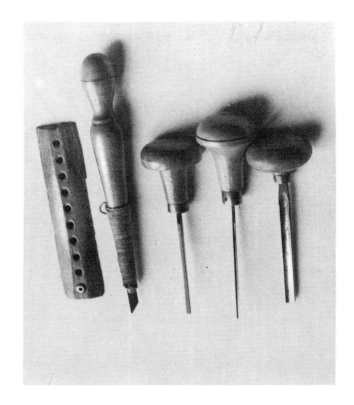

Vocabulary

Contour: to outline the drawing with a knife.

Rout: a term which clearly defines the woodcutting process, i.e. to scoop or gouge out the wood from the board, leaving only the drawing standing proud.

Champlevé work or *hollowing out:* making depressions in a surface to leave a pattern visible, i.e. by eliminating the background field ("champ").

Working on the plank or side grain

Use a board about 1.5 cm thick, planed to a smooth surface and finished with fine glasspaper. Draw out your design on a sheet of paper of the required size and then transfer it onto tracing paper, which is reversed on the piece of wood since it must be borne in mind that the design on the wood will be reversed when printed. As you are cutting the wood, the design on paper will have to be kept within sight as a reference. Lightly trace out the design on the wood itself.

(The entire surface of the board can also be coated with white gouache and the design drawn in black gouache. The white areas are then to be routed and the black ones left.)

Contouring

Contour the design with the penknife or the Japanese knife (i.e. define each line by cutting away the wood at an angle between the black line and the white one). For this work, the board is held in the left hand and pivoted to suit the cutting requirements. The knife is held like a pencil with a very hard lead or, if you can position the board against a bar secured to the work table, both hands can be used. The knife is then held in the right hand and pushed with the index and middle fingers extended away from you along the knife blade.

This first incision is known as the *cut.* Next, turn the board and with the knife perfectly upright insert it in the cut from the opposite direction and lift out the chip. Make a cut the other side of the line, at an angle away from it, turn the board again and remove the chip: a line is now left standing proud as a result of these four operations.

Hollowing out

Before starting this work, the bottom of the triangle on which the line just engraved is located is cut with the knife perfectly vertical. This ensures that the graver will not lift the line since its movement will end against this cut.

With the hands resting on the small piece of wood (8 x 5 cm), the wood is hollowed out with gouges of various sizes to suit the surfaces, i.e. the areas to be left white when printing will be dug out. The depth of the hollows is about 2 to 3 mm, although it can be as much as one centimetre.

Large surfaces are removed with a chisel, a strong, flat tool struck with a mallet. The larger the areas of white, the more deeply they have to be dug out.

Hold the gouge in the right hand with the mushroom-shaped handle against the palm, thumb stretched along the blade, and the other fingers curled towards the hollow of the hand; the left hand holds the piece of wood. The chisel is held and controlled by the left hand and pushed along by the right. The thumb of the right hand rests on the left thumb. If the cut is deep, the chisel is moved forward by the mallet. (See End grain work.)

When the cutting is finished, the design can be printed.

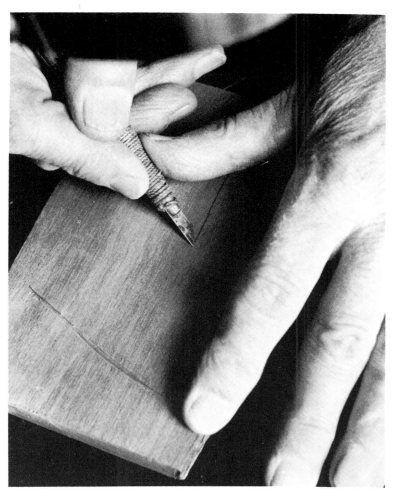

Contouring (1st operation). Cut.

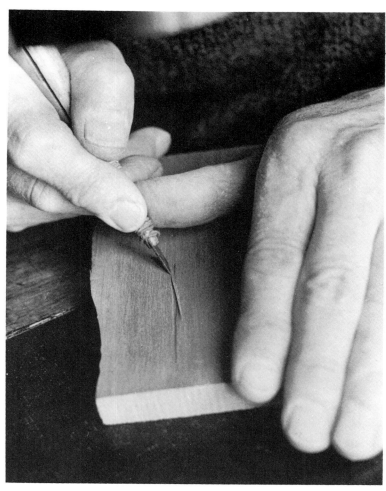

Contouring (2nd operation). The engraver lifts out the chip.

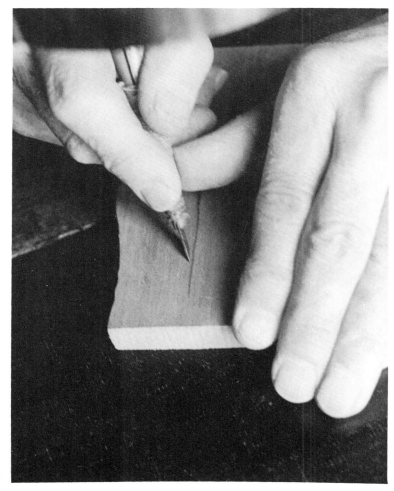

Before hollowing out (knife perfectly vertical).

Hollowing out.

Lines in side grain of a colour print.

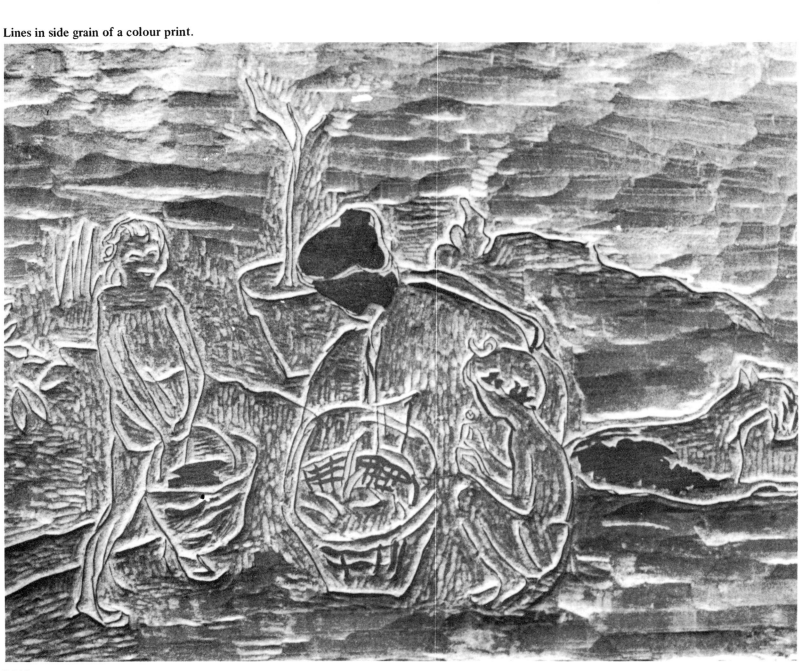

Printing

Woodcuts have a major advantage in that you can "pull" your own prints to assess the progress of the work.

Spread the ink (a creamy paste) on a piece of glass with a spatula and move the printing roller (leather, rubber or plastic, with a handle like a rolling pin) so that the ink is evenly distributed over its surface, i.e. the roller movements cross, once along the length, once along the width.

Pass the roller impregnated with ink over the engraved wood, again in both directions.

Take the sheet of paper to be printed (when hand printing, fine, good quality paper containing very little size, such as Japanese paper, should be used). Locate the paper on the board, having calculated the margins and marked precisely where the corners of the board are.

Using a polisher, burnisher or baren (in fact any object, provided it is hard and rounded off: a spoon, for instance, or a wooden doorknob), rub the back of the paper with some pressure to ensure that the sheet adheres well to the relief of the design.

Gently raise the paper at one corner and briskly peel it away. Your design has now been transferred from the wood to the paper as a mirror image. As many copies as required can be taken of these hand-printed or burnished proofs.

Alternatively, you can take the board to a typographic printer. The prints obtained are usually more definite, the black more even and the white brighter because of the preparation, which involves placing very thin bits of paper torn by hand behind the areas where the weak parts of the wood will print.

Good results testify to a good printer who knows how to deal with all areas of the wood without eliminating the slight differences which are the very essence of the woodcut.

Baren.

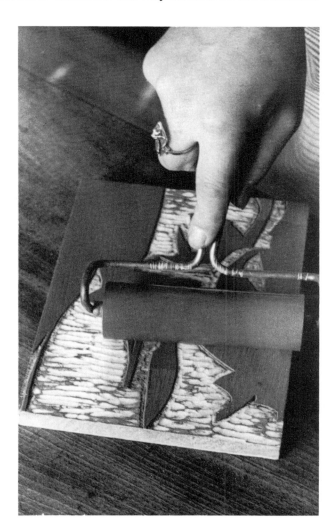

Woodcut by Sophie Leroux.

Printed sheet (Sophie Leroux).

Colour woodcut by Pierre-Eugène Clairin.

"The barn", side grain woodcut. (Notice the sky effect produced by the pattern of the oak.)

II ENGRAVING THE END GRAIN OF THE WOOD

The board to be engraved has been sawn across the tree or branch, then cut into small cubes which, when carefully assembled and stuck with strong glue, form boards. Once polished, the surface of such boards is hard and smooth like marble or metal.

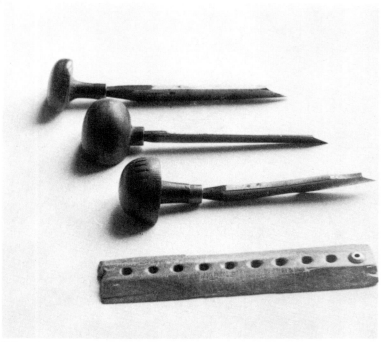

EQUIPMENT AND MATERIALS

The table or bench is the same as that used in side grain work.

— magnifying glass;

— gravers: the graver with lozenge shaped cross-section is similar to the burin used by the etcher (engraving on copper), except that the cutting angle is more acute: it is therefore sometimes referred to as a burin;

— spitsticker: available in about 6 widths of blade: its sides are convex: a very versatile tool;

— scorper: principally used to clear away pure white areas;

— gouge, chisel;

— multiple cutter: grooved graver with several parallel tips with which multiple scores can be made (rarely used today).

— sandbag or round leather cushion filled with sand on which the board is placed so that it can easily be tilted or pivoted.

Woods: as a rule, box or fruit trees.

End grain work

It should be recalled that end grain engraving is mainly done with the graver or burin and that the tool does not alter its position when following the design, but that the design is turned so that it is offered to the burin, which always points in the same direction, i.e. from right to left towards the inside. Great skill has to be acquired to move the hand and not the board.

The woodcutter holds the burin so that the handle (which looks like half a mushroom) is hard against the palm of the hand. The tool is held with the fingers but controlled by the wrist and even the shoulder. The other fingers are curled around the tool handle towards the hollow of the hand.

End grain work means cutting away from the body, in contrast with side grain work, when the knife is pulled towards the body.

Sprinkle talc on the board and wipe with the hand. The design will thus stand out clearly against a white background.

The wood engraver should see his work before the board is finished, so, just as in the case of side grain work, trial proofs should be pulled.

SHARPENING THE TOOLS

In the case of both side and end grain engraving, the tools will have to be sharpened often, which requires a fine-grained oilstone.

The quality of the cuts and the ease with which the engraving can be done are governed by the effective sharpening of the burins.

1) Place the burin perfectly flat on the oilstone having given the stone a few drops of oil.

2) Push on the burin with the forefinger and move in a circular action from right to left, first on the ordinary stone, and finishing on Arkansas stone.

3) Complete sharpening by trimming the sides of the burin. Place each side absolutely flat on the stone and rub lightly to remove the burr, moving the tool backwards and forwards lengthwise.

Check the keenness on a fingernail; holding the handle between the thumb and forefinger, allow the point to drop on to the nail: the point should dig and be held. If not, re-sharpen. Burins must be sharpened often to prevent burring.

ENGRAVING IN LINOLEUM or LINOCUTS

This type of engraving uses the same processes as those adopted for wood, but the linoleum is much easier to cut. We recommend its use as a way of practising handling various tools. Because of the softness of the material, the line is normally less firm than in the case of wood. Nevertheless, some modern artists have made outstanding use of the lino-cut, with which they have obtained beautiful effects. The process is very suited to the so-called "white cut" i.e. the line is cut in instead of being left proud. The board is then completely inked so that the line appears in white or colour against a black background.

Linocut by Henri Matisse. Illustration of "Pasiphaé".

COLOUR PRINTING

The *original* colour print is never an engraving in black to which colours have been added.

The original colour print starts in colour.

The design of the colour print has to be broken down into several prime colours, the superposition of the various coloured areas producing the required result. A dark line is sometimes added at the end to achieve a particular stroke or strong value.

1st colour.

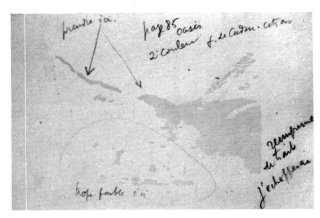

2nd colour.

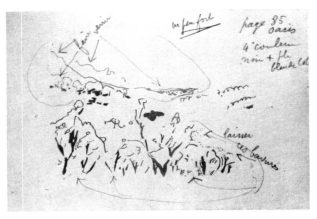

4th colour.

3rd colour.

Let us imagine peach trees in bloom in a hollow between reddish-brown mountains with greenery and a blue sky (white clouds).

1st colour: the mass of the mountains, a mixture of:

> Mars yellow,
> cadmium red,
> dash of madder red.

2nd colour: lemon cadmium yellow.

(Applied underneath the greens to come and over parts of the mountain to reinforce the warmth of the first colour.)

3rd colour: madder lake, which produces the pinks of skin and further modifies the first shade.

4th colour: outlines the shapes and prepares for the final dark colours:

> ash grey,
> cobalt blue.

5th colour: the blue of the sky, which provides shadows for the fishermen and the green trees (to come):

> cobalt and cerulean.

6th colour: the green of the trees.

7th colour: a darker ochre (with the end grain board used for the pink, having gouged out everything which is not required):

> ochre,
> burnt sienna,
> dash of madder red.

8th colour: ash grey,
> dash of blue.

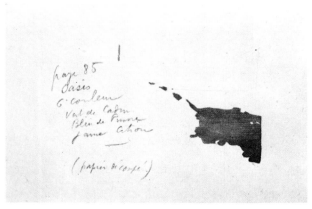

5th colour.

6th colour.

 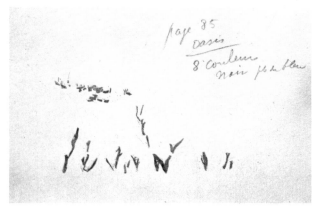

7th colour.   **8th colour.**

Final print.

"Immouzer des Ida Outanan, Morocco".

Woodcut by Pierre-Eugène Clairin
for "An adventure in the Sahara" by Montherlant. 200 prints taken by the "Société des XXX" of Lyons.

Original French text by
Guita Mileva

Dry point

Dry point. Proof.

This craft is close to that of the painter or the sketcher. The principle involves drawing on the copper with a point held as far from the horizontal as possible so as to raise burrs on each side of the line, which will give the print its velvety blackness.

Lines which are to remain definite and light are deburred.

The equipment is the same as that used by an etcher, except that the burins are replaced by points of all sizes secured in a holder.

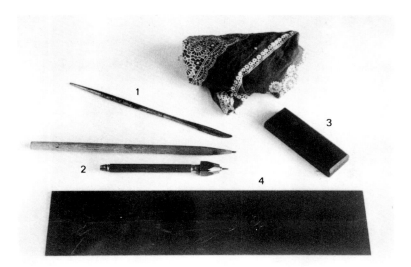

Sharpening the point.

1 Burnisher, 2 Points, 3 Sharpening stone, 4 Copper plate.

The work. Draw on the copper with the aid of the point, the surface penetration being determined by the intensity to be given to the line. The point must be firmly held to ensure that the line is deliberate and that clean, rigid burrs are raised on the copper on each side of the line.

It is always difficult to assess the work without a trial print, yet the precarious strength of the burrs prevents more than about ten prints or so to be taken from a dry point engraving. An attempt can also be made to judge the progress of the work by occasionally wiping the plate with a piece of rag dipped in ink. The ink is then retained by the burrs, thus providing a rough idea of the effect in print.

The drawback of dry point is its fragility. If more than a dozen prints are to be taken, the copper is steel faced, whereupon any number of prints can be pulled. (Engravings and etchings from which a very large number of prints are required, e.g. for books, are also steel faced.)

Some dry point artists remove the burrs from their plates, so that the result closely resembles an etching.

Electroplating with steel is resorted to if a considerable number of prints are needed, or if the dry point plate is very delicate.

When the last print has been taken (i.e. the 50th of a run of 50), the engraver scores the plate with a burin incision right across it, or in the form of a cross, after which he takes one more print to show that the plate is useless for further printing.

Dry point. Proof.

Engraving the plate with a point.
Notice the position of the fingers and of the cloth used as protection.

Engraving the plate with a point.

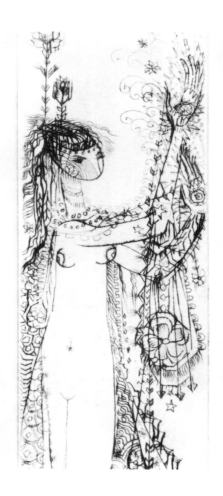

Original French text by
Robert Cami
Teacher, head of the engraving studio at
the *Ecole Nationale Supérieure des
Beaux-Arts* in Paris.

Line engraving

Line engraving by Dürer.

The oldest of the engraving processes is that which involves the use of the burin. Prehistoric man, who has left us his works of art on the walls of caves, also worked as an engraver and produced engravings on objects made of reindeer horn. The points of their flint burins already had the shape of our steel burins, and their works reveal a science of form and a sensitivity of line which are not always among the attributes of the modern engraver. Anyone intending to take up line engraving would do well to study the technique of these early engravings.

Engraving print underwent tremendous development when the invention of the printing press provided the means for disseminating knowledge, thus creating a climate of intellectual and artistic curiosity. The almost simultaneous discovery of papermaking in Europe (brought from China by the Arabs), and the subsequent ease with which proofs could be run off, promoted this growth of the engraving.

Thorough comprehension of a technique presupposes an insight into what can be expected of it: the purpose of engraving is to obtain a large number of prints. Before the requirements and imperatives of the engraver's technique can be understood, the method of printing engravings must be explained first.

PRINTING

Let us start with the copper plate engraved by the intaglio process, either with the burin or with acid, the printing procedures being the same.

Principle

Fill the crevices (incisions) with ink. Clean the surface of the copper and, by applying pressure to the paper, transfer the ink in the crevices to the paper, so that the drawing is reproduced.

The copper-plate engraving press

The press comprises two rollers side by side which are subjected to a very high pressure. A perfectly flat plate known as the "bed" travels between these two rollers. The inked copper plate, the moist paper and the blankets (i.e. thick felt which, because of the pressure, virtually moulds the paper into the hollow of the crevices in the plate) are positioned on this bed.

The shaft of the upper roller, supported in bearings, is equipped with arms which, when turned, move the press. The bed passes between the two rollers where, under the effect of the high pressure, the paper is forced into the inked crevices.

Inking the plate with a pad. In the foreground: the three pieces of muslin rag.

Inking the plate

According to the treatise of Abraham Bosse (17th century), the ink then used was made up of carbon black crushed in nut oil, which had been boiled to thicken it. Today, printing inks are sold ready for use.

Inking means first filling in all the incisions, then wiping the copper to ensure that the surface is perfectly clean.

The copper is then placed on a heater plate and gently heated from underneath to liquify the ink. The inking pad consists of a rolled strip of cloth, not too tightly coiled, to which a handle is fitted.

Spread the ink over the entire engraved surface until it has penetrated into the slightest crevice, and in sufficient quantity so that the incisions are well covered. The excess must be removed to rid the surface between incisions of all ink. The clean areas will be white on the print. Three pieces of rag (muslin) are needed to wipe the ink: one dirty, one less so and a third clean, which are successively rubbed over the surface of the copper in a circular motion. Final cleaning is done with the palm of the hand, the strokes being as far as possible perpendicular to the incisions. As soon as the palm is heavily covered with ink, this should be removed with whiting, which is itself carefully wiped off the hand to ensure that it does not enter into the incisions.

The edges of the plate (bevels) must also be carefully wiped. (At some stage before printing, the copper plate has to be bevelled along the edges with a file and polished with a scraper to prevent the paper from being cut by rough edges.) The copper is then placed directly in the middle of the press bed, being positioned lengthwise. The location of the paper and of the copper are outlined in pencil beforehand on the press bed to determine the width of the margins.

Wiping with a muslin rag.

Final wipe with the palm of the hand.

The printed engraving is carefully peeled off with mittens to prevent any damage.

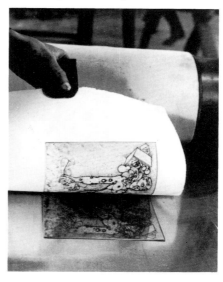

The paper

The paper must be made of pure rag, soaked beforehand by immersion in water; the excess water is absorbed by blotting paper. Stroking with a soft brush softens the size in the paper again.

The paper is then positioned on the inked plate.

Lower the blankets over the plate and the paper, and roll the bed through the press by turning the wheel.

Raise the blankets and peel off the printed paper with the aid of cardboard "mittens" (i.e. a piece of cardboard folded to form pincers) to prevent damage to the print.

The prints should be dried by exposure to the air rather than stacking them on top of each other, to prevent crushing any lines printed in relief.

Once dry, the prints can be flattened again by inserting them between board, each print separated by two sheets of tissue paper, over and under, and two sheets of blotting paper.

ENGRAVING

1. Tallow.
2. Cushion.
3. Oil.
4. Scraper.
5. Burnisher.
6. Oilstone.
7. Burin in its traditional handle.
8. Scriber.
9. Burin.

MATERIAL AND EQUIPMENT

Table or bench.

This must be placed underneath a window. A drawer is useful as a place to keep tools.

Subdued light.

The light should be subdued by tracing paper or calico stretched in a frame to prevent glare from the copper. Legibility of the work and restfulness for the eyes depend on this screen. Optimum illumination with artificial light is obtained by directing the source of light onto the surface of the frame, which should be next to the engraver: the light will then be filtered on to the copper.

Chair.

The chair on which the engraver sits should not be so high that he has to bend over the work.

Copper plate.

Copper is preferable to zinc, although it costs more.

Burins.

Burins with square or lozenge cross-sections are used; their cutting angle should not be too sharp.

Handles.

Short handles for long burins and long handles for short burins. The handle has a part sawn off, and looks like half a mushroom.

Fitting a handle to a burin (see sketch).

The end of the burin which is not tempered must be bent and inserted into the handle, dead in line and underneath its centre close to the copper ferrule. A hole has to be drilled into the handle for the purpose.

When the tool has been correctly connected to its handle, it is hammered home with the burin held vertically, with its point on a piece of wood.

Scriber.

A needle in a holder, or a dry point graver.

Oilstone.

This is needed to sharpen the tools. The stone used can be either an artificial "India" stone or natural stone.

Oil.

Edible or machine oil can be used. Linseed oil should not be used since this leaves a film on the stone when dry, spoiling it.

Sharpening the burins.

Perfect sharpening is essential. A badly sharpened tool cannot be used for engraving.

The two bottom surfaces of the blade have to be sharpened first. For this, the burin must be held absolutely flat against the whetstone and moved backwards and forwards lengthwise, polishing the surfaces until the point has a sharp angle. Then sharpen the bevelled edge of the burin to a perfect angle.

Any burrs (small particles of steel left along the cutting edges just sharpened) have to be removed by honing, in the same way as for the two bottom faces.

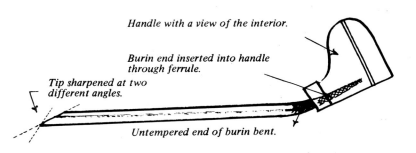

Handle with a view of the interior.

Burin end inserted into handle through ferrule.

Tip sharpened at two different angles.

Untempered end of burin bent.

1. Screen to diffuse light.
2. Tallow.
3. Polish.
4. Oil and oilstone.
5. Sheet of copper on cushion.
6. Scraper and burnisher.
7. Burins.

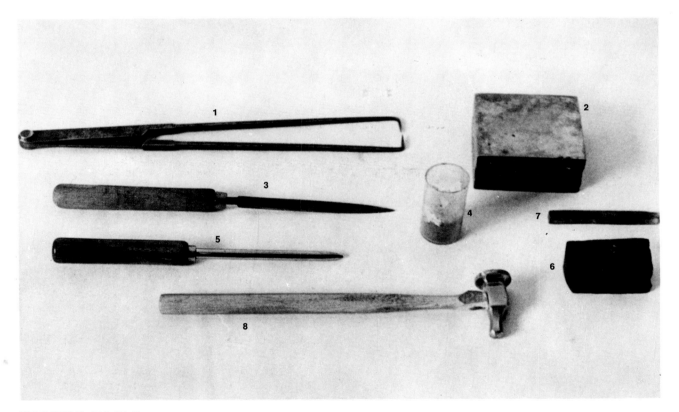

1. Outside calipers.
2. Dolly.
3. Scraper.
4. Polish.
5. Burnisher.
6. Willow charcoal.
7. Ayr stone.
8. Planishing hammer.

ERASING TOOLS

Scraper.

The scraper must have a cutting edge, being sharpened on all three faces.

Burnisher.

The burnisher must be kept well polished (with very fine polishing powder); do not allow it to rust.

Outside calipers.

These are used to locate the area of copper to be hammered at the back of the plate.

Planishing hammer.

A light hammer of special design for "repoussé" work.

Dolly.

A small steel block with a polished top used as anvil.

Ayr stone (natural stone) and willow charcoal.

These must be kept immersed in water.

Polish, mutton tallow, rag.

The above three products are also needed during engraving.

Some engravers prefer to draw on the actual plate, either with a soft pencil, a lead pencil or a pen. The drawing is then defined with a very light line drawn with a scriber. Nevertheless, the simplest way to transfer a drawing exactly is to draw it on ordinary architect's tracing paper with a lead pencil, with only the contours of shapes being indicated. It should be remembered that a second tracing on the reverse is necessary so that the engraving on the plate faces the same way as the drawing.

Having lightly greased the surface of the copper with mutton tallow, place the tracing on the copper, folding the paper over the back of the plate to keep it in place. Rub the surface of the paper with the burnisher, and fix the outline to the copper by means of a light score drawn with the scriber.

The burin handle is held in the hollow of the hand, the palm pushing the tool and the fingers guiding the blade. The forefinger is placed close to the point while the other fingers hold the blade.

The engraver now faces his plate and the adventure can start.

To engrave, the tip of the burin is lightly dug into the copper and, whilst pushing the tool, the appropriate angle is found between the tool and the copper which enables an incision regular in depth to be made.

To make curved incisions, the plate is swivelled on a cushion, so that the hand holding the burin can remain almost stationary. The left hand guides the work by turning the plate so that it is always being offered to the point of the burin. The incisions are always made from the outside to the inside. "From the hand to the heart" said Cournault, and we cannot improve on this quotation of his words: "A joy, a strength emanates from the mind through the heart into the right shoulder; the shoulder transfers this strength through the arm as far as the palm which, as soon as the angle of attack has been found, pushes the tip of the burin, which enters the copper like a ploughshare. At the end of the furrow the burin removes the raised chip of metal and the scraper cuts away all trace of burr, since the incision must be perfectly clean and pure. The difficulty does not lie in the effort of cutting, but in obtaining a controlled cut with the burin.

"All the freshness and freedom of this art result from the range of this push, which varies from the lightest pressure on the tool, producing incisions shallower than a hair's depth, to a powerful action for the widest and deepest cuts.

"Infinite flexibility must maintain or support, reduce, taper or broaden the ever variable incision.

"Emotion guides; breath controls and regulates. Depending on the quality of the man's soul, the incision is born dead or alive, and reveals everything. The very life of the engraver seems at stake."

Half-tones or blacks can only be obtained by successive cross-hatchings made with the square burin, the lines being closer together to obtain a darker value.

The burin, when more or less pressure is applied, will produce different crevices and consequently various shades of black. Very fine lines are engraved with the lozenge burin, with the hand pressing very lightly on the tool.

Position of the burin in the hand.

When making the incision, the burin raises a sliver of metal.

Deburring.

The play of the cross hatchings, the spacings and varying values of the incisions, together with the choice of points, introduce a diversity in the technique which is very useful as a means of expressing objects and colours.

During the work, a piece of rag impregnated with soot is rubbed over the incisions, thus making them darker and easier to see by suppressing the shine of the metal.

Before printing, the burrs must be very carefully removed with the aid of the scraper, held very flat to prevent scoring the metal. All traces of the scraper can be eliminated by polishing the plate, followed by cleaning with white spirit.

Successive prints enable progress of the work to be checked and reveal where corrections have to be made.

It should be borne in mind that the first print is always somewhat faint.

The print should be corrected with a lead pencil to determine exactly what effect is to be obtained, without the risk of confusing the correction with the engraving. This is the best way of saving time since, with all the values evident, the artist can more surely pursue the aim he has set himself. A second proof, which is not retouched, bears witness to the work already done.

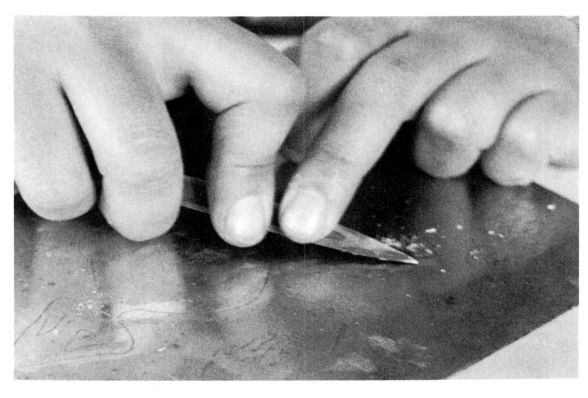
Scraping the copper.

Erasing and correcting.

A very light line can be erased by simply passing the burnisher over it in the direction of the incision.

Deeper incisions have to be eliminated by means of a very sharp scraper, which has to remove slivers of copper. Metal must be removed up to some distance from the incision to prevent creating a hollow.

Traces of the scraper can finally be obliterated by first rubbing down with Ayr stone, followed by willow charcoal, both kept very wet.

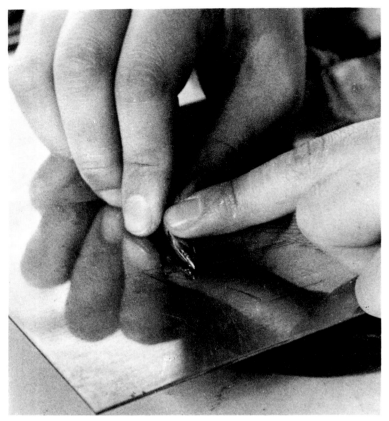

Holding the burnisher.

Each stroke must cross the previous one at right angles so as to make the effectiveness of the action evident. The traces of the willow charcoal are then removed with polish, which is applied dry and at right angles to the charcoal strokes.

If, in spite of everything, the hollow left by the scraper is still there, with the risk of holding ink during printing, the metal will have to be raised. For this purpose, the area of the hollow is defined on the reverse of the plate with outside calipers and outlined with a scriber.

The plate is now placed with the engraved side on the carefully polished dolly and the outlined area is tapped with the planishing hammer, starting with the edge of the hollow.

The hammer blow on the copper must produce a full sound, the copper being held absolutely flat and firmly on the dolly.

When the copper has been satisfactorily planished (i.e. the hollow has been removed), all traces of the operation are eliminated by means of willow charcoal and polish.

Wiping with willow charcoal.

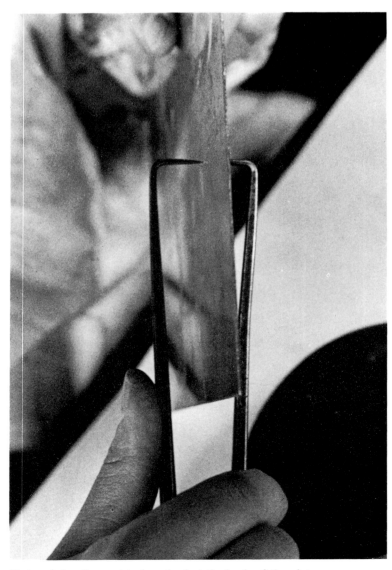

Determining the part to be raised at the back of the plate.

Hammering the back of the plate, which is held absolutely flat against the dolly.

The slowness of work with a burin leaves ample time for thought. The exactness of the medium suits carefully considered and detailed compositions, and the temperament of those artists who leave nothing to chance.

It is not an easy medium to use, but the discipline and order involved will result in the production of rewarding work.

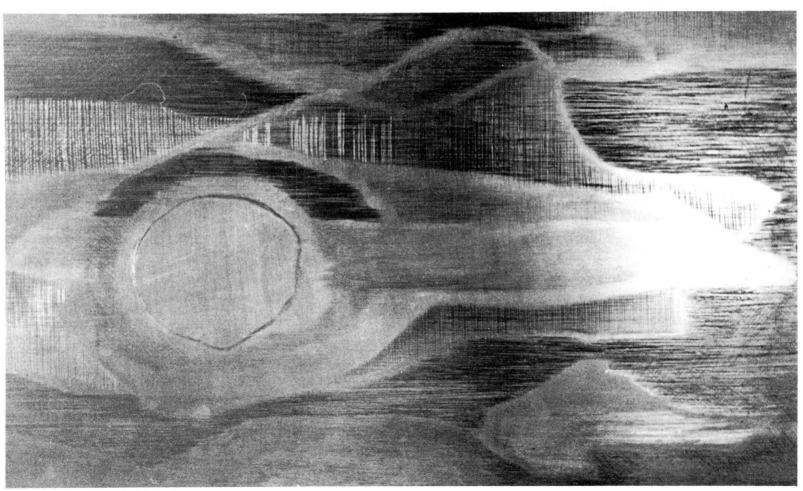

Copper plate engraved with burin.

EMBOSSING

by Sophie Leroux

There is another technique between line engraving and etching whereby metal objects can be decorated with the aid of the same processes, although in this case the engraving must be more deliberate and deeper.

Examples:

I   Silver chalice engraved by the etching process using nitric acid. The "stripped" effect is emphasized by the speed of the mordant attack (acid diluted to 50%). The cavities have different depths because the chalice was partly revarnished twice during the work.

II   Plate engraved with the burin and embossed. Embossing tools have no cutting edges and raise the metal instead of cutting it.

Original French text by
Lucien Coutaud
Painter and engraver.
Founder member of the *Comité du Salon de Mai.*
Designer of décor and costumes for 17 plays, ballets and operas.
Originator of 30 tapestry cartoons.
Titular member of the *Peintres-Graveurs.*
Teacher, head of the etchings department at the *École Nationale Supérieure des Beaux-Arts* in Paris.
Grand Prix des Beaux-Arts: City of Paris.
Chevalier of the Legion of Honour.
Officier des Arts et des Lettres.

Etching

Etching is often the engraving method adopted by painters.

The process, more flexible than the burin, allows for richer modulations: there are as many ways of using the etching needle to trace through the ground (varnish) as there are ways of drawing.

The principle involved is simple. A carefully cleaned copper plate is coated with a thin layer of ground. When this is dry, an etching needle is used to draw on the surface, scoring through the varnish and exposing the metal. The copper is then dipped in acid, which corrodes those parts where the ground has been removed. Ground is then used to stop further corrosion of parts where only shallow etching is required, and the copper is re-dipped in acid to deepen other parts to the required depth.

1. Magnifying glass.
2. Dry points.
3. Ruby-tipped etching needle.
4. Etching needle.
5. Oilstone.
6. Roller.
7. Scraper.
8. Two burnishers.

Equipment and material

The etcher requires a real little laboratory, kept clean and tidy at all times, equipped with a gas stove and running water and a work bench with the following:

— metal plate (copper or zinc),
— etching needles (diamond or sapphire-tipped),
— a sharpening stone,
— cups containing oil for the sharpening stone,
— a burnisher,
— a scraper.

Next to the tap used to rinse the plate after its removal from the acid, the workshop also contains an oblong tank (photographer's tray) in which the copper is etched. Nearby are the bottles of acid, ferric chloride, methylated spirits, and white spirit, and sticks tipped with cotton wool or feathers which are used to stroke the copper as it is being etched to remove any bubbles.

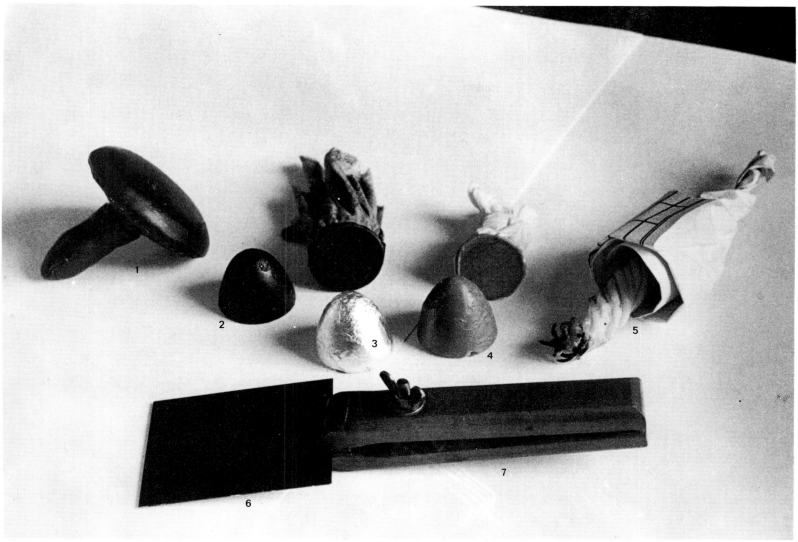

1. Leather pad.
2. Black ground.
3. Transparent ground.
4. Soft ground.
5. Wax taper for smoking.
6. Plate with ground.
7. Hand vice.

Method of working

Cleaning the plate. The metal plate must be thoroughly de-greased, otherwise the varnish will not adhere well. Rub it with a mixture of salt and vinegar, or with whiting applied with a damp rag. You can check that all grease has been removed by wetting the plate: the water should cover the entire surface and not form small puddles.

Thoroughly rinse and dry the plate.

Applying the ground. The ground can be applied in one of three ways, as follows:

A *The simplest and quickest method: liquid ground*

This ground is available in either brown or transparent forms and is ready for use. Using a soft brush, the ground is applied as a thin coating by means of regular strokes, but without passing over the same area several times.

The amount of drying time required depends on the type of ground being used.

— When ground is being put on a plate which has already been etched, this second coat will have to be thicker to ensure that the incisions are well covered. A transparent ground should then be chosen so that the previous etching is more easily seen.

Lucien Coutaud at his workbench.

Using a pad to spread the hard ground by melting it on the heated plate.

Plate prepared with ground by means of a pad.

— The stop-out varnish dries quickly but cannot be scratched with the etching needle. It is used to cover areas which are not to be etched further after an initial biting. It can also be applied to the edges and the back of the plate which must, of course, be protected.

B *The time-honoured, classic method: hard ground (ball ground).*

This ground is hard and takes the form of a dark ball (which can also be cone-shaped). It is applied hot. It can first be wrapped in a piece of cloth (taffeta, silk).

Position the base of the ball in the middle of the cloth, fold up the edges and tie with strong thread (thus forming a handle). Use the same cloth to make a pad filled with cotton wool to smooth out the ground.

Heat the plate over a flame (holding the plate with pliers or a hand vice to prevent burning the fingers). Move the pad over the entire surface of the plate. Watch the plate temperature: the ground should melt slowly. Use the cotton-wool pad to even out the varnish. If the ground has to be very black, the plate is inverted over a taper whose wax contains soot. Such a taper produces thick smoke which completely blackens the ground.

C *Soft ground.* (See also p. I-157.)

Soft grounds, either black or white, are also available (the two can be mixed); the black ground dries more quickly.

Prepare the ground on a glass plate by flattening it out with a rubber (or leather) roller, altering direction to ensure that the varnish is evenly spread. Then push the roller in all directions over the plate to obtain a very thin and perfectly homogeneous layer. The etcher first presses down on the roller, then he lightens the pressure to spread out the ground The plate has to be slightly heated from underneath to ensure that the varnish is bonded to the metal.

Once the plate has been prepared with ground using the pad, it is smoked with a wax taper.

Engraving on copper or zinc plate.

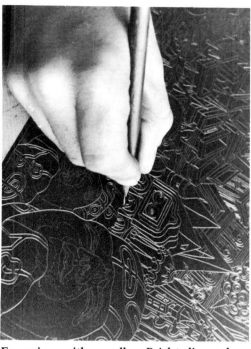

Engraving with needle. Bright lines: bare copper ready for biting. Matt lines: tracing of drawing (sketch).

Applying soft ground with a cloth pad.

All these grounds can be removed with white spirit.

Once the plate has been prepared and has cooled so that the ground is hard, the etcher draws on it with a steel point in a holder, as he would with a pencil. Depending on the drawing, the etcher either barely scores the ground or pushes hard to cut not only through the ground but into the copper as well. As a result, a single biting will produce various thicknesses of lines, thus introducing diversity into the drawing.

Before the plate is immersed in the acid, the etcher eliminates lines he considers unnecessary, mistakes, etc. by covering them with stop-out varnish.

Painting protected areas with stop-out varnish.

Biting. Nitric acid or ferric chloride are used, both diluted in water in a ratio from 30% acid — 70% water to 50% acid — 50% water, depending on the strength of biting required. The solutions have to be strengthened after use since they become reduced.

Nitric acid, which is almost colourless, has a more erratic bite. Place an open ammonia bottle close by; avoid breathing in too much of the vapour produced by the bottle.

Ferric chloride is dark brown and less dangerous. Its bite is also more regular, so this is the mordant used for industrial etching.

Immerse the engraved plate in the tray of acid (use rubber gloves). If nitric acid is being used, the incisions gradually become covered with bubbles, which have to be gently removed with the aid of a swab of cotton wool or with feathers.

The corrosive action of the ferric chloride is less evident, but the liquid should be stirred from time to time.

When the bite appears to be sufficient (the depth of the lines can be checked with an etching needle), the plate is withdrawn and rinsed thoroughly under running water.

Once the plate is dry, certain areas where the mordant action has been sufficient can be re-varnished with stop-out, and the process continued.

A reverse procedure could also be adopted: initially only the lines to be etched deeply are drawn and the shallower lines are drawn in later. The first incisions will be attacked again while the biting action is starting on the second set of incisions. The drawing is then finished by etching the light lines during a third immersion.

In any case, the condition of the work can only be assessed by taking successive proofs from the plate.

Practical hints. Avoid using the same acid as the mordant for different metals, since this could interfere with the biting action.

(Some precautions have to be taken when disposing of used acid: these acids are normally still active and can therefore cause serious damage to drains. They should be neutralized by adding soda crystals, and diluted with a lot of water.)

After the first etching, the etcher re-covers his plate with transparent etching ground to ensure that he can see the work already done. He then engraves again and takes another trial print from which to assess his work and so on. Rembrandt often had to take ten or fifteen proofs to obtain a certain deep black or to produce some subtle value.

A mistake, a wrong line, or an unduly strong value can be made good by means of the burnisher or the scraper and neat nitric acid, the areas not to be bitten being protected. The burnisher can be used to soften an incision or remove it completely if it is not too deep. Care must be taken, however, that the area to be burnished is given a drop of oil to prevent scratching. In the case of deeper incisions, the scraper can be used to greater effect on the metal; the area to be corrected is blended in with the aid of the burnisher and willow charcoal.

Lastly, the etcher often uses the burin to vary the effect or to accentuate a line; dry point etching can also be used.

The amateur will find it somewhat difficult to tell the difference between an engraving and an etching, but a magnifying glass will easily reveal the clean, sharp cut of the former and the slightly ragged edges of the incisions of the latter.

The soft cut is readily recognizable because the line stands proud, and this can be seen and felt.

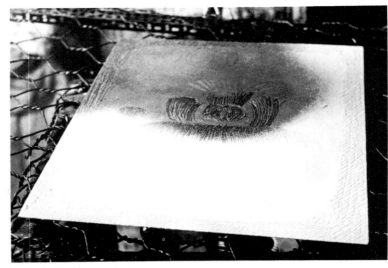

Resin being baked: it becomes transparent.

Remove bubbles with a goose quill to ensure that the acid attacks the copper evenly.

I-148

Removing the sheet from the soaking tray.

Preparing the paper after soaking. Wiping and drying with a sponge.

Finally, after the paper has been sponged, it is lightly brushed to make it "receptive" (on the side to be printed next to the copper).

The plate is inked on the heater plate with the aid of a muslin pad before printing.

The copper-plate printer turns the wheel. The plate, covered by the paper to take the engraving, is fed between the rollers and the blankets.

Removal of the print after passing through the press.

Taking prints. The artists of the past took very few prints from their etched plates or, if a large number of prints were required, they reworked their plate with a burin or needle. Or they simply took prints until the plate was completely worn. Thus, the quality of old etching prints varies considerably: the first prints (newer, with the fresher incisions) are the best.

Today, however, the artist gives the printer a proof, i.e. a print he considers satisfactory, and annotates the margin with the words "ready for printing", and the number of prints he requires.

The artist has a few special prints taken for himself, adding the words "artist's proof" in his own hand on the left-hand side beneath the image. As a rule, original etchings are printed in fairly small numbers (30 to 80).

The artist signs each print in pencil in the right-hand corner below the image, and numbers the print in the left hand corner, the actual number of the print being written above a line under which appears the total number printed, e.g. 3/50.

Lucien Coutaud's engraved plate.

Print from Lucien Coutaud's plate.

Original French text by
Avati
To date, his output comprises over 500
engravings of all types, those of the last
ten years being almost all mezzotints.
He has illustrated six quality books.
Member of the *Peintres-Graveurs
Français.*
Winner of the *Prix de la Critique.*
Gold medal of the President of the
Republic at the international exhibition
of Graphic Art in Florence.

Mezzotint

Avati. "Still life with timid leaf", 1961. Editor: Sagot-le-Garrec gallery, Paris. (Size: 32 x 26.)

The engraving process known as mezzotint was invented more than three centuries ago by a soldier, Ludwig von Siegen. He was a lieutenant-colonel of Hesse-Cassel in the service of the Palatine Prince Rupert. The first known technical success achieved with this process was the portrait of the Landgravine of Hesse, which was executed by von Siegen in 1643. From Germany, the process rapidly spread to Holland.

However, the process reached its apogee in England. Even though it did not produce any major masterpieces at the time, the mezzotint enabled some spectacular technical works of art to be performed.

The greatest artists of the 17th century were perhaps deterred from using this technique because of its difficulty, and the time it takes to prepare a mezzotint plate. Rembrandt and several of his contemporaries knew the technique but, although they did make use of it, they only did so occasionally, and it never became one of their principal methods of expression. The mezzotint is a means of expression, fraught with technical difficulties, which calls for patience, skill and a true sense of vocation. Yet it represents a source of keen enthusiasm and delight to those artists who are determined to master the technique.

Avati at his workbench.

A mezzotint engraving is usually made in copper. The main tool used is the *rocker,* so called because of the rocking motion adopted when moving across the plate. This movement is caused by the convex shape of the bottom of the tool. The rocker is finely grooved, which gives the curved base a serrated edge. The tool is made of very hard steel and, when its base is properly sharpened, the rocking movement will mark the plate with a series of dots which will hold the ink.

The mezzotint technique involves two separate operations. The first phase prepares the texture of the plate with the aid of the rocker, which leaves a countless number of minute dots in the copper. Each dot and its associated burr will hold ink when a print is taken from the plate. The rocker enables you to cover the entire surface of the plate by working systematically in all directions: horizontally, vertically and diagonally. Eventually, the whole plate is evenly covered.

Adequate preparation means rocking the entire surface of the copper at least 80 times, and the artist with the patience to do this will be amply rewarded. The finer the rocker (e.g. 80 to 100 grooves per inch), the wider the range of grey shadings obtainable.

This first operation is not only tedious but very exacting. It requires sustained physical effort and attention, and involves a repetitive movement which, although monotonous, never becomes completely mechanical. Anyone tempted to get someone else to do this work for him will be disappointed with the results. Only the artist himself must obtain the quality and intensity of black he needs for his particular work.

One solution is to listen to music while performing the endless rocking motion of the tool. Although "Rock around the clock" could be the ideal theme for the mezzotint artist, it is advisable to listen to classical music rather than rock and roll for a sustained effort.

The second operation in the mezzotint technique is the reward for the patient performance of the first, since the chosen subject can now be engraved in the prepared copper. The magic quality of this technique becomes evident at this stage. With all the other intaglio engraving processes, the artist starts with an area of light and creates shadows, whereas mezzotint means bringing forth light from the shadows by creating whites and greys. Using scrapers and burnishers the artist flattens the roughened surface of the plate, the degree to which he does this enabling him to obtain all possible shades from the purest white to the most velvety black, passing through the entire range of greys.

For some time after its invention, mezzotint was mainly used to reproduce paintings. To improve output, the texturing procedure for the plates was frequently mechanised, and several machines for the purpose were developed during the 19th century. These machines did not, however, enable the beautiful mezzotint process to be exploited to the best advantage. The results of this mechanisation were always poor, producing greyish blacks and undue regularity in the rocked surface, making it lifeless. Such expediencies must be avoided if the engraving is to remain a major form of expression and an original work of art at all stages of its execution.

The story goes that, a few decades ago, a better method than the texturing machine was available in Paris. Apparently, mezzotint plates were being prepared by members of the Garde Républicaine. These soldiers, we are told, were boosting their pay by texturing plates during their spells on watch at night. (They now have either better pay or more pleasant ways of passing their leisure hours!) An enterprising etcher, who had had enough of rocking his plates, visited their barracks a few years ago with a stack of 25 copper plates under his arm. He scuttled out very quickly and explained, indignantly, that the military authorities thought he wanted to join up. Since then, he has turned to lithography.

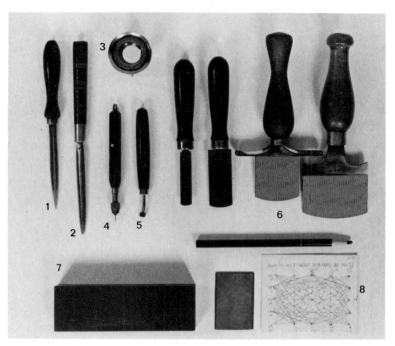

Tools:
1. Scraper.
2. Burnisher.
3. Magnifying glass.
4. Etching needle.
5. Roller.
6. Four rockers.
7. Sharpening stone.
8. Rocking diagram.

Preparing the copper with the rocker.

Sharpening the rocker.

Numerous experiments have been carried out with processes akin to the mezzotint technique in an attempt to achieve comparable results with shorter preparation times. None of these experiments has, however, been very conclusive. Although there is no reason why these substitute processes should be condemned, the final result differs drastically from the conventional mezzotint, whose purity compels admiration.

Taking a print from a mezzotint plate poses no special difficulty, provided the plate was properly rocked. But the pressure applied must be greater than that used for other engraving processes with intaglio plates, and the press blankets must be thick and of good quality, to ensure that the paper properly absorbs the ink held in the plate incisions.

Inking and wiping are done in the usual manner, using either a pad or a roller. A little more oil than usual is added to the ink. The plate is then wiped with a piece of muslin, followed by the palm of the hand. To obtain purer whites, however, it is advisable to wipe these areas with a piece of silk as well before the final wipe with the hand.

The prints must be left suspended in air to dry for as long as possible, then they are dampened, placed between two sheets of blotting paper and thick cardboard, and weighted down. Air drying is intended to harden the ink, thus making the prints less fragile: fragility of the print is the only weak point of the mezzotint process. Collectors must be warned to handle these engravings with even greater care than the others, since the slightest scratch causes irreparable damage. Unfortunately, the appearance of deep velvet easily tempts exploratory fingers, which inevitably leave a glistening trail on the blackness of the print.

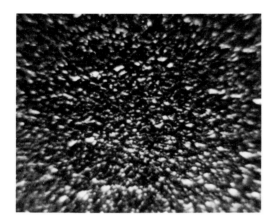

Rocked copper ready for engraving, seen through a magnifying glass.

Use of the scraper to obtain pure whites; these areas will next have to be polished with a burnisher.

Use of a burnisher to crush the texture.

The best paper for mezzotint prints is rag paper. As a rule, printing on Japanese vellum does not produce very good results, although beautiful prints can be taken on Chinese rice paper glued to a sheet of ordinary rag paper.

Normally, a mezzotint plate can only produce about twenty very good prints, but a greater number can be obtained by steel-facing the copper. Once again, however, the frailness of the mezzotint print poses a problem. The textured copper plate is so delicate that electrolytic steel-facing has to be done with special care. Unfortunately, this process is often carried out by firms whose main activity is the chrome plating of taps, and they sometimes find it hard to see the difference between a tap and a work of art!

Avati.
"Fruit and pitcher", 1966.
(Size: 28 x 22.)

Original French text by
Philippe Lelièvre
Premier Grand Prix de Rome de Gravure.

Soft ground

First proof from copper plate.

This process involves drawing on a sheet of paper which is positioned on a copper plate that has been degreased with whiting and water or salt and vinegar, then coated with a ground (or varnish) which remains soft because it contains one third grease (e.g. beef tallow). The ground comes off onto the paper wherever the artist has drawn. The plate now only has to be bitten with acid (preferably ferric chloride, since nitric acid entails clearing the bubbles with a feather, with possible damage to the ground, which is delicate).

Two types of soft ground are commercially available. One type is applied warm with a pad. Place the copper on a heater plate; put the ball of ground on it and, when it begins to melt, spread it all over the copper, smoothing it out (in small quantities at a time) with a piece of muslin in a criss-crossing motion; allow to cool. The copper is now ready. The other ground is applied cold with the aid of the gelatine roller. These two grounds must be applied as evenly as possible in a very thin layer, free from dust.

The papers most suited to this technique are the most flexible ones, which contain little size. Cloth can also be used. It is better not to draw on the paper itself but on thin tracing paper, placed over the paper to retain its texture. This enables progress with the drawing to be checked at the time of the second proof. At this stage, the tracing paper is placed on the copper. Provided two pin holes were made in two opposite corners of the tracing paper when the first proof was taken, these two holes only have to be made to coincide with those left in the copper to ensure that the tracing is correctly located. The tracing paper is then secured along the top with adhesive tape and raised to slide a fresh sheet of paper underneath. The tracing paper is now secured along the bottom as it was along the top. Now you can continue the drawing.

The "soft ground" process is characterised by the fact that the different values of the print are usually obtained more by the differences in pencil pressure rather than by difference in the bite of the acid. Nevertheless, the acid bite can be varied by carefully applied stop-out varnish.

1. Pad-applied soft ground.
2. Pad.
3. Roller-applied soft ground.
4. Roller.
5. Burin, scraper and burnisher.
6. Copper plate.

Tracing
operation (1).

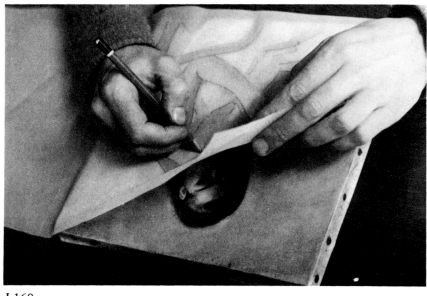

Tracing operation (2).

1. Applying the ground with a knife.

2. Spreading the ground with a roller.

Drawing: the prepared copper is under the drawing.
When the paper is lifted, the ground adhering to it
because of the pencil pressure is removed from the plate.
Above: the painting is reversed in a mirror.

"A process for decorating wood which involves engraving a design with the aid of a metal point at red heat. Engraving performed by this process."

Pyrography

Original French text by
Daniel Legros
Creator, editor; stained glass windows, decorative ware in wood, engraving.

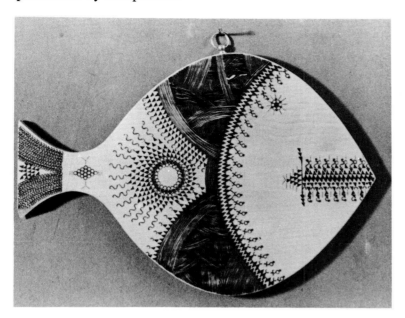

Detail.

EQUIPMENT AND MATERIALS

— pyrograph instrument (electrical),
— tips of various shapes which are screwed into the holder,
— wood, preferably beech, although any wood can be used.

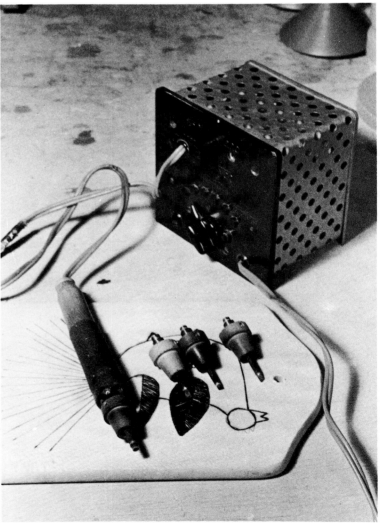

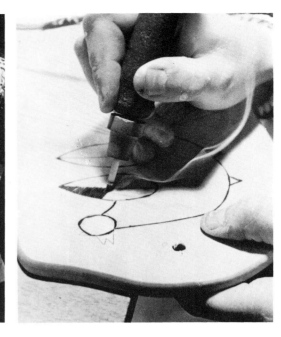

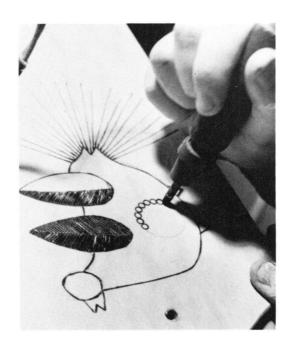

METHOD OF WORKING

Start by making a template, i.e. a cardboard cut-out whose shape is transferred to the wood by drawing round its outline with a pencil. This shape will serve as the basis for ornamentation, which must remain free and inspired by decorative spirit if the best use is to be made of pyrography.

Next, the line-drawing is inserted and, having selected the required temperature, the outline is followed with the stylus held in the same way as a pencil. The wood is grooved by the red-hot tip, a brown line being created and slight smoke produced.

Other tips are now selected to draw circles, triangles, semi-circles, etc., filling the area of the work to be decorated.

A small piece of wood should be kept handy to try out the grooving effect of the various tips.

When the work is finished, glass paper is rubbed over the entire surface to polish it.

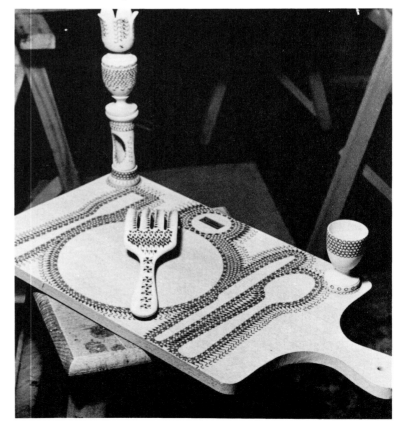

Original French text by
J.P. Froidevaux

Enamels on copper

Enamelling is a technique whereby powdered, coloured glass is fused onto a metal support. The vitreous glaze is coloured with metal oxides and is specially treated for enamelling on metal; it is fired at a temperature of 800° to 900°C.

Materials

1) *The metal:* copper or silver, as available.

The thickness of the plates used varies from 3/10 mm to 3 mm, depending on what the artist intends to do. Enamelling can also be applied to mild-steel sheet providing special steel enamels are used.

2) *The enamel:* this is available in various forms:
— in powder form, ready for use,
— in powder form, unwashed,
— in lumps, rods or plates.

In the two last cases the enamel has to be prepared.

Tools

1) *For firing:*
— a kiln,
— pliers and a furnace shovel,
— refractory brick panels.

2) *For working the metal:*
— snips, hacksaw,
— metal file,
— hammers,
— burnisher,
— tweezers and pliers,
— gas stove.

3) *For working the enamel:*
— pliers,
— porcelain pots,
— fine strainer or sieve,
— atomiser,
— spatulas.

1. **Sieve.**
2. **Metal file.**
3. **Spatula (narrow).**
4. **Spatula (wide).**
5. **Tweezers.**
6. **Flat-nose pliers.**
7. **Snips.**
8. **Hammer.**
9. **Agate burnisher.**
10. **Metal burnisher.**

PREPARING THE METAL

1 *Cutting to size:* cut the size of plate required from the sheet of metal, using either the snips or the hacksaw, depending on the thickness. If the metal is between 3/10 and 5/10 mm thick, it distorts easily during firing. To prevent the metal from buckling during cooling and thus cracking the enamel, the piece of sheet has to be slightly hollowed and counter-enamelled (i.e. enamelled on the reverse side). Counter-enamelling may be sufficient if the plate is small; the larger the plate, the greater the stress and the more it will tend to buckle during firing.

2 *Hollowing the copper:* heat the copper over a flame until it becomes red; this makes it easier to work.

Thin copper (3/10 to 5/10 mm) can easily be curved with the aid of the burnisher but, if the copper is fairly thick, this has to be done with a hammer.

Hammer regularly, working out from the centre in concentric rings to the edges of the plate.

The hollowing effect must be even, ensuring that the four sides of the plate remain in the same horizontal plane.

3 *Volume shapes:* if a really hollow shape (small bowls, ashtrays, etc.) is required, the same procedure is adopted,

but the operation will have to be repeated several times. The areas with the greatest curvature will also require more hammering.

After a certain amount of hammering, copper work hardens and can no longer be worked. It will then have to be reheated to a red colour, this annealing being done as often as necessary.

4 *Cleaning the metal:* if the plate of metal is not perfectly clean and degreased, the enamel will fail to adhere properly during firing.

The metal can be cleaned by heating it until red to burn off all impurities and grease. On cooling, the copper oxidises, and the film can be removed by immersing the plate for a few minutes in an acid bath containing a very dilute nitric acid (about 1 part of acid to 8 parts of water) known as *pickle.* (Take care when using concentrated acid. Always add acid to water, never the other way round, to avoid dangerous splashing. Store out of the reach of children.) Rinse the plate afterwards with copious amounts of water while rubbing it with fine sand or pumice powder.

As far as possible, the plate should not be touched with the hands after it has been cleaned.

PREPARATION OF THE ENAMEL

Enamel ready for use has been reduced to powder and washed.

If unwashed enamel powder is used, or if it is bought in the form of plates, lumps or rods, preparation is needed beforehand.

1 *Crushing:* a porcelain pestle and mortar are used. Place the lumps of enamel to be crushed in the mortar filled with water and break them up by tapping the pestle with a hammer (the mortar should be stood on a piece of cloth). Once the lumps have been broken up, crushing can be completed by hand, grinding with the pestle until the enamel powder is fine.

2 *Washing:* fill the mortar with distilled or rain water. Stir with the pestle. When the enamel has settled in the bottom of the mortar, the water is emptied, fresh water poured in and the operation is repeated until, after successive washings, the water remains perfectly clear. Then remove the enamel, spread it on paper or aluminium foil, and dry it in a warm, dust-free place. Enamels are stored in glass jars with close-fitting lids, suitably labelled.

The enamels do not have the same colour in powder form as they do after firing. It is therefore advisable to make samples on small plates of metal, taking care to mark the back of the plate with the reference number of the corresponding jar (with enamel paint or by engraving). These check samples can then be consulted when one is selecting colours.

ENAMEL WORK

General rules

Enamels do not mix: they are applied in layers.

It is preferable to fire between each layer of enamel. The enamels must be perfectly dry at the time of firing. Thus, if you have applied the enamel in the moist state, the plate will have to be dried before inserting it in the furnace. Drying can be done by placing the enamelled plate on a refractory base and heating it on the stove.

Dry enamel does not adhere to the plate, which must therefore be handled carefully and inserted into the furnace without shaking it.

The different types of enamels

There are two types of enamels: opaque enamels,
                                 transparent enamels.

They can be placed directly on the metal, although it is preferable to apply them on a *flux* fused during an initial firing. *Flux* is a transparent, colourless enamel which adheres well to metal; it is also used for counter-enamelling. Silver requires a special flux.

Enamelling and counter-enamelling with flux

Brush enamel glue (based on gum tragacanth, a vegetable glue which disappears during firing) on the prepared metal plate. Using a sieve, sprinkle the flux over the entire surface area of the metal. The plate should be placed on a clean piece of paper so that the flux which falls next to the plate can be recovered.

When the layer of flux is uniformly white, spray water over it to make the flux stick firmly to the glue. Dry thoroughly before firing.

Applying the enamel

1 *With a sieve.* This method does not enable a definite design to be achieved and is mainly adopted to lay a base, or when using a stencil.

2 *With a spatula or brush.* The enamel is applied when moist. Place the enamel in a porcelain cup with a little water. Spread the enamel, more or less wet, to the required thickness.

When working on a surface which is not horizontal, the enamel will have to be moistened with water to which gum tragacanth has been added.

Firing the enamel

Enamel is fired at a temperature of 800° to 900°C for about three minutes. The window in the furnace enables the firing to be monitored, since times vary according to the particular enamel, the effects wanted and the size of the plate. In general, the enamel is fused when the plate is cherry red. Trial firings should be made beforehand. As a guide, enamel which remains granular has not been sufficiently fired, and excessively fired enamel shrinks, and takes on a stippled appearance (which can be interesting).

During firing, enamels tend to mix as they vitrify, so that the design may not be very clear.

The *champlevé* and *cloisonné* enamelling techniques separate the enamels by means of a raised surface or wire. These techniques therefore not only allow for a more definite design but also for an interplay between the enamel and the metal.

Note: As work progresses, the copper parts not covered with enamel oxidise during firings. These parts will therefore have to be cleaned with a brush or nitric acid before applying further enamel.

CHAMPLEVE ENAMEL

This technique involves making cavities in the metal to receive the enamel. The copper sheet used has to be about 1.5 mm thick to allow for cavities 0.5 to 1 mm deep; these can be made either with a tool or with acid.

1 *Using a tool*

Gouges are used, either manually or with a hammer. In the latter case, the plate must be secured in a bed of mastic compound. Engravers use a container filled with the compound into which the plate is set. These techniques call for a certain amount of engraving practice.

2 *Using acid*

The areas of the copper not to be hollowed out are protected by a layer of acid-resistant varnish.

When the plate is ready and adequately protected at the edges and on the reverse, it must be dipped in a bath of ferric chloride diluted by 50%. The acid bath has to be stirred frequently to prevent deposits of oxide which would stop the mordant action. Nitric acid could also be used, but although its bite is faster than that of the ferric chloride, it is less regular and must be used with great care as it gives off poisonous fumes. Once the plate has been thoroughly cleaned under hot, running water to remove all traces of resist and acid, the enamel is spread on with a spatula.

Should the enamel overflow on to the copper surfaces, or if the enamelled surfaces have to be at exactly the same level as the surrounding metal, the plate will require *stoning*, i.e. rubbing down with an abrasive stone, after firing. A

Hollowing a plate with a hammer (preparation of the metal).

Hollowing out a plate with a burnisher (preparation of the metal).

Counter-enamelling (1st operation).

Spreading the flux (2nd operation).

Wetting (3rd operation).

The cloisonné technique.

Enamelling technique using a spatula.

Stoning the enamel.

Firing. Insertion into the kiln.

carborundum stone is used, and this is kept wet during rubbing. Stoning leaves the surface of the enamel matt; its shine can be restored by firing the enamel again or it can be given a matt lustre (enamelling technique of the Middle Ages). For this purpose, the enamel has to be carefully polished with pumice powder, then whiting. Polishing can be finished by hot-waxing the enamelled surfaces.

CLOISONNE ENAMEL

This technique involves separating the enamels with copper or silver wire secured to the metal plate so as to form divisions ("cloisons"). These wires can have round, square or flat cross-sections and are of different thicknesses, so varying effects can be achieved.

Preparation of the divisions. A convenient method is to stick the drawing underneath a piece of glass, so that the wires can be shaped without tearing the paper. If copper wire is used, it should first be heated until red to make it more flexible.

When all the wire divisions are ready, the design is transferred to the plate, which has already been flux-enamelled. The wires are then positioned and provisionally secured with gum. During firing, the wires will be firmly fused into the flux.

After this second firing, the enamelling process is carried out normally with the aid of a spatula.

When the enamelling is finished, the plate can be stoned, or the wires only can be cleaned with a carborundum stone.

Copper oxidises fairly quickly. If the metal is to retain its shine, the copper parts can be coated with a colourless metal varnish or lacquer, or can be gold plated. (This plating is done by gilders using the electrolytic process.)

ENAMEL PAINTS (Limoges technique)

These paints are more convenient to use than enamel if fine brushwork is preferred.

The colours can be mixed and are usually applied to a pre-enamelled base and then fired in the kiln in the usual way.

Preparation of the colours. These have to be mixed with a specially produced painting medium such as oil of lavender or of cloves. Mixing should be carried out on a piece of frosted glass, using a wide spatula until the paint has the consistency of gouache.

The colours can only be mixed after the above preparation. Ensure that the paint is really dry before firing.

"Saint Gabriel", cloisonné enamel by J.P. Froidevaux.

GLASS BEADS
by Lozach

This is an old craft which is dying and is only being practised by a few skilled artists, such as Mme LOZACH, who hand-craft glass beads and other small items made of wire-cored glass.

MATERIALS
— glass rods,
— a gas and compressed-air torch (approximately 1200°C) and a pipe to exhaust the fumes,
— a support for the glass rods,
— oil to quench the beads,
— a caliper gauge to measure the beads,
— shaping pincers,
— brass (or silver or gold) wire.

1 The brass wire is held in the left hand and the glass rod in the right.

2 The heat (at about 1200°C) from the torch melts the glass rod, of which one drop falls on the brass wire.

This drop of glass must then be skillfully rounded off into a bead of the required size. The considerable dexterity needed for this is not attained overnight. A clever artist can manufacture objects of wire-cored glass in many colours by successively using glass rods of different colours, giving the desired shape to the creation merely by the way in which he locates the fused glass, draws it out and turns it in various directions. The entire procedure is very fast.

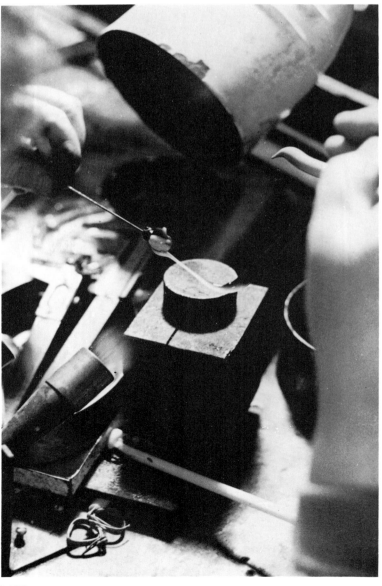

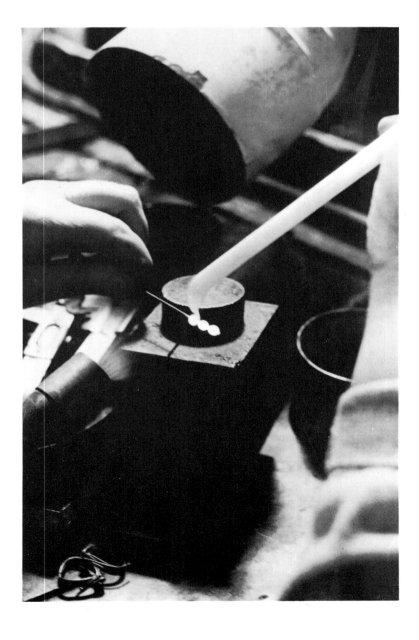

Original French text by
Henri Plisson
Chevalier du Mérite national.
Croix du Combattant.
Chevalier des Arts et des Lettres.
Chevalier du Mérite agricole.
Grande Médaille d'Argent: City of Paris.
Laurier de Terres Latines 1964.
Bronze medal of the City of Mantes
1964.
Grand Prix de la Biennale de Deauville
1965.
Médaille du Salon de la Marine 1965.
Médaille du Salon de la Marine 1968.
Grand Prix de l'Exposition de Taverny
and the *Médaille de Vermeil 1969.*
Vice-President of the *Salon de Saint-*
Guénolé.
Vice-President of the *Syndicat autonome*
des Artistes Peintres Professionnels.
Member of the *Commission de la*
professionnalité des Arts Graphiques
et Plastiques.
Member of the *Salon d'Automne:*
Peinture, Sculpture et Art monumental.
Former member of the *Comité du Salon*
des Indépendants.

Ceramics

PREFACE

Ceramics, as with all the decorative arts which are based on complicated techniques, have reached a dead end, from the artistic point of view.

But it is not because we have gone as far as possible that our fate is sealed. I am not able to predict the future – I cannot say whether we will solve the problem by simplifying the technique or by changing it completely, but I personally am trying to change its course. There is an endless range of exciting prospects which can be used to make ceramics a worthy art form again.

H. Plisson.

A craftsman's studio.

Let us begin by listing the various processes needed to convert the clay into the finished product.

1 *Manufacture of the aggregate.* The composition of this varies according to the finished product and the firing temperature.

a) 800°C: earthenware, bricks, flower-pots (ordinary clay).

b) 900°C: china (white clay, silica, chalk).

c) 1200°C: stoneware (clay and silica, as little chalk as possible).

d) 1410°C: porcelain (kaolin, no chalk).

The hardness of these ceramics will also depend on the manufacturing technique used: sculpture, turning, moulding, stamping out.

2 *Drying.*

3 *Finishing.*

a) Polishing.

b) Scraping.

c) Sculpting.

4 *Firing.* In general, a preliminary firing is given to non-glazed material, which is called *biscuit.*

5 *Cleaning of the pieces.*

6 *Preparation of glazes.* We are not concerned with their manufacture, but with making them suitable for application with a brush or a spray-gun, by dipping, or in powder form.

7 *Glazing.*

8 *Glost firing.*

9 *Secondary firing.*

10 *Temperature control, possible refiring for special effects or for repairs.*

THE HISTORY OF CERAMICS

The manufacture of ceramics is one of the earliest — if not the earliest — manufacturing technique invented by mankind.

To solve transport problems, early man made use of basketwork, and for liquids he tried to create basketwork vessels hardened with a covering of clay. This mixture happened to be placed in a fire, and man discovered a new material: hard, non-melting, porous earthenware. It certainly took a great deal of time to produce a vessel, and even then it was not practical, as it would not hold water, or even oil.

Glass had to be invented first, and the great step forward was the application of a special sort of glass, called glaze, onto the surface of the earthenware.

The need for vases, amphorae and pots led to the invention of the potter's wheel, the machine which enabled man to produce with ease all sorts of circular vessels.

Ceramic objects have been found all over the world: Asia Minor, India, China, Peru, Mexico, Tunisia and, of course, in Egypt, Greece, the rest of Europe and, in particular, Spain.

All these different ceramics were decorated either by incision or engraving, originally done with the fingers, then covered very rapidly with a material coloured differently from the body of the vessel, which could be scratched to reveal the underlying colour: red on white, white on red, and later black was used, as in certain Greek vases. Decoration was also applied later with a brush, using cobalt, iron or manganese oxides. Only in the case of majolica was success achieved with coloured glaze covering the whole body of the vessel. This technique was very difficult to master, and was achieved by Bernard Palissy.

More recently, in the 18th and 19th centuries, porcelain, a carefully guarded Chinese secret, made its appearance.

Porcelain is made from kaolin (pure clay), which is fired at a high enough temperature to fuse the basic molecule.

Hispano-Moorish Pottery (16th century)
(Decorative Arts Museum, Paris)

Asia Minor (18th century)
(Decorative Arts Museum, Paris)

Ming Period (14th—16th centuries)
(Guimet Museum)

Persian Tile (13th—14th centuries)
(Decorative Arts Museum, Paris)

I-175

EQUIPMENT

This is simple but relatively costly. You will need a very large studio, well lit and ventilated, with a ceiling high enough to prevent the opening from the kiln chimney causing a fire. The floor must be strong enough to hold the kiln and possibly a wheel and a compressor. There must be a water supply and enough electricity to supply the kiln. (There are also gas and oil kilns available which give excellent results.)

So you will need:

> an electric kiln;
>
> a wheel, if you want to produce pottery
>
> a compressor for glazing with a spray-gun.

Not much else is needed, apart from sculpting tools, chisels, pointing tools, knives, supports (pieces of wood and plaster) and buckets for the clay.

If you wish to use plaster moulds, you will need a marble slab to which, when it is well greased or soaped, the clay will not stick. The moulds can be made from modelling clay. They are either very simple for stamping out, or made in different sections for more complicated pieces.

An electric oven — open and empty.

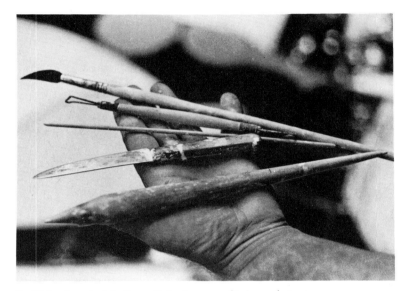

Sufficient materials for satisfactory results in sculpture.

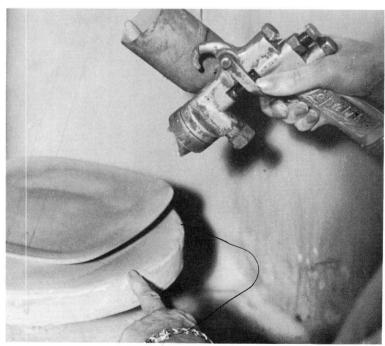

A spray-gun: the spray-gun should be used in a very well ventilated room, as glazes are very toxic.

1 THE CLAY

This is made from various combinations of clay (aluminium silicate Al_2O_3), silica (sand SiO_2) and calcium (chalk CaO).

This formula can be modified by the addition of small quantities of potassium (K_2O) and sodium (Na_2O).

Red clays are coloured by the addition of ferrous oxide (Fe_2O_3), dissolved in clean water.

Water is already present in the clay molecule and it evaporates during firing. This water cannot be recovered and it establishes the difference between raw clay and fired clay. The greater the quantity of chalk and ferrous oxide, the lower the firing temperature, as in the case of bricks.

Silica provides the strength of the pieces. It fuses at 1600°, and therefore presents no risks of melting at the relatively low firing temperatures used.

Most glaze manufacturers also produce clays suitable for their products, and sell them in small quantities. Complete instructions for use are supplied free by the manufacturers or their representatives.

METHODS OF USE

a) The simplest process is when the clay, of plastic consistency, is used in balls stuck to each other with a little water.

b) To make a vase, you flatten a ball of clay to form a round base. You then take a larger piece of clay and roll it out into a long sausage shape. Attach this piece to the base, then continue by coiling it round on itself to form a vase of the desired shape. Then smooth it, first with your fingers and finally with a sponge.

c) *Stamping out.* A mould is used which bears the imprint of the piece in reverse. The clay is inserted into the mould and takes the detailed imprint of the mould. As many pieces as are necessary can be obtained from one mould.

d) *Turning.* This involves a professional technique. Some training should be obtained from a potter's studio. The potter's wheel is a machine, which is attended by technical problems, but it can be used to produce works of art, as demonstrated by the artist, Beyer.

The potter's wheel is a spectacular piece of machinery, as you watch the piece being created by your hands. It takes shape, spreading, contracting, lengthening, thickening, swelling — all under your control. The technique gives great satisfaction and can be easily learnt with a little patience and a good teacher.

e) *Moulding.* Moulding has become simple since the discovery of the property of sodium carbonate (Na_2CO_3) in retaining the plasticity of clay although it loses most of its water. Plaster can also be used as, being porous, it absorbs water. If you put some slip (a liquid paste containing the smallest practical quantity of water) into a plaster mould, the mould absorbs the water from the paste, leaving a covering of clay on the surface of the mould. The longer you wait, the thicker the covering becomes. The surplus of liquid paste should be removed, allowing the remaining covering to become solid enough to remove it from the mould.

2 DRYING

The pieces must be very dry before being placed in the kiln, as the smallest degree of humidity can cause a disaster. The water, converted into steam which cannot escape, causes the pieces to explode. If the explosion is violent, it can damage the neighbouring pieces in the kiln.

Working the clay with the fingers.

Stamping out.
The piece shows the hollow design of the mould in reverse.

I-178

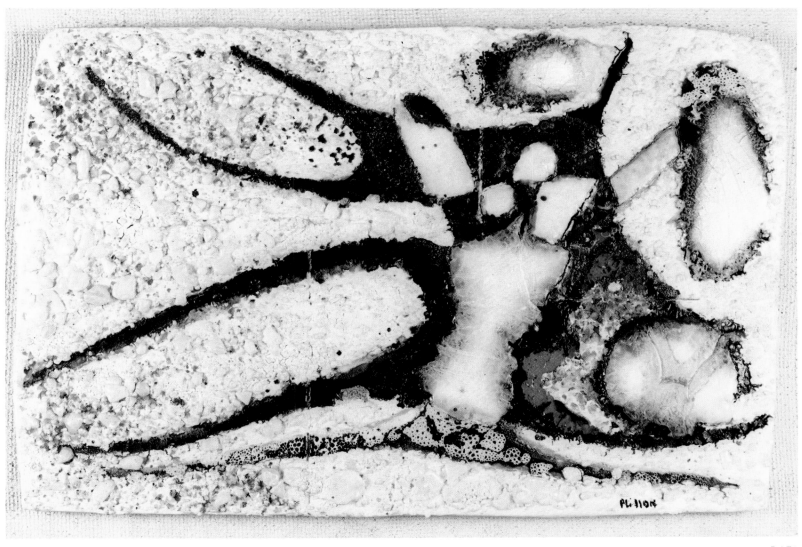

I-179

Adding
decoration
to a piece.

Various
sections of
a composite
mould.

Pouring the liquid slip into the moulds.

Removing the piece from the mould. As the piece is still pliable, it must be handled with care.

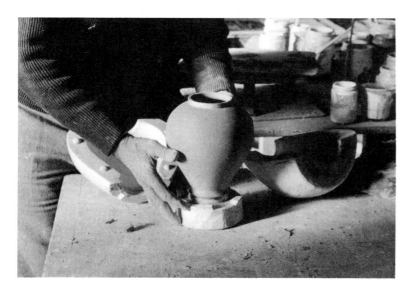

Vase being removed from a composite mould.

The thickness of the crust.

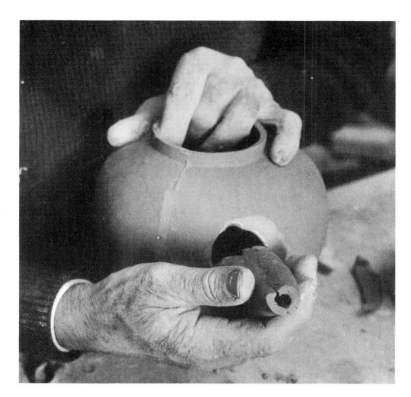

The various parts of a complicated piece are stuck together with slip. The illustration shows a spout being added.

The door of the kiln must be opened with care.

3   FINISHING AND POLISHING

Once the pieces are dry they should be inspected, polished with glasspaper, and the lumps removed. A piece which has not been fired can be remade.

Drying changes the proportions to some extent, as the pieces shrink during drying and they often need to be retouched.

4   FIRING THE UNGLAZED CLAY

There are no special precautions needed for firing non-glazed pieces (biscuit). They can touch each other, or be piled up, but you must not forget that they are very fragile, as they are still nothing more than dry mud. So take care, and allow each piece to be fired in safety. Two pieces which are closely touching react as one piece with the thickness of both. Water is the number one enemy.

The temperature is increased in two stages. Firstly, the temperature is slowly raised to about 300°. Then, it is increased more rapidly. Generally, unglazed clay is fired at a slightly higher temperature than glazed.

The interior of a kiln, with objects in biscuit placed near the opening.

PREPARATION OF GLAZES

To add colour, there are three techniques available:

a)   underglaze painting,
b)   overglaze painting,
c)   self-coloured glazing.

In earthenware, pieces are usually covered with a transparent glaze. This allows the colour of the body to appear, whereas coloured glazes are usually more opaque.

a)   If you take a fired piece of biscuit and add decoration (various metallic oxide colours) diluted with either linseed oil, turpentine, size, or glycerine, and then cover it with·a glaze, the result will be underglaze painting, visible through the glaze.

b)   You can paint oxides on top of majolica — an unfired tin glaze which fires to an opaque white. The result will be overglaze painting.

Note that this overglaze can be fired at a much lower temperature than underglaze, as you do not need to melt the top surface.

Mme. Jeannette Aubrière decorating plates.

Glazing with a brush. The various containers hold glazes ready for use.

GLAZING THE BODY OF THE PIECE

Buy your colours according to reference numbers, since grinding techniques and the addition of various products, such as minium, have modified colours considerably.

The colours need only to be diluted with water and size, which is usually a concentrate of seaweeds, obtainable commercially in a powder form called *alginate*.

The glaze can be applied to the piece:

1 By brush — taking care to double up in those parts which need thick application.

2 By dipping — the piece should be dipped in a bath or, preferably, glaze should be poured over it.

Glazing with a brush on a decorative work on the floor.

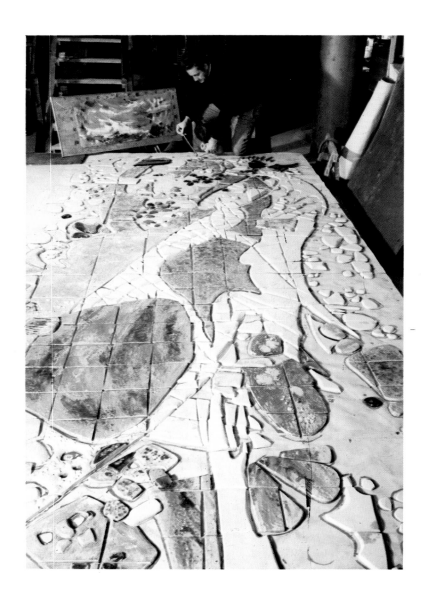

Glazing a plate with a spray-gun.

3   By spray-gun — this method is most regularly used, giving the best commercial results.

4   Sgraffito — another decorative technique which is done by covering the body of the piece before it is fired. The piece is covered with a thin layer of slip of a different colour: red, black or yellow on white, for example. If a design is scratched on this, the original colour is revealed and the result is very effective. The ancient Greeks brought this technique to perfection.

Glazing a decorative plaque with a brush.

5 FIRING OF GLOST PIECES

A glazed piece should not touch either the walls of the kiln or any neighbouring pieces, and should be raised on the oven shelves by triangular blocks of earthenware.

The pieces must be dry before placing them in the oven, and firing is done in two stages: the heat is low at first, then increased rapidly. Glazes for commercial earthenware can generally be fired between 920° and 980°. Temperature control can be arranged in two ways:

a) With a pyrometer, which indicates the internal temperature of the oven, avoiding any checking problems.

b) With melting indicators. These are cones which melt at given temperatures. For example, earthenware is fired when cones 0.9 and 0.10 melt. The cones are placed behind the inspection window in the oven. Before closing the oven you should ensure that the cones are visible. The cones only indicate the temperature when they melt, so you should check the firing process very carefully.

The inside of a kiln prepared for glazing. Note how carefully the pieces are arranged, so as not to touch each other.

RE-FIRING

If a piece is badly fired or the colour is not good, you can re-fire it as long as it is not broken, since repairs create difficulties. The defective parts should be generously re-glazed as the glaze does not spread during firing.

We have limited ourselves here to what is generally known as ceramics, that is, glazed earthenware with coloured glazes applied to the body. Stoneware needs a much more expensive oven because of the higher temperatures demanded. The technique is very interesting but, while the greys and browns can be very attractive, there are fewer possibilities of using decoration and colours. The only colours possible are blue cobalt oxide, red ferrous oxides, a chalk-based white, and black manganese and ferrous oxides.

Porcelain is too technical a subject for us to discuss in a few pages. Equipment is also very costly, and, if the pieces are good, decoration (glazes applied at a low temperature to pieces which have already been fired) is often used only to conceal faults. Fine pieces are usually white with simple gold lines of decoration applied at a low temperature.

However, there is an industry which prospers on decorating white porcelain, bought regardless of quality from manufacturers.

The technique is similar to overglaze painting; the painting is raised and offers certain possiblities.

Firing is carried out at a low temperature — between 600° and 700°.

Amateurs could therefore be interested in this technique as impressive results can be obtained with little equipment, the main problem being that of the kiln.

As a general rule, work with care and keep a log book noting work details, the origins of your materials, and the mixtures you use.

Causes of accidents:

1   Raw materials may be:

   a) impure (plaster in the clay);

   b) incorrect granulation (too coarse or too fine);

   c) incorrect mixtures.

2   Pieces insufficiently dry — the biscuit base may crack and the glaze have a rough surface.

3   Dust preventing the glaze from adhering to the piece.

4   Too rapid an increase of temperature in the oven.

You should, therefore, retrace your steps carefully, and discard any faulty material in order to achieve successful results.

Original French text by
Mme Nicolas Untersteller,
née **Hélène Delaroche**
Member of the *Salon d'Automne.*
Chevalier des Arts et Lettres.
Creator of numerous frescoes and mural
decorations.
(among others, the church of Saintes-
Anges de Saint-Maurice de Gravelle, in
collaboration with Nicolas Untersteller,
her husband).

Decorating paving stones

Fresco decoration is often impractical to create for several reasons.

— Situation: the decoration needs to start at floor-level and consequently is exposed to damage outside from bicycles and tyres and, inside buildings, from bumps by chairs, furniture, etc.

— The walls themselves may not be suitable for mortar application.

Large scale ceramics are similar to frescoes in many ways. I refer here only to mural ceramics which have paving stones as a base.

These stones are mostly made from *Volvic* — blocks of lava taken from quarries and often cut on site to the necessary measurements.

Of varying grain and density, these stones are more or less regularly pitted and are chosen to obtain different effects.

The stones are heavy: a stone measuring 30cm x 30cm x 1cm thickness weighs about four pounds. They should be laid flat on the ground and painted while you are standing on them. They are very solid, unless they are incorrectly laid.

The paving stones should be numbered before being laid on the ground as they will be mixed up during transport or firing. A simple system can be used: the horizontal stones should have letters and the vertical ones numbers, or vice versa, according to the size of the work. In this way, each stone will have a letter or number painted on the reverse and they can then be easily put into order.

The cartoon of the design is prepared as for a fresco.

The cartoon is marked with squares or rectangles corresponding to the paving stones, and is placed vertically in front of the stones. The design is transferred to the stones by copying it, using the squares as a guide.

The drawing should be executed in charcoal, or with a brush impregnated with a colour you wish to keep in the finished work.

The colours are ceramic paints, bought from specialist suppliers and fired at 970°. They are dangerous to inhale as they contain lead.

You will need several china or plastic bowls to dilute the colours into liquid pastes.

The brushes used should be the same as for oil or fresco painting. A large amount of white should be prepared as this is used as an undercoat. The powder is diluted in water, with a little gum tragacanth added to prevent the dry paint from disintegrating into dust when the stones are moved. To obtain white, the colour must be thickly applied, and every shade of grey can be obtained by using this white in dilution.

It is important to know that certain colours cover more than others, and that certain of them need white as an undercoat to give them body. If painted directly on to the stone, they will have a dark, greyish tone, and the reds in particular need to be applied thickly. If used as a wash, they disappear or leave a sulphur yellow trace.

You should be aware of possible reactions in order to make suitable compensations.

Fig. 1

Fig. 2

Fig. 3

You can paint a medium-thick layer of white over the stones, allow it to dry, and then paint the design over the white with a ceramic paint. Although the colours you wish to apply over the white may be diluted with water and gum tragacanth, I prefer to dilute them in turpentine with a few drops of oil to fix them. (See Fig. 1.) In Fig. 2, you see the container of oil, turpentine, the colour chart and some bags of colour.

Fig. 3, 4 and 5 show that you can also trace the drawing straight onto the stones in charcoal, without any preparation. You then apply the diluted whites in the necessary areas, and also where other colours applied over them will need to be luminous. Those areas of stone remaining natural will of course have no colour applied. If it contains ferrous oxide, the lava stone (Volvic) often acquires a reddish tone during firing.

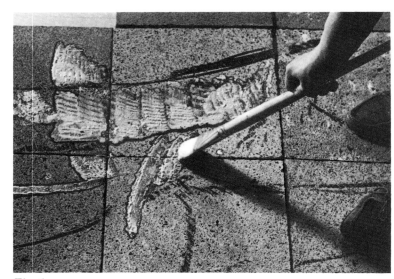

Fig. 4

The rapid drying of the colours presents one of the difficulties of application. If they are dark, they become much paler, and bear no relation to the colours obtained after firing. For example, the darkest brown becomes pale yellow.

When you have placed the stones carefully in the kiln, the temperature should be raised gradually to 970° for about one night. The stones should be allowed to cool before you open the kiln.

Then comes the surprise and pleasure of seeing how your design has turned out. A clear drawing with positive colours becomes even clearer and more positive; the beauty of the lava stone appears through the colours, and you are anxious to piece the whole design together.

You should allow a professional to lay the stones, either in cement or plaster, or with an epoxy-resin glue, allowing the joins to be visible.

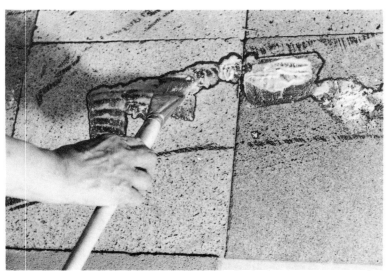

Fig. 5

Original French text by
Albert le Normand
Teacher of fresco painting at the *Ecole
Nationale Supérieure des Beaux-Arts* in
Paris.
Teacher of chromatology at the *Ecole
Estienne* in Paris (Graphic Art section).
Member of the jury of the *Prix de Rome
de Peinture.*
Advisor at the Centre of Oriental Music
Studies (Institute of Musicology at the
University of Paris).
Chevalier des Arts et Lettres.

Mme Nicolas Untersteller,
née **Hélène Delaroche**
Member of the *Salon d'Automne.*
Chevalier des Arts et Lettres.
Creator of numerous frescoes and
mural decorations
(among others, the church of Saintes-
Anges de Saint-Maurice de Gravelle, in
collaboration with Nicolas Untersteller,
her husband).

Frescoes

The word *fresco* comes from the Italian word "fresco", meaning fresh, and has for many centuries described the painting applied to a surface freshly laid on a wall. In strict painting terms, the use of the word fresco should be reserved for this technique and not applied to any mural decoration, as is now generally the case.

A description of the fresco technique follows, and will explain why the use of the word should be limited.

The fresh covering, the mortar, made of slaked lime and sand, is applied to the wall and then covered shortly afterwards with additional layers of mineral colours made from pastes containing varying amounts of liquid.

These layers of paste are fixed to the mortar by a thin layer of crystalline carbonate of lime, which is formed by carbonic acid from the air combining with the calcium hydrate of the mortar. This layer of crystalline carbonate of lime or *lime crust,* constantly rises to the surface through evaporation, and hardens very rapidly.

To understand the mysterious technique of the fresco, you must realise the importance of this waterproof crystalline covering which protects the mortar when it has been formed. Colours applied after this formation take on a rather white appearance when they are dry, and become a powder which falls away when touched.

This waterproof layer must be broken down by light pressure from a trowel. The moisture comes to the surface again so that a new layer of paint can be applied which will again be penetrated by the calcium hydrate and fixed by combining with carbonic acid from the air.

This combination of metallic oxides with the calcium hydrate and the carbonic acid produces practically a layer of marble. When the painter, at the end of his day's work, presses hard with his trowel on the work he has finished and sees a slight vapour escape, giving life to his colours and transforming them into a thin layer of marble, he feels a sense of exultation.

At the beginning of the 16th century, this technique, which had been the means of expression for the painters of ancient Egypt, Etruria, Rome, Byzantium and the entire Middle Ages, fell into disuse and was completely forgotten. When Puvis de Chavannes, wishing to paint frescoes, sought out the technique in the texts of Vasari and Cennino Cennini, he failed to make it work.

It was only in 1858 that Victor Mottez translated the "Book of Art" by Cennino Cennini, as published in Italian in 1821 by the Cavaliere Tambroni.

Paul Baudoin was passionately interested in frescoes and created the first studio for fresco painting at the Ecole des Beaux-Arts. In 1914 he wrote a treatise on the fresco.

Baudoin, like Mottez, failed to find details of the original techniques in the old texts. He taught how to use watercolours on the fresh mortar, a technique which existed to produce certain effects, but which was only a small part of the art of fresco painting.

By studying and copying the frescoes of Pompei, which looked like marble, and the work of Giotto, Chirlandaio, Pintorrichio, and the Roman frescoes, painters became certain that the rich colours of these frescoes were not due to retouching, as Paul Baudoin thought, but the result of a powerful technique. This was finally confirmed by a Roumanian, Costin Petresco, son of one of the last Balkan zoographers. He studied the genuine tradition in his youth by accompanying his father on visits to convents and monasteries. He lectured in France in about 1930, taught at Lyon, and, in 1932, published a treatise on his experiences, which included invaluable information on the techniques used by his father and companions.

The durability of the fresco depends on the quality of its support. If the wall is solid and free of saltpetre, then it makes no difference if it is of stone, brick or cement. The fresco can even stand up to rain on the painted surface. But penetrating damp and saltpetre spell disaster.

A brick wall provides the best support, since the moisture of the mortar is sufficiently absorbed to allow it to adhere easily. On cement however, which is practically non-absorbent, the mortar takes many hours before it is ready. Mortar which is applied to cement in the evening can still be too fresh to work on the following morning.

To ensure that the mortar adheres to the wall perfectly, it is an excellent idea (and essential in the case of a cement wall) to first use a very liquid mortar of hydrate of lime and sand, applying it to the wall with a small broom.

To help the mortar to adhere, the wall can also be roughened with a pickaxe. If a wall is of rather impermeable cement, the best solution is to use the liquid mortar described above and then add a mortar consisting of two parts coarse sand to one part of lime. This should be allowed to dry before applying the mortar which will be used for the fresco.

The life of a fresco also depends on the type of colours used. Lime will completely destroy colours with an aniline or organic base. The best colours are mostly metallic oxides and silicates, the most reliable being the ochres and earth colours:

yellow ochre,
red ochre,
Pozzuoli red (which produces a very pretty pink),
earth reds,
natural sienna and burnt sienna (the latter sometimes sets badly and powders off),
umber, natural and burnt,
cadmium yellow, red and purple,
cerulean blue,
cobalt blue,
ultramarine blue (not always very resistant — may bleach out in the polluted air of cities),
cobalt green,
emerald green,
lime green,
Mars brown and red,
slate grey (powdered slate is difficult to use mixed with white),
oak black (produces a magnificent bluish grey, like indigo),
vine black and peach black,
soot black (not advisable due to its intensity).

Certain finely powdered colours are insoluble in water unless they are previously soaked in vinegar.

The white colour known as "bianco Sangiovanni", or St John's white, and used in former times, was made from lime which was soaked, dried in the sun and crushed several times until it was completely inert. We have, however, found it simpler to buy carbonate of lime from the chemist, as it is completely inert and gives a beautiful white.

Colours are sold in powder form in packets varying in weight from 50g to 1 kilo. Some colours are up to 40 times more expensive than others if they come from specialized makers who guarantee them resistant to lime and light.

The colour mixtures are prepared dry, then enough water is added to make a liquid paste. When a large cow-hair brush is dipped into the colour, it should, when lifted out, allow a few drops to fall off.

To check on the colour, you should draw the brush across a piece of umber. The colour will dry immediately. However, personal observation is important. You will notice that some tones get paler while others remain strong. Burnt umber produces very powerful tones.

Preparation of the wall by roughening with a pick.

Wetting the wall with a bowl in readiness for work.

Sieving the sand.

Mixing, dampening and pounding the mortar in the trough.

Application of the mortar on the damp wall.

Smoothing the mortar with the mortar-board.

Applying the coating on the fresh mortar.

Smoothing the coating.

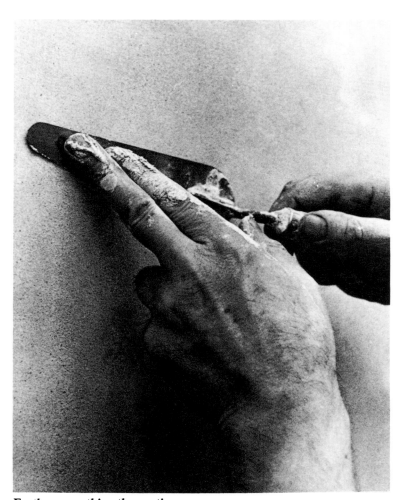

Further smoothing the coating.

Pouncing the tracing on the smoothed coating.

I-194

Detail of a mural called "The Three Graces" by A. Le Normand.

Materials should be ready — sand, lime and tools. You should choose a river sand which feels gritty. Quarry sand is not advisable, and beach sand should definitely not be used. Check that the sand is clean and without any earth, especially if it has been stored outside, where it can be dirtied by cats and dogs. It is wise to wash the sand, put it in a sieve and then dry it.

It is now possible to buy inert, finely sieved lime for the fresco, or you can render lime inert yourself. You take pieces of quicklime and plunge them in water for a few moments in a wire sieve. As soon as you remove the lime from the water the pieces break up into a dazzling white powder. This should then be carefully sieved. (It is wise to protect your nose and mouth with a mask and your eyes with glasses, as the lime dust is very caustic). Remove any remaining pieces, as these, not being inert, could, even months later, explode in the mortar. Small holes would then develop with disastrous results.

To be sure of avoiding these problems, you should put either the purchased or the treated powdered lime in a large barrel where you soak it with a few buckets of water, mixing it well with a long stick and allowing it to rest, protected from the air, by covering the barrel with a sheet of nylon. After some weeks you will find extremely clear water covering a thick paste of completely inert lime. Remove the water carefully and replace it, when you have taken out the amount of lime you need for the mortar. Slaked lime can be kept for months (or, even better, aged for years in a special storage pit), as long as it is covered with water. Otherwise, it will absorb carbonic acid from the air and slowly return to limestone.

If possible, place your supply of sand near the wall, in a sheltered position. Have a heap of fairly finely sieved sand for the first layer of mortar and one of very finely sieved sand for the second layer. There must be no pebbles present to spoil the application of the mortar. You will need several hods for the mortar, especially if the fresco is large. Two large, two smaller and one very small hod are advisable.

You will need several containers to work in comfort — thirty, for example, in varying sizes. Large white china bowls are practical as they can be easily washed. Square plastic containers are also suitable, and lighter. Large deep plates could be used. While working, you should have clean containers ready in reserve in case you wish to dilute a colour for glazing, or vary a shade.

The wall must be well soaked the day before you apply the mortar. The degree of soaking should depend on the absorption of the wall (bricks, for example, need to be saturated). A wall which is insufficiently wet will dry too quickly and the mortar will not adhere. If there is saltpetre in the wall, you will have to build a thin brick partition wall with a few centimetres between the two to allow the air to circulate. You will then apply the fresco to the brick wall. The mortar used in the latter must be made from lime and not plaster.

When the wall has been well prepared, you add the first coat of thin liquid mortar. You are then ready to apply the mortar for the fresco.

Tools you will need:

— a large, short, non-flexible trowel.
— a longer flexible trowel to apply the mortar.
— a large metallic and rectangular mortar-board or float is also excellent to apply the mortar.
— a large rectangular wooden mortar-board or float to smooth large surfaces of mortar.
— a very small wooden mortar-board or float, narrower at one end, to integrate the new layer of mortar with that applied the previous day.
— a pliable metal smoothing trowel for polishing.
— two similar measuring bowls for the sand and lime, or, even better, two large ladles (A ladle will allow you to take the lime from the barrel without putting your fingers in it. You must be careful with the lime, as it is still caustic. You will, in any case, need to touch the mortar often while painting the fresco, and the grains of sand in it can be very painful in any cracks in your fingers.).
— two or three buckets.
— a very large round brush to wet the wall.
— a vaporiser to moisten the join between mortar painted on different days without letting water run over it.

You now have at hand the sifted sand, the lime in a barrel, and a large trough. Let us start by making the mortar, which should be prepared two or three days before work begins.

The wall should already have been covered, two or three weeks previously, with a rough cast or scratch coat of thin liquid mortar composed of 2 parts coarse sand to 1 part hydrate of lime. When this was dry, you should have already applied a brown coat, a layer of coarse mortar composed of 2 parts coarse sand to 1 part of slaked lime.

We want to produce a fresco with a smooth, marble-like surface: we shall, therefore, now add two further layers of mortar, one, the sand finish, very early in the morning and the second, or *intonaco,* some time later.

In the proportion of 5 parts of sand to 3 of lime, we shall put into the trough:

    30 measures of sand (finely sieved),
    18 measures of lime.

As the lime is in paste form, it would seem impossible at first to make mortar by using the dry sand. Don't be discouraged. By mixing the lime and sand well with a trowel and by adding a few glasses of water little by little, you will obtain a superb paste. This mortar should be held in reserve in a large container, either a trough or non-rusting washing tank with a well-fitting cover. You will find that, in due course, the mortar has become thick and covered with a little water. Take as much mortar as you need and mix it without adding any water. You will soon obtain a pliable consistency.

The second layer of mortar, the intonaco, on which you will paint the fresco, should be prepared in the same way, but in reverse proportions: 3 parts of sand to 5 parts of lime. The sand should be very finely sieved and the lime taken from the bottom of the barrel, where it is thickest. Do not add any water. As the proportion of lime is greater you will obtain a very pliable mortar.

You should mark on the wall the limit of the area you wish to paint in a day, giving an extra hand's breadth for good measure. Place a trowel-load of mortar on the metal mortar-board. Press it firmly against the wall with both hands, starting at the bottom. Do not hesitate or reduce the pressure. Refill the mortar-board and cover the area you intend to paint in a day. Next, smooth it over with the wooden mortar-board, which should be quite wet, but not dripping with water. You should use semi-circular movements from right to left over the entire surface, taking care to apply constant, firm pressure, otherwise you will have pockets of air beneath the mortar-board. If these develop anyway, you should pierce them with a pin and smooth them over again. This operation should be carried out swiftly to avoid drawing the lime to the surface. The mortar should have the colour and texture of a large piece of natural linen.

Later, when you cannot press your finger into the mortar, you should apply the second coat of mortar, on which you will paint. The second coat will be softer and contain more lime than the first, and should be applied very thinly (not more than 1 cm in thickness, whereas the first coat can be 1.5 cm thick). Applied and smoothed skillfully and rapidly, the second coat of mortar will be ready for painting when the finger does not penetrate when pressed lightly on it and no water rises to the surface.

In spite of natural impatience, especially if it is late in the day, you should avoid painting on mortar when it is too fresh. Even the softest brush will disturb the mortar, and the colours, mixed with the mortar, will become whitish and unattractive. (If this happens, you should smooth it over with the trowel and wait for the mortar to be well set before starting again.)

Let us assume that the mortar is ready for painting. Place your large scale sketch, or cartoon, where you can see it easily. Your colours should be ready in their pots, with numbers or letters for easy recognition. Your brushes should be in a bucket of water. Have another bucket of water ready to wash them and a further container of clean water for diluting colours.

Take the tracing of the section you intend to complete in the day. (This drawing has been perforated with an embroidery wheel.) You will need a helper to hold the drawing in both hands while you tap, or *pounce,* the drawing with a small bag of fine cheese cloth or muslin filled with powdered colour (red or blue umber are the favourites). The powder goes through the holes in the drawing. You can then subsequently retrace the drawing with a pointed sable brush.

A better process is to copy the drawing with charcoal on the reverse of the tracing paper. You then press the paper against the mortar and pass your hand lightly over it so that the charcoal is imprinted on the damp surface.

Next, the metal smoothing trowel is passed over all the mortar. This is very delicate work, and must be stopped immediately if you feel the surface is too wet. No lime should come to the surface, only transparent moisture. Painting can then begin. The main colours should be painted in, taking care not to graze the mortar. You must then wait for the colours to take. By touching them very lightly, you can feel if a slightly rough crystalline crust has formed, and you should check that no colour is deposited on your finger.

At this stage, the important process of polishing is begun. Using the pliable trowel (and waiting if you see the drawing becoming distorted under the pressure of the trowel), you use a light pressure to break the crust, allowing the humidity underneath to come to the surface.

Once you have done this, you should hastily apply another layer of colour, as the dampness will lose no time in absorbing carbonic acid from the air and changing into impermeable carbonate of lime, preventing subsequent colours from becoming fixed. The colours should therefore be applied as quickly as possible so as to form a screen between the calcium hydrate in the mortar and the carbonic acid in the air, delaying the calcification of the former. You can then continue to paint for some time, applying very light coats of paint, using glazes of colour in the most wonderful uninhibited way. The colours do not run on the surface of the mortar as in water-colours, since they are gently absorbed, and the brush achieves a more exact effect than in oil or water-colour painting. This freedom is, however, relatively short-lived, and lighter and lighter glazes are used. The trowel may be applied again to areas where you wish to continue to work. If you leave the fresco in this state, it will remain matt.

It is wise to pass the trowel again over the entire area at least once so as to ensure that all the colours are properly fixed. To obtain the brilliance, feel and appearance of marble, you can, at the end of the day, pass the trowel over the surface several times, applying light pressure. The polished fresco will appear darker, as the colours are protected by the crystalline film, and the mortar will not crack, even when pressed hard. The fresco treated in this way is very resistant to adverse conditions. It should be remembered that not only has lime carbonate been formed on the surface, but also a real cement, formed by the layers of coloured clay and hydrated silicates of aluminium which have bonded with the lime in the mortar and the silica dioxide from the sand.

The work is very demanding, lasting as it does from early morning to late evening if the mortar is slow to set, and conditions are tough, as you are standing on scaffolding covered with lime and sand. Nevertheless, it can be very rewarding.

It is always difficult to blend one day's work with the next. It is best to use the darker paints for continuing. You can obtain a clean join by using a putty-knife to cut the mortar and obtain a bevelled edge. You place the cutting edge of the knife on the line you wish to cut and you remove the mortar by pulling the knife towards you. You should do the cutting as soon as you have finished painting. The next day you sprinkle water over a few centimetres of the previous day's painting at the join. Care should be taken to avoid allowing water impregnated with mortar to run over the painted area, as the caustic lime in it will leave unsightly, indelible marks. New mortar should therefore be applied with a little gap between it and the previous day's work to avoid touching it when using the mortar-board. When the new area of mortar has been applied and you are waiting for it to set, you should fill in the gap with a very small trowel and the pointed mortar-board. This needs to be done carefully, and it is better to do it yourself. With the trowel, you polish the join and the few centimetres of painting from the previous day. The damp mortar will react well to the polishing and you can eliminate the join. If you use the correct pressure, there will be no crack visible when the mortar dries.

Notes:

Depending on the character of the building where you are working, you can use several variations in technique to achieve different results.

You can use water-colours on mortar which has only been smoothed. You should paint rapidly and not let the paint get sticky. For this technique, you can use mortar with sand containing grains of equal size, obtained by sieving several times and discarding those grains which are either too large or too small. A good mortar results, and you could keep some of the mortar to use as highlights. Some quick work with the trowel at the end of the day is very helpful in fixing the colours and shades.

You can also use rather thick water-colours, and paint rapidly on fine polished mortar, leaving it when you have gone over it with the trowel. The mortar appears beneath the colours and makes them brilliant. You should judge the thickness of the colours very carefully.

A polished fresco can be further polished with white wax. It then becomes darker.

One small practical hint: a damp covering placed a few centimetres away from the mortar which has been painted, but not finished during the day, will delay calcification by keeping the same air in front of the fresco. You can then continue painting the next day.

Fresco by Mme. Nicolas Untersteller.

Original French text by
Pierre Castelnau
Honorary Gold Medallist of French
Artists.
Lauréat de l'Institut de France.
Maxime David Prize 1946.
Rowland Prize 1962.
Levallois Silver Medallist.
City of Bordeaux, Bronze Medal.
Salon Violet Bronze Medal, 1962.
Bronze Medallist of the Prefecture of the
Seine.
Bronze Medallist of the General Council
of the Seine.
Silver Medallist of Art, Science and
Letters.

Myriam de Monneron
Member of the *Salon des Artistes Français.*
Honorary Gold Medallist.
Maxime David Prize.
Rowland Prize.
Lauréate de l'Institut.

Miniatures

The word miniature comes from "minium" (red lead): the first illuminations were carried out with minium on the parchment of sacred books.

Letter illumination gradually gave way to full pages, painted in gouache and heightened with fine gold, representing scenes from the Bible, the lives of the saints and scenes of everyday life.

In the 18th century, water-colour and gouache painting was performed on the lids of ivory cosmetic jars. It was noticed that flesh tints acquired a marvellous transparency when produced by water-colours on such a support.

Ivory was gradually substituted for parchment and vellum. Nowadays, water-colours are practically always used instead of gouache, which is employed only for certain highlights and pure whites (spots of light reflected in eyes, fabrics, lace).

This art is always on a small scale, because of course the pieces of ivory never exceed certain dimensions (elephant's tusks).

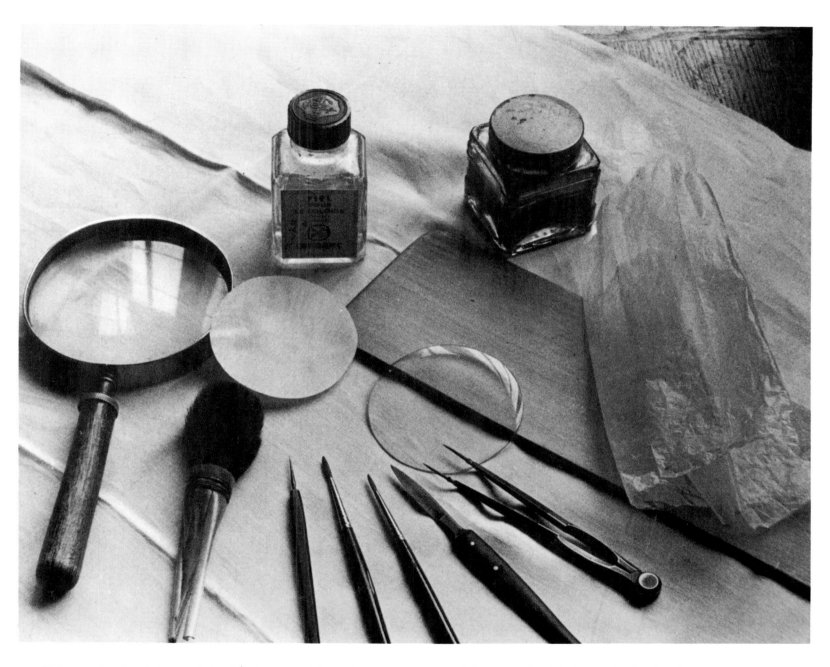

— Take a sheet of ivory 4 to 5/10 mm thick and sawn lengthwise off the tusk. Select ivory which shows the fewest possible veins, particularly in the centre.

— Palette: a large ivory sheet 4 to 5 mm in thickness.

— A small wooden board covered with paper, for putting the ivory on during the work.

— Sandpaper of different grain, even well-used, for rubbing down the ivory.

— Gum arabic (thin and very light-coloured).

— Sable brushes of different thicknesses, but always with a good point.

— A magnifying glass to check work in progress or completed.

— A scalpel for scraping thick parts.

— A needle attached to a handle for removing dust.

— A large squirrel-hair brush, for dusting purposes.

— Dividers for measurements and a compass with a pencil point for drawing circles.

— A piece of bent plate glass of the required size to protect the miniature.

— Goldbeater's skin to fix behind the finished work.

Three qualities of glass are used:

— shaped glass: bent over a wood fire,

— fine glass: ground after bending,

— french glass: this is bent and ground, but completely transparent, without any bluishness. This type of glass is the best and dearest.

Sometimes the glass over old miniatures becomes opaque, in which case the glass simply has to be changed.

Enlargement of detail from Pierre Castelnau's miniature, reproduced overleaf.

Water-colours making up Pierre Castelnau's palette.

Veronese green	Naples yellow	Mars brown
Ash green	Light cadmium yellow	Ventian red
Bladder green	Indian yellow	Madder brown
Cobalt green	Cadmium orange	Vermilion
Hooker's green	Yellow ochre	Saturn red
Prussian blue	Natural sienna	Carmine
Ultramarine	Burnt sienna	Madder pink
Cobalt blue	Natural sepia	Cherry madder
Indigo	Coloured sepia	Burnt carmine
Cerulean blue	Blackish-brown (bistre)	Lamp black
Ash blue		
Mars violet		
Cobalt violet		
Payne's grey		

N.B.   As they age, the pinks become effaced and the blues come out more strongly. This must be allowed for during the work. Use as little blue as possible in flesh tints, giving preference to cobalt violet which, when Veronese green is superimposed, produces very fine bluish greys.

WORKING

Cutting.   First of all, the miniaturist cuts out the selected sheet of ivory to the exact shape he needs, always reckoning in millimetres, tracing the outline with dividers if it is round, and using the glass which is to cover the miniature if it is oval.

This is an extremely delicate operation because, when using shears for cutting, you must make sure that the ivory does not split along the grain. To prevent this, cutting is performed at an angle to the grain of the ivory (which can always be detected by the slight streaks on the surface); when necessary, the piece of ivory must be rotated to facilitate cutting.

If absolutely necessary, the ivory can be immersed for several minutes in cold water until it becomes highly transparent, when it cuts as easily as a fingernail. Nevertheless, follow the preceding instructions. (See the sketch on the right.)

Then dry the ivory in a press.

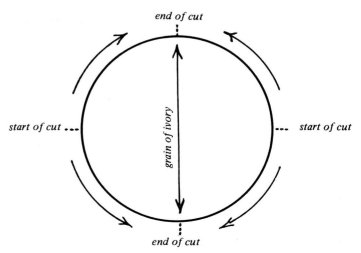

I-203

A word must be added about the use of water, since the miniaturist does not use much of it, as a rule preferring spittle! In this way, he gradually learns how to gauge the minimum liquid for mixing with the gum arabic. His glass of water will be used mainly for cleaning his brushes.

Once the finished drawing has been transferred, the artist comes to the actual painting work, using his colours and the gum arabic as a binder.

Use a larger amount of gum arabic for the large surfaces (hair, clothing, backgrounds, etc.). Distribute the gum (mixed with colour) with the tip of the brush skimming the ivory, until it is almost fully dried, applying only the slightest pressure at the places which are to remain lighter.

In other cases, work with the tip of the brush or by quick successive coats on a dry lower layer.

It is preferable not to mix your colours on the palette, but on the ivory itself; the colours are transparent, and they can be superimposed finely until the required effect is obtained. When the work is completed, the brush strokes must be invisible. Work can be performed using a magnifying glass. Extremely fine operations require satisfactory diffuse lighting, without hardness, to save your eyes. It must never be electric lighting (even blue lighting), which changes the colours.

Polishing. Once the piece of ivory has been cut up, it is polished with a rotary movement, using progressively finer emery papers (the paper is rolled around a stopper placed lengthwise). The face which is to be treated is carefully polished. Polishing is very important and calls for some patience, since the ivory was sawn, and streaks are visible. They must be completely eliminated, since the colours would accumulate in greater thicknesses in the streaks and would be visible in the completed work.

Working with the brush. When the ivory is well-polished, place it on the workboard; slide the Indian ink drawing between the ivory and the board. Reproduce the drawing on the ivory, using a sable brush in a neutral water-colour (a mixture of cobalt blue and vermilion, for instance); never use pencil. The ivory must be so placed that its grain runs north-south in relation to the artist.

You can also start to paint directly on the ivory, but it is preferable to have a drawing to which you can refer, if only to get the setting exactly right at the start of each session.

If gouache is required for a highlight or a more opaque surface, neither the same brushes nor the same palette must be used (sable brushes for water-colours and squirrel brushes for gouache).

Finishing. Before the glass is placed over the miniature, examine it through a magnifying glass. Gently remove the dust, using (for instance) a sewing-machine needle fitted on-to a handle. Scrape away excessively thick portions of paint, using the scalpel, and finally dust down using a thick, very soft squirrel-hair brush which is reserved exclusively for this purpose. You must never blow on the miniature to remove the dust, as you might be inclined to do, since the slightest drop of saliva would stain the work. When handling the ivory, use paper, since your fingers might make it greasy. If you should make a greasy mark with your fingers, use "ox-gall" mixed with the colour, or clean using alcohol at 90°.

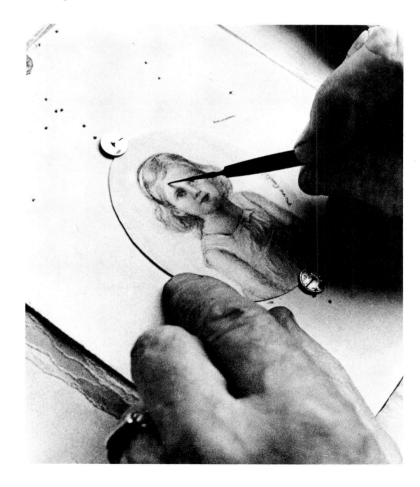

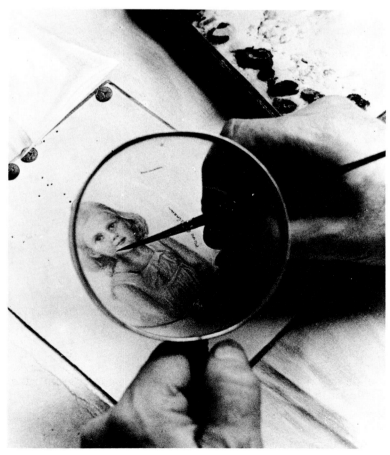

When the miniature is finished, glue it onto a paper selected with reference to the effect of transparency to be obtained and the overall tonality required: either very white, or slightly yellowish. People used to use a "wisp", which was a sheet of silver paper: some old miniatures show grey stains due to its oxidation. To restore the freshness of the miniature, just remove the silver paper and substitute white paper.

To fix the new paper, place the miniature on it, trace its outline with a crayon and then withdraw the miniature. Coat the edge of the paper inside the traced area with gum arabic. Place the ivory on this and place the whole in a press or under a pile of books. Then cut the paper all round, taking care not to touch the ivory.

APPLYING GOLDBEATER'S SKIN:

This is an important operation for sealing and therefore protecting and preserving the miniature; it holds the glass and miniature together to prevent the entry of dust and damp.

Cut out the goldbeater's skin to an area much larger than the actual format; place on it the miniature covered with the glass; brush on gum arabic (fairly thick, but in very small quantities) all around before folding the goldbeater's skin down on to the glass (about 1.5 to 2 mm) so that it sticks satisfactorily to the perimeter. Once it is properly glued, cut off the surplus skin. The miniature is then completed and ready for its frame.

N.B. *A miniature must never be cleaned with water, but it can be cleaned with alcohol at 90°. Neither must the glass of a framed miniature be cleaned with water, since a little moisture might enter the miniature and spoil the work.*

Portrait of Gilles Colleville. A miniature by Myriam de Monneron.

Original French text by
Georges Delplanque
H.C. Gold Medallist and member of the
Comité du Salon des Artistes Français
and of the *Salon Comparaisons.*
Chevalier of the Legion of Honour.

Andrée Gavens
Painter of the frescoes at the Chapelle des
Carmes, Avon.

Murals

ANDRÉE GAVENS

Of all mural painting techniques, there can be no doubt that the noblest, longest-lasting, as well as the most difficult and the one nowadays least practised, is fresco painting. It is the genre preferred by any painter who has ambitions in the direction of large-scale architectural decoration.

In everyday use, the word *fresco* is applied to any mural painting (we speak of the frescoes of Saint-Savin, the frescoes of Lascaux, the frescoes of the Ajanta caves), and rightly so if we mean painting with the use of water on walls or vaults. Actually, the term *fresco* strictly refers to painting using pure water and performed on fresh mortar. However, there are various ways of painting on dry wall surfaces and, in general, such techniques may be described by the term *fresco secco*.

The paintings at Assissi, Saint-Savin and Arezzo are certainly frescoes, while the Indian wall paintings were carried out on dry renderings, but it often takes a practised eye to detect the difference.

Whilst it remains true that painting on fresh mortar is superior to any other method, this is not always possible. We may therefore settle for painting on dry mortar, cement, stone or plaster, or even on such surfaces as timber, canvas or paper.

Fresco secco entails painting using water with an added fixative, such as glue, wax or casein (only fresh mortar supports firmly ground colours diluted solely with pure water). This method of painting, performed on a dry wall, is not an imitation of frescoes, but is authentic in its own right and has produced great works of art. Indian treatises on painting explain the use of buffalo hide glue to fix colours on dry walls "which may last a hundred years". In fact, these paintings are several centuries old; they were carried out on stone or mortar renderings. In Central Europe, use was made of cheese glue or casein on plaster renderings covering walls or timber panels. Elsewhere, the use of wax is recommended for dry mortars or woodwork.

Very careful preparations are indispensable in every case. First of all, the surface to be secco-painted must be completely dry, smooth and firm. If it is a mortar rendering, it must be prepared as carefully as for frescoes: two parts of perfectly clean, sieved sand, and one part of slaked lime, slightly wetted and smoothed with a trowel as evenly as possible. If it is a plaster wall, it must be in good condition: smooth, and without cracks. If it is a wooden surface, it must be coated several times, glued using animal skin glue, and covered with several very thin layers of very even plaster. If it is a canvas panel, it must be of a strong, close texture, preferably herringbone, glued, and covered with a coating of whiting (Spanish white) which is smoothed with a knife to cover the surface evenly. The quality of the support of the painting ensures its long life and also prevents the performance of the work from being impeded. If painting is carried out on a large surface of paper, it must be firm, without grain, and attached to a strong gauze.

If it is decided to paint a wall or ceiling, vaulted or flat, on a dry coating, the work will still be performed in accordance with the general laws of frescoes; more or less the same thing applies if painting is performed on a wooden, canvas or paper surface. All that matters is to observe the spirit of mural painting — i.e., ensuring that the painting suits and complements the architecture, and does not merely provide a decorative element, or a picture.

The advantage of a dry wall over a "fresh" wall is that there is no need to do the work piecemeal in order to finish the prepared surface in a few hours. The cartoon can be spread over the whole wall and rubbed down, the whole composition can be designed, and even the "verdaccio" (a light preparation of an even tone: ochre or terre verte) can be applied beneath the painting. The work can be distributed over larger surfaces, and retouching is possible to a certain extent. All the same, just like frescoes, secco work must be carried out quickly with only a small amount of retouching if it is to retain all its freshness. The drawing must be enlarged to full size (by squaring) on to strong paper and pricked out. (Brown paper is more suitable than drawing paper for this as it is more flexible, and strong tracing paper is best if you are painting on canvas or paper.) When the cartoon has been attached to the wall by adhesive plaster, a fabric bag (a knotted sock) filled with lamp black is lightly knocked against the cartoon, so that the lamp black passes through the pricked-out holes and fixes a thin outline on the wall. When the paper has been removed, the outline is retraced very lightly with a brush or with sepia, and the surface is painted with ochre or terre verte (verdaccio) with very broad brush strokes, so as to bring out the general shape of the image. Almost the same colours are used as with frescoes: earths or metal oxides (good quality prepared powdered ones can be obtained). They must be wetted with pure water, ground using a muller on thick glass, and mixed into a thoroughly smooth, homogeneous paste. You then fill a closable jar with the amount needed and remove the amount you require every day in a shell. A thick glass plate will do as a palette.

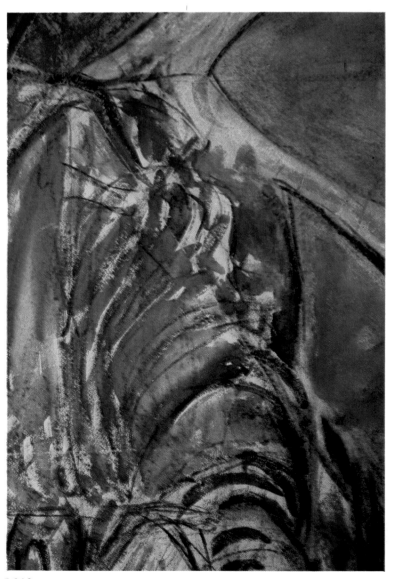

You do not create any shadows, but this does not mean that you cannot use a variety of shades. There is a method of bringing all the colours into play by superimposing fine streaks of another colour on top of the first, which produces subtle nuances and avoids a flat effect. If the colour powders have been wetted and ground using pure water, they are not subsequently diluted. Nor are they mixed with pure water at the actual moment of application as in the case of frescoes.

Preparation of the glue (size) paint or distemper. Animal skin glue can be obtained in slabs from drysalters and chemists. It must be immersed in tepid water until it has become soft, after which you melt it by heating about three parts of water to one of glue, the result being a rather thick solution which no longer hardens, can be clarified as required, and mixes well with the colours without altering them. One disadvantage is that sometimes this glue may go mouldy or break; it may be preferable to use a glue generally used by the painters of building firms for ceilings or colour washes. Kelose is excellent, or any other similar composition (powders which can be diluted with cold water). The object is to obtain a fairly thick liquid which gives the colours a smooth, sliding consistency and does not stick to the brush; spreads out transparently; enables fresh layers to be superimposed, and does not become detached if a wetter brush is passed over impasted portions. These resin glues do not spoil colours, but leave them fresh and intense; the glues do not whiten, but give the work a very good velvety quality. The dried painting must be retouched as little as possible – this applies to all mural painting. However, fresh colours can be superimposed to show up through each other; this is a subtle device which produces fascinating effects.

There is no point in having a very large number of colours. The following list is generally adequate:

— yellow ochre,
— two tones of Naples yellow,
— natural umber,
— burnt umber,
— red ochre,
— Puzzuolli red,
— terre verte,
— oxide green,
— German ultramarine (true lapis lazuli),
— cobalt blue and green,
— cadmium red,
— lamp black,
— St. John's white (bianco sangiovanni, the most transparent of all – produced from lime),
— Mars violet,
— Indian red.

A palette can be produced which is muted, delicate, shimmering and irridescent. If the wall to be decorated cannot be painted itself, because it is in a poor condition or of a consistency unsuitable for a rendering, or if the ornamentation is to be only temporary, painting can be performed on large pieces of canvas: a technique known as *painted tapestry.* These are not attached to stretchers, thus avoiding enormous pictures, but are left flexible: when sewn by a saddler and sized with glue and Spanish white mixed with glue, they can be painted with gum tempera or distemper (size or glue paint), and suspended from rings on rods attached to the wall; when taken down, they are carefully rolled up.

Although, from a distance, the painted canvases seem to be tapestries, care must be taken not to make them sham tapestries, but to retain the characteristics of paintings.

The canvas is glued and sized very carefully with animal skin glue and allowed to dry properly. The composition is set out on paper, and transferred by means of tracing paper to prevent the direct application of too much charcoal. It is then painted with the glue paint mentioned above. The paint must not be too wet, or the canvas will be spoiled (even though the canvas is protected by the glue). If the intention is to use a wider range of hues to produce a highly coloured style, using Chinese vermilion, madders and emerald green, then the palest of Naples yellows must be substituted for St. John's white (which is a product of lime and is dangerous to these colours).

A large canvas painted in this way and loosely attached to a severe wall can be dazzling. This method of painting has very considerable resources, so long as it is not turned into "the poor man's tapestry"; it is a technique with which very artistic qualities can be expressed. More subtle and intimate decorations can be produced by large panels of paper with which you can cover a whole wall or large surfaces between woodwork or fabrics.

When we think of the panoramic papers of the Romantic period, some of them printed, others painted, we may well feel that this form of decoration could be more widely used today to add charm to our homes. The papers, pasted on canvas, are firm enough to be fixed to walls without glueing. Or the design can be transferred to the wall and painting can be done direct with tempera or water-colours; the result has a freshness, clarity and transparency which wears very well.

We must say something about painting with wax, which attaches very satisfactorily to dry mortar and pre-glued timber prepared with plaster. You must use beeswax, the genuine article being obtainable only from beekeepers; there is no point in using candles, tallow, paraffin wax, or any other substitute. Beeswax, therefore, is placed in a water-bath to melt (6oz water to 1oz beeswax); when the wax is liquid and well mixed with the water, pour in $\frac{1}{3}$oz ammonium carbonate; the mixture immediately decomposes into a soft, greenish, smooth paste which is then further diluted with water, and mixes very satisfactorily with the colour. It is very pleasant to paint in this way on a smooth, perfectly dry wall; the painting tarnishes a little as it dries. When the work is finished and properly dried (it is advisable

to wait for several weeks), a light layer of white, highly liquid wax is vaporised and gently applied with a soft rag. The result is a very slight brilliance which brings up the colours and is very attractive (and also has the advantage of keeping down dust which might spoil the painting). It looks particularly good on woodwork, and can be used for panels and painted furniture.

Clearly, in all its techniques, wall painting requires a mastery of the painter's art.

You can practise by working on strong paper, using flexible brushes with thick, pointed hairs, brushes cut askew, and water-colours. It is no good whatever to practise oil painting in order to acquire a mastery of mural technique. A picture is almost the opposite of a wall painting, and you cannot transfer from one to the other without a change of register and optical approach. Various exhibitions and excellent reproductions have demonstrated the nature of wall painting, fresh or dry, and it is clear that these techniques have contributed greatly towards perfecting large-scale decorative religious art.

It is a demanding art which calls for hard work, a lot of application and care, extensive knowledge, and a fair amount of humility (one always has to learn and adapt oneself to the demands of the location of the painting, the subject, and any variations in technique demanded by often unforeseeable circumstances, such as the climate, the light, the state of the walls, the material of the surfaces to be painted, and the local technique, which it is always useful to study and advantageous to use). Any painter taking up mural work should never forget to learn from the painters of building firms who, particularly in Italy, Spain and other countries in which trades are handed down from masters to apprentices, and not in schools, possess knowledge and recipes which no artist should fail to study.

Even though painted canvases may have the advantage of being cheaper than tapestries, and are quicker to make, they must not be turned into imitations of their renowned rivals. Tapestry is a marvellous, inimitable art, but a tempera-painted panel, which is not a picture, is also a means of creating a work of art of a particular kind which has its own qualities and does not need to imitate anything else.

TEMPERA IN MURAL PAINTING

G. Delplanque

There were very few painters of my generation in the 1930s and 1940s who did not dream of an indelible distemper which would enable them to reproduce as faithfully as possible on a wall the drawing which they had carried out with gouache (the process generally used for this purpose).

What was left but frescoes? A noble means of expression, with a glorious past, but a terribly demanding one. Painting with glue, wax, egg or casein involved complicated preparation which was off-putting and discouraged a great many of us. Oil painting was far from giving us what we wanted. In the first place, it was dull, and we had a few notorious examples showing us that great painters had been betrayed by that technique. The fact is that, on a wall, oil undergoes oxidation, which gives a leaden, yellowish look to the work, which it progressively destroys. The main drawback with gouache was that it was impossible to retain in the work itself the quality of the colour of the sketch — it no longer had transparency, and was no longer either airy or luminous. I remember the comment made about the late Robert Rey, who was at that time the General Inspector of the Beaux-Arts. He had come to my studio to see how work was getting on, and told me wistfully: "I much prefer the material and colour of the drawing. Why don't you look for an indelible distemper which would suit a wall much better? Thin painting, both matt and opaque, diffuses the light so much better . . ."

This aspiration was to be realised a few years later. A start had been made with the introduction of a wax-based emulsion known as Ceracolor. It was a simplification of an old technique, but its new form was to give us a great deal of satisfaction. A little later it was followed by Flashe. I shall not go into detail about the nature of this latter discovery since my main object is to emphasise the facilities provided by tempera. I shall therefore merely quote the opinion of the chemist Marc Havel, who lays emphasis on its virtues in a brochure which was published recently.

"Flashe is the modern form of the famous 'tempera' which the old masters prepared with the milky sap of certain plants. Its basis is an emulsion of high polymers, microscopic particles separated from one another by water. When the water disappears during drying, the particles come close together and become welded to one another, enclosing the pigments which had been mixed with them. The actual plastic material thus formed, which is chemically inert, unlike a film of dried oil or rubber, is remarkable for its flexibility, firmness and resistance to ageing and light, and the fact that it does not yellow in darkness."

Tempera quickly became successful since it served the required purpose and could be applied to practically all supports: cement, lime, plaster — and also canvas, so long as it was not prepared with oil. Moreover, it is very easy to use; like gouache, it can be diluted with water and does not change during the rapid drying, which enables it to be corrected within a few hours without reducing the quality of the colour or sacrificing any of its brilliance. Tempera also permits very careful execution and satisfies painters who are fond of precision in their outlines and shapes.

Detail: Left-hand wall.

Detail: Right-hand wall.

I should add that the palette is rich and possesses a wider spectrum of colours than fresco, so that it is closer to the taste and demands of our age, in which colour is all-important. However, means of expression are not everything. Although we owe a lot to the progress of modern chemistry, which relieves us of the work of colour preparation (too much so in the view of some people), we must admit that chemistry does not facilitate the production of a work of art all that much.

The spirit of creation remains and will be the first element of the study of a project calling for imagination, and it will be the final arbiter of the value of the work performed. We must remember that the main quality which mural decoration must possess is integration with architecture. The scale of the surroundings will therefore be respected by the painter, who will organise the surface to be decorated in relation to its dimensions. Moreover, the constituent elements of the composition (even if they are only rhythms and patches of colour) must harmonise completely with the dimensions of the premises. This is a matter of the personality and taste of the artist who is to complete or complement the architect's work. A large hall can seem diminished, and thus lose its original character, if the elements of its decoration are too large (and vice versa). *This balance between architecture and painting is the prime condition of any incorporated pictorial work.*

Following the above basic observations, we must consider the general principles which enable the actual decorational work to be successfully carried out.

The support. As already stated, indelible gouaches accommodate themselves to a large variety of supports (on condition that they are sound and thin). The painter must therefore examine the state of the wall and supervise its preparation carefully. Any holes or cracks must be stopped up, and it must be lightly rubbed down to obtain a matt bonding surface. If the wall is too absorbent (Isorel or plaster, for instance), size must be applied. Ready-mixed products can be obtained from suppliers of building materials.

If, on the other hand, the wall is not porous, it will be primed with diluted white Flashe. Whatever the preparation used may be, it must under all circumstances be applied as a liquid, since this improves impregnation and adherence. If the support is a canvas, it must never be primed with oil, but must be thin and absorbent.

The drawing. For the reasons already stated, the drawing (generally to a scale of 1/10) must be carried out extremely carefully. (In this way, mural painting clearly differs from easel painting.) In working out the design, the artist will avoid perspective which is too pronounced for this plane of the surface, and destroys the balance of the architecture. The painter should find two dimensions enough to express himself, unless he deliberately chooses to transform the architecture by using eye-deceiving (trompe l'oeil) painting. We have many examples of this, from the Renaissance to the 19th century.

But it is better to remain faithful to the great principles of Byzantine and Romanesque work, namely flat surfaces without optical distortions or perspective.

The cartoon. The finished drawing is enlarged in the conventional way (squaring) and then copied full scale on to the wall using a sturdy piece of charcoal. Some painters, anxious about the quality of the shape and outline, produce the cartoon on manila paper or tracing paper, before reproducing it on the final support. In that case, it is indispensable to place the cartoon on the wall beforehand, in order to make sure that it harmonises perfectly with the architecture of the premises. When the cartoon has been finished, the painter will transfer it to the support by tracing or "pouncing". If the support selected is a canvas, it will be sized before the work is performed. We have often noticed that, if the final work is carried out in the studio, it is disappointing, as the surrounding light and atmosphere are not the same as in the final location. The painter often has the tendency to overload such work with useless details or elements which complicate the composition and therefore destroy its unity. Moreover, the lighting of the premises is of great importance and may have a considerable influence on the selection of values and the harmony of colours.

Finally, the design is fixed. The painter then distributes large patches of colour in accordance with the drawing. If certain colours are mixed ones, he will make enough of them to last the work, keeping them in properly closed jars, and will use at least two layers: the first layer will be diluted with water and will be more fluid; the second will be richer.

As in the case of frescoes, the painting must, of course, start in the upper part of the panel. A few colours will certainly run, but these can be covered after the application of the second layer.

A lot of time will be saved if this work is carried out with great care and precision.

The particular technique and talent of each artist will do the rest, as tempera allows a great variety of execution. Moreover, the painter will find in this means of expression the same pleasure and facility which he experienced when painting with gouache. He will also have the satisfaction of having discovered a very simple technique which is particularly well adapted to being worked on a wall and has, in addition, all the advantages of oil painting, with the added freshness and light of a fresco.

Between the classic gouache and acrylic colours (satiny or glossy), there is a category of opaque and matt colours: Ingres, Tamma... They can be diluted with water and have the advantage over gouache that they are indelible and dry slightly more quickly, enabling covering or transparent colours, according to their dilution, to be superimposed.

Original French text by
Jack Chambrin
Winner of travel scholarships from the
state and the Maison Descartes of
Amsterdam.
Fénéon Prize.
Abd el Tif Prize.
Descartes Prize.
Prix de la Signature cachée.
Painter, engraver, mural artist.
Teacher at the Academy Frochot.

Sgraffito

A sgraffito is a mural cladding carried out "al fresco" which enables limited colour effects to be obtained, along with light relief which is achieved by "engraving" or hollowing out the cement.

Its principle is very simple: three (at the most four) successive coatings of coloured cement are applied to a wall prepared in the normal manner for this purpose and thoroughly wetted. These coatings used to be made up on the spot, using lime, fine sand and powdered colour, but nowadays ready-mixed coatings can be obtained in a fairly wide range of colours, which are produced in Germany under the name of Terranova.

When the mason has applied the three differently coloured coatings on top of one another, a scraper or any instrument suitable for creating the desired effect is used to engrave the intended design and to reveal the required colour.

A surface of four to eight square metres can be treated in one session, depending on the setting speed of the cement and the simplicity or complication of the design. Each individual part of the composition must be completed in one session.

Like all techniques which must be performed freehand and without retouching, a great deal of practice is necessary.

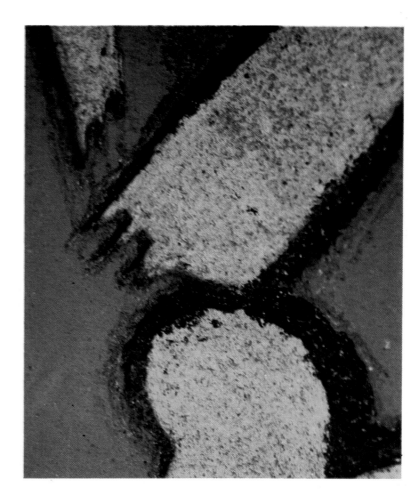

Details of execution.

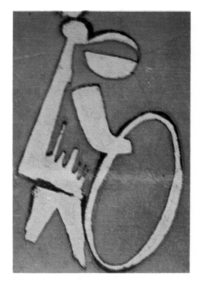

Original French text by
Jacques Le Chevallier
Glazing artist.
Former teacher at the *Ecole Nationale Supérieure des Beaux-Arts* in Paris.
Former director of the *Centre d'Art Sacré*.
Member of the *Salon d'Automne* and the *S.A.D.*

Jacques Loire
Master glazier.

Stained glass

Glass slabs

Jacques Le Chevallier.
Glazing artist.

Rose window in one of the bays of the high naves of Notre Dame, Paris. J. Le Chevallier

A stained glass window is a translucent mosaic suited to the light of western countries and more particularly to 12th century French architecture, which is characterised by a simplification of the supporting structure, and the consequent building on a strong framework of lightweight vaults whose thrust is cancelled out by the flying buttresses, which transfer all stresses to the external abutments. The result of this architectural development was the possibility of bathing the interior of large religious buildings in light; the large bays made space available for decorative compositions which took advantage of the transparency of glass and the brilliant light effects which it transmitted.

One of the oldest treatises on painting and stained glass windows, written by the monk Theophilus, shows how clever the French were at producing coloured glass in sheets. Be that as it may, it is certain that the 11th and 12th centuries saw the birth in France of a novel method of decoration effected by the assembly in cast lead rods of fragments of coloured glass, cut in accordance with the outlines of a drawing, with a view to a harmony of colours. The fashion for certain colours in different periods brought about changes in the processes of producing coloured glass.

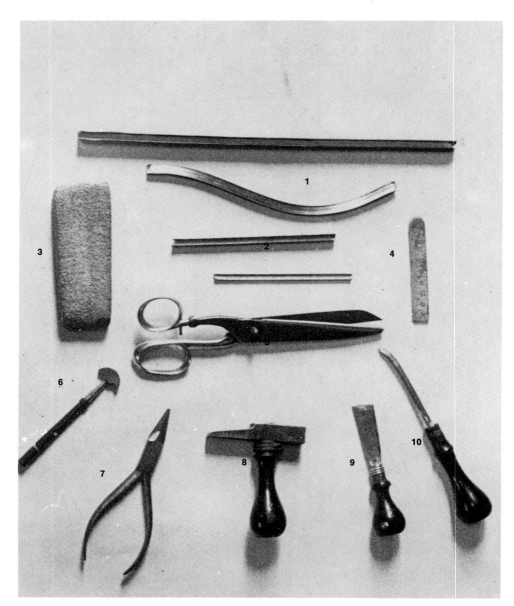

1. 8 mm leads.
2. 4 mm leads.
3. Whetstone.
4. Piece of wood for turning down the lead flanges.
5. Double-bladed shears.
6. Diamond.
7. Pliers.
8. Hammer.
9. Cutter.
10. Tool for opening up the lead flanges.

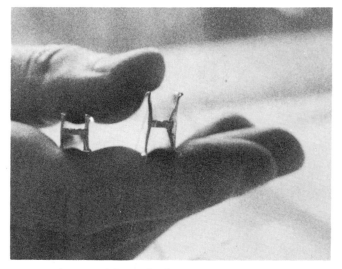

4 mm and 8 mm leads.

The artist designing a stained glass window must, above all, have a thorough knowledge of the intended location of the window in the building. He must be familiar with its surroundings and their architectural style, and with the amount and direction of the light which will fall on his work.

After the model has been made, taking account of the basic principle, which is to define the colour arrangement in a frame of lead (the model is generally to a scale of 1/10), a full-size cartoon is made. A highly accurate list of measurements is required for the cartoon, which shows, exactly the same size as the final window, the placing of the leads which will separate the colours and emphasise the outlines of the design.

A piece of tracing paper is placed over the cartoon, and lines are marked showing where the pieces of glass will be cut.

The tracing is transferred to "template" paper (quite strong manila), and the paper is cut up following the lines of the tracing, each piece bearing a number.

The work of cutting up the template must allow for the thickness of the lead.

As regards the selection of the glasses, stained glass technique does not consist in putting colour on glass, but in selecting colours from a range of manufactured glass. The technique of making stained glass has hardly varied since the 12th century; the glass is blown in the form of a cylinder, which is then opened up. The basic colours of the glass have remained practically unchanged, but they have acquired a considerable variety of shades.

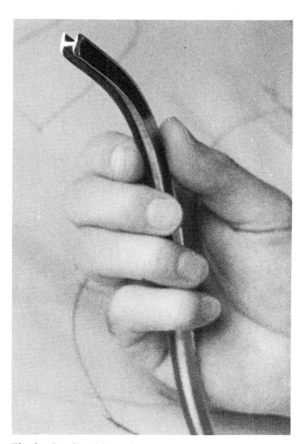

The lead is flexible and remains ductile indefinitely.

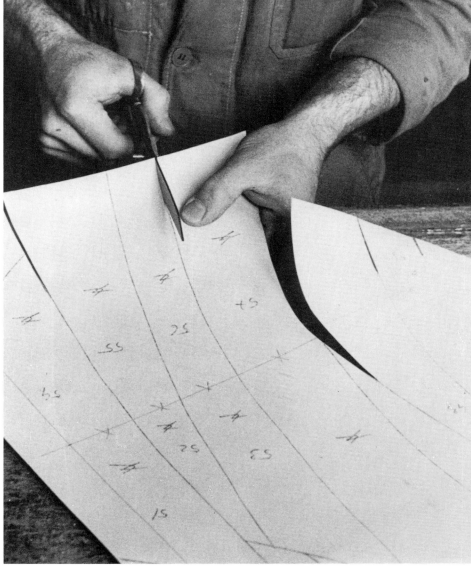

Cutting the templates using double-bladed shears. A number and a conventional sign on each template enables it to be located.

The glass is cut with a wheel (or diamond), following the shape of the template accurately.

When the glasses have been selected, the technician cuts them very accurately in accordance with the templates, using a diamond or a cutting wheel.

Provisional setting is carried out with a narrow lead when *grisaille* (explained below) is in hand — otherwise the glass is immediately mounted in the final leads (8 or 9 mm). The leads are retained by being soldered with tin at certain points, the overall panel as a rule not exceeding sixty to eighty square centimetres.

Setting the pieces of glass in the lead. The pieces are provisionally secured by headless nails.

The end of the lead is cut off flush with the glass and then flattened for insertion in a transverse lead.

The pieces of glass are assembled with the templates after cutting.

Glasses of different colours.

Fragment of ancient glass (13th century).

"The Labourers of the Eleventh Hour",
a stained glass window by J. Le Chevallier.

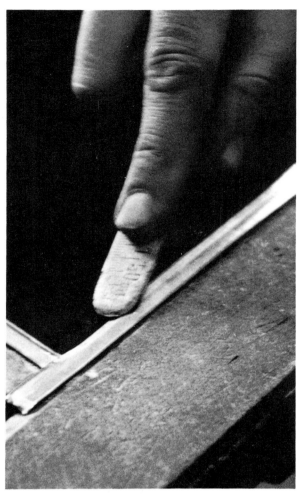

Pushing the lead flanges down.

Soldering the lead joints, using an electric (or gas) soldering-iron and an 80% tin rod.

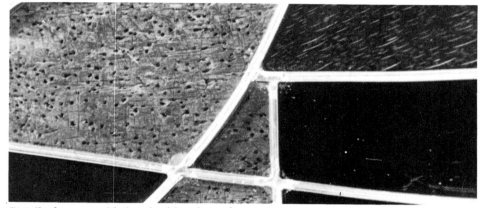

Detail of an assembled and soldered panel.

Manoeuvring a panel by tilting it on the table edge. The panels are always handled and stored on edge, not flat.

Grisaille work: grisaille is the name given to producing a design on glass with iron oxide. Once the panel of glass has been mounted in the provisional leads (the pieces of glass can also be attached to plate glass by spots of wax) the grisaille must be very freely worked, using a brush, fingers, or a sponge. When the required effect has been obtained, the panel is taken apart and all the pieces which have been coated in grisaille are placed in a furnace at 600° and fired for 24 hours (followed by 6 hours heating and 18 cooling). The pieces are then reassembled and the stained glass finally remounted in heavy leads.

The panels are then sealed with putty, which ensures that they are rigid.

The completed stained glass window is introduced panel by panel into the openings, where T-iron (glazing) bars have been sealed. The panels are retained by tringlettes (glazier's rods).

The assembly of iron fittings contributes towards the general effect of the stained glass window.

Applying grisaille with an ordinary brush.

Producing grisaille with a badger-hair brush, enabling work to be performed vertically.

After the panels have been unset, the pieces with grisaille are laid down on plates and separated from each other by plaster. The plates are then put into the furnace. Firing is carried out at 600°, and the pieces are then set in 8 mm lead.

I-227

Jacques Loire
Master glazier at Chartres.

The art of stained glass making has been renewed by the coloured glass slab, which is like a precious stone, 25 mm thick, embedded in concrete.

This material can be used for producing entire coloured walls, which are less fragile than leaded windows and fit perfectly into a modern architectural setting.

When the artist prepares his model, he will be as much concerned with the concrete surround as with the glass itself because the thick or thin lines of concrete surrounding the glass slabs emphasise the design and are an important part of the overall effect.

Apart from this different consideration, from the model onwards the work is the same as with a leaded window, involving the making of a full-scale cartoon and templates.

The glasses can be selected from 400 to 600 differently coloured samples so that the model can be reproduced with a high degree of accuracy.

The selected glasses (slabs of 30 x 30 cm, coloured throughout the body of the glass) are cut up into the required shapes in accordance with the templates, using a small hammer. The glasses can be skillfully chipped by the hammer to create a play of light on the resulting uneven surface.

The cut glasses are placed on the numbered cartoon so as to form the design of the panel.

Around the pieces of glass an iron armature is then placed which follows the outlines of the design and reinforces the concrete.

The glasses are secured with putty, and liquid concrete is poured between the pieces of glass. When the concrete has dried, the panel is lifted to assess it in the light (after the putty has been removed and the glasses have been cleaned). If there is an error in comparison with the model, the panel must be broken up and a completely new start must be made.

One can ensure that the concrete seals tightly either by incorporating a special product when mixing the cement, or by the application of a protective film after casting.

Research is being carried out in stained glass workshops with a view to substituting opaque or transparent epoxy resins for concrete.

M. Guy Soleille makes a coloured polyester, which is not used in place of glass, but its properties allow effects which would be difficult or even impossible in glass.

This new material affords great possibilities: it can be used over large surfaces; it can be sawn, screwed and glued with a resin; it is light and very firm, and can be specially processed to produce the appearance of bubbles, streaks, and flash effects.

"The Bluebird". Glass slabs. Private collection (Jacques Loire).

Cutting up cardboard to obtain the templates.

Cutting up the glass slab in accordance with the templates.

Preparation for concrete casting.

Concrete casting.

Chipped glass slab.

Original French text by
Riccardo Licata

Mosaics

Detail of a mosaic produced in the studio of Riccardo Licata of the Ecole Nationale Supérieure des Beaux-Arts, Paris.

Mosaics are a very ancient form of art. Excavations have revealed the remains of many beautiful examples dating from the Sumerian period (3rd millenium B.C.). In ancient times, many peoples used mosaics, particularly in the form of inlays.

From the 5th century B.C., mosaic floors laid in Greece and Sicily, representing figures or geometrical patterns, were made: first from small round pebbles and, later, cubic ones. During the Alexandrine period, mosaics were widely produced in the Hellenistic world. Roman art blossomed and took over mosaic-laying techniques from the 2nd century B.C. onwards. Subsequently, the use of mosaics spread through all the provinces of the Roman Empire.

The Romans used mosaics in all public buildings, and each private house had at least one mosaic floor. Some wonderful examples have come down to us almost intact, even where the houses have fallen into ruins. The classical Roman mosaics continued to be laid, in different ways and at different periods, right up to the 6th century A.D.

Early Christian mosaics developed after the Edict of Constantine (313 A.D.): at first used mainly as a mural art, they subjected technical perfection to mystical expression and preferred esoteric gold and bright colours to the muted colours of Roman marble floors. Throughout the Middle Ages, mosaics were used to create works of great beauty in

Details.

Christian art, in accordance with its successive styles: Early Christian, Byzantine, Romanesque and Gothic.

In the East, Islamic iconoclasm gave rise more particularly to inlay, with geometrical motifs, while in the 6th century, Jewish art created extraordinary mosaics.

The Christian art of the Middle Ages also gave us marble floors with figures and geometrical inlays. From the 16th century onwards, the art of mosaics declined, just like those of tapestry and stained glass. The reason was the misuse of mosaics as a means of reproducing paintings, the result being flat and lifeless, the work generally being a mechanical copy and not an original work of art. The craftsmen were obsessed by effects and multiplied colours to an unbelievable degree to imitate faithfully all the light and shade effects found in Renaissance painting.

Contemporary criticism, by re-evaluating primitive art and interpreting Roman art fairly, brought mosaics to the attention of modern artists. For about twenty years, the art has flourished again, due to numerous painters who use this means of expression to free themselves from the constraints of Mannerist and Neoclassical art.

Mosaics are an essentially monumental art, lending themselves to integration with architecture, and particularly suitable for the decoration of walls and floors.

Mural decoration must be understood to be an original work of art which has been conceived as an authentic and autonomous means of expression, philosophically and historically of its time, and integrated with architecture while retaining its individuality and "presence". It must never become an anonymous cladding.

Mosaics are work formed by an organized assembly of *tesserae* fixed by cement. *Tesserae* are parallelepipedic cubes of varying sizes, as required by the design: the tesserae, of stone, marble, limestone, flint, pebbles, glass paste, enamels, gold, or brick, are produced by using a hammer to cut the material, which is placed on a cutting edge fitted on to a block.

The assembly of tesserae can be carried out in different ways, so that the mosaic maker expresses his message as follows:
— by his method of laying and his materials,
— by the arrangement and size of the tesserae.

The Romans gave names to the different kinds of mosaics.
— *Opus Tessellatum.* Mosaics produced using small regular cubes measuring about 1 cm.
— *Opus Sectile.* Mosaics built up of very large tesserae, sometimes arranged in a clearly defined manner — a process sometimes resembling inlay.
— *Opus Alexandrinum.* Geometric dual-tone opus sectile.
— *Opus Vermiculatum.* This differs from opus tessellatum by the different shapes of the very precisely cut tesserae. The very small tesserae are organized in wavy lines.
— *Opus Segmentatum.* Formed by the insertion of larger, very long segments into a tessellatum carried out in quincunx.
— *Opus Incertum.* A laying technique in which the tesserae are cut and then deliberately arranged at random.
— *Opus Signinum.* A floor comprising a base of cement and crushed brick which is enlivened by white pebbles arranged in lines forming a geometrical outline.
— *The Barbaricum floor.* A beaten floor of a mixture of cement, crushed brick and pebbles of different colours.
— *The Venetian floor.* Similar to barbaricum, but having small pieces of crushed marble in the mixture: it can be in compartments or scattered.
— *Opus Pellae.* Typical of certain classical Greek floors, this results from the assembly of small round pebbles forming clearly defined configurations as a result of metal partitioning.

These terms of the Roman period can be applied to modern works.

There are also new styles and manners of expression which have been invented. All these techniques are carried out using hand-cut stone or marble, or enamels and slabs of glass, but never with 2 x 2 industrial tesserae of glass paste or ceramics.

Artistic mosaics must not be confused with claddings carried out in industrial mosaics, although there are some interesting examples of the latter, produced by talented designers.

Mural mosaics (walls, ceilings, apses, arches, columns, panels, icons, etc.) must be distinguished from floor mosaics (pavements, basins, swimming pools, tables, slabs, etc.). There are differences in conception, since the floor is viewed from a close distance (the height of the human being), while a wall is often viewed from far off.

Usually, a floor mosaic is carried out in marble, so that the colouring is muted.

Mural mosaics can be carried out in glass, enamels and gold, thus widening the colour range. As a rule, mosaics are fixed decorations of a wall or floor, but transportable mosaics can also be made.

In the ancient world, people were very fond of emblems, which were small polished mosaics produced on a sheet of slate and set in the middle of the floor. The Byzantines had mosaic icons, often on a wooden support, which could be carried about.

At present, wall panels are produced on sheets of different materials, and polished floor mosaics in cement slabs. A table or floor can be produced by assembling a number of slabs.

When producing a wall mosaic or a floor, the site where the work is to be carried out must first be studied: its surroundings, the lighting, the purpose of the building, and other aspects. Sketches and studies are done with a view to elucidating artistic problems in order to produce an important work, a landmark in the history of the art.

These minor sketches and studies will result in coloured maquettes (models) reflecting the quality, laying and size of the actual tesserae selected.

A final drawing, showing the colours to be used, will be produced, usually on a 1/10 scale. This is then enlarged to full size. The result is the cartoon, which can be coloured, although black and white is adequate, indicating the outlines and showing the boundaries of the coloured zones.

Basically, the mosaicist himself makes the maquette and the drawing, and carries out the mosaic himself, but he may need assistance when producing large murals. He will find collaborators to put his ideas into effect, continue his work, and lay the tesserae in accordance with his instructions. If a painter has to design a mosaic, without being familiar with its technique or demands, it is preferable for him to have his work interpreted by a mosaicist, who should be free to choose the materials and method of laying, rather than simply imitating and reproducing the model.

DIRECT LAYING TECHNIQUE

When the maquette and cartoon have been prepared, trace the outline of the cartoon on to glassine paper, and retrace on the reverse side of the paper, using an ink which will come off with water, so that when the paper is placed on the fresh, moist cement, the tracing will print clearly. Lines can also be traced directly on the fresh cement using a nail or a knife, or else the old method can be adopted of using paper with the outline of the cartoon perforated with a pricking-wheel. The paper is laid on the fresh cement, and a sachet of colour is sprinkled through the holes.

Having decided on the quality of the tesserae to be used, the necessary amount of materials must be obtained (marble sheets, glass slabs, etc.) and cut to form tesserae of the required size.

A hammer and a cutting edge fitted on to a block are required for cutting the tesserae.

The stone (or other material) must be held in the left hand, flat on the cutting edge. Give a sharp blow with the hammer (it is advisable to use the force of your wrist). The blows of the hammer and the cutting edge itself must always be square and well aligned. To cut square or rectangular tesserae, the cuts must be parallel and perpendicular, while to obtain triangles or trapezoidal shapes the material must be rotated on the cutting edge so as to produce the required shape. You must be able to cut tesserae properly (this needs a lot of practice) if you wish to master the technique of mosaics.

You must also obtain the materials for the cement and take into account the preparation of the support. If it is a wall, there must be neither plaster nor paper on it. If it is made of brick, which is too absorbent, prepare it by applying a thin mortar.

If the wall is of cement or stone, the only preparation needed is to notch the surface slightly to roughen it.

If the intention is to produce a portable wall mosaic, a panel must be prepared which has an absorbent base, and the same characteristics as a wall. It can be made from reinforced concrete panels about 1.5 cm thick, or using Eternith. It can also be prepared by using other building material made up of cement and asbestos bonded chips and measuring 2.00 x 0.50 x 0.002 m. Héraclite can easily be sawn up and used without a frame for small panels (up to 0.50 x 0.80 m). For larger panels (the material is not heavy enough for more than 2 x 2 m), attach the Héraclite panels to a frame of timber, or preferably iron (which is stronger and less noticeable).

As soon as everything is ready — maquette, drawing, tracing, tesserae and support — laying can begin. Wet the wall or panel properly, and prepare the mortar, which can be of various kinds.

The mortar is a mixture of lime with one or more materials, such as cement, sand, crushed marble or brick, etc., used in different combinations and proportions in accordance with local traditions. The ordinary mortar in current use is made up of:

— 1 part of lime paste,
— 1/2 part of normal grey Portland cement,
— 1/2 part of sieved river sand.

Prepare it on a table, using a trowel (cat's tongue), first mixing the lime and the sand. Then add the cement in small quantities without water. The result will be a consistent workable paste which will remain cool and suitable for laying tesserae for about 4 hours. It then hardens and at the end of a month becomes as hard as stone. For several days it remains soft enough to allow modifications. Another mortar, namely 861, which has the same qualities as the preceding one and is also used nowadays, is very satisfactory, but harder to use, as it hardens by the following day, and it is therefore difficult to make adjustments. Experienced mosaicists who can work with confidence are advised to use 861 because:

— it is sold in bags,
— it can be used immediately,
— it is easy to mix,
— it is a substantial material.

Mortar 861 is made up of:

— 3 parts of Lafarge 861 powdered cement lime,
— 2 parts of sieved sand,
— enough water to form a paste of adequate consistency.

Mix it all in a plastic trough, using a large square trowel (you are advised to mix the 861 and sand first). The fresh mortars are grey in colour but turn white as they dry, enabling that colour to be used for the gaps.

As soon as the mortar is ready and the support has been properly wetted, apply the mortar: first of all a thin preparatory spread, immediately followed by a layer approximately 1 cm thick — sometimes thicker, sometimes thinner, as required. The surface to be coated must be calculated in relation to:

— the number of tesserae which can be laid in 4 hours,
— their dimensions,
— the difficulty of the design,
— the skill of the mosaicist.

If the mortar is laid on too large a surface, it will dry out, and the part which has not been used will have to be removed. Once the mortar has been smoothed with the trowel over the required surface, trace the appropriate part of the design, using glassine paper. Then start the direct laying of the tesserae, following the outline of the tracing. Press the tesserae down into the mortar beside one another at the desired angles and intervals. To lay the tesserae in the mortar, push them down by 2 mm (further in the case of large tesserae) so that edges are formed which will retain them.

Usually, tesserae are half embedded in the mortar, the other half being visible. However, very thick or long stones can be used which are pushed in to a distance of 1 cm, the remainder being allowed to project by several centimetres. Rather flat tesserae can also be used which are pushed right in, so that the mortar overflows, forming a rim. There are nowadays no rules or restrictions, but any different approach or change must be deliberate (meaning that every approach and action must be governed by a need for expression). Cover the working surface with tesserae (the mosaic can be designed with portions of mortar left visible) as dictated by the particular style selected. You must always give the tesserae a logical sequence, and never "fill in" afterwards.

Lay marble tesserae so that the hammer-cut side can be seen. The same thing applies to ceramics, except for thin ones, and gold.

Finish the laying sessions when the whole surface of fresh mortar is covered, taking care to leave a margin of 1 cm free from tesserae at the edge of the surface covered; this is done to prevent an unwanted inclination of the tesserae due to the sagging of the final portion of the mortar.

As soon as laying is completed, or on the following day, remove the mortar margin perpendicularly, flush with the tesserae. This operation can even be performed a few days later, but will then be more difficult, since the mortar will have hardened.

Detail of a mosaic produced in the studio of Riccardo Licata of the Ecole Nationale Supérieure des Beaux-Arts, Paris.

Corrections can be made during the work or immediately following its completion. The procedure is as follows:

— Remove any tesserae which are out of place or are the wrong shape or colour and replace them, adding a little mortar.

For corrections on dry mortar:

— Remove any unsuitable tesserae.
— Hollow out the mortar down to the support.
— Wet the area.
— Introduce fresh mortar into the hollow.
— Lay the tesserae.

The mosaic must be sprayed with water before and after work, and for at least ten days afterwards, so as to make sure that the mortar sets properly.

When resuming an unfinished mosaic, it must be well sprayed with water, to prevent the dry mortar from absorbing all the water from the fresh mortar to be laid alongside.

About ten days after a mosaic has been finished, it can be washed to remove the skin of lime which may have formed. If the work has not been done cleanly, use a heavily diluted solution of hydrochloric acid and water, or water and vinegar in the case of certain limestone which may be attacked by hydrochloric acid.

The solutions must be applied with a dog-tooth brush; then the mosaic should be washed down thoroughly.

Mixing the mortar.

INDIRECT LAYING TECHNIQUE

This means that the mosaic is produced on a temporary support and then transferred to the final mortar. This procedure is easier than direct laying, as there is no need to worry about the mortar drying out.

In this method, the tesserae are glued upside down onto strong packing paper; then the whole assembly is transferred onto fresh mortar.

For this purpose, the prepared cartoon must be redrawn upside down or reversed, otherwise the finished mosaic will resemble an image viewed in a mirror. Once this has been done, the paper on to which the tesserae are to be glued must be cut up into sections measuring 30 x 30 cm, and each sheet must be numbered.

The tesserae are then glued, using a water-soluble flour glue, remembering that the glued part will be what is revealed when the mosaic is finished.

On completion of the glueing, proceed to laying (on wall, ceiling or floor). If it is a wall, it must be wetted beforehand. Then apply the mortar (half cement — half sand) over the required surface and lay the mosaic down with the paper upwards (this must be detached half an hour later). When laying, you can either leave the surface flat or create some movement by tapping the tesserae lightly with a hammer to give them different inclinations. A grout of premixed cement of a rather liquid consistency is now spread across the surface and worked well down between the tesserae. The layer of surplus grout is then wiped off.

Original French text by
Yvette Cauquil-Prince
Artist, diploma of the *Académie*
Royale des Beaux-Arts of Belgium.
Tapestry maker.
Founder of the *Atelier du Marais Y.C.P.*

De Brus

Sophie Leroux

Dinah Relange

Tapestry

Tapestry by Sonia Delaunay (les Gobelins).

Tapestry by Mathieu (les Gobelins).

"The Night" (detail).

"The Night". Low warp tapestry by Yvette Cauquil-Prince, produced at the Y.C.P. Studio (250 x 180 cm).

What exactly is tapestry? It is the translation, in variously coloured threads of wool, silk, flax (or gold thread), of a composition (cartoon) conceived, drawn and painted by an artist. Sometimes, artists do not make their own cartoons: they use instead a work whose spirit is in harmony with tapestry technique (Rubens, Goya, Jean de Bruges, Picasso, Miró, Chagall, etc.). The artist and the tapestry maker establish the cartoon between them (or else the tapestry maker does it on his own). This will be different from a cartoon made by "artist cartoon-makers", a term used for the first time in this sense by Lurçat. Usually Lurçat made neither a drawing nor a painting, but directly produced a numbered cartoon. Both methods are used nowadays by different artists.

Tapestry is actually the hand-weaving of a work on a loom, so an original work is therefore produced. Today, 3 to 6 copies of a tapestry are usually made (if it is a unique work, this is marked in the weave on the back).

A clear distinction must be made between embroidery and tapestry. Embroidery is needlework carried out on a fabric backing, sometimes superimposing one fabric on another.

In tapestry, all you have at the start is a collection of bare threads forming the warp; the weft yarn constantly inter-sects the warp yarn at right angles to produce both the weave and the design. The threads are almost always cotton. Cotton or flax were formerly used. At one time wool was used, giving a kind of frog-skin effect, with puffed-out sections occuring every 3 to 4 cm.

When were the first tapestries made? Several thousands of years before our time, the Egyptians, Greeks, Chinese, Pre-Columbian Americans, etc., were already familiar with the art of textiles and all dyeing processes. The paintings of the Beni-Hassan hypogeum (3,000 B.C.) show a loom similar to those used today.

Originally, only woollen and cotton yarns and flax were used; subsequently, silk and gold threads added a sparkling effect. We think of Oriental luxury, but we must also remember Oriental patience, which was not put off by any work, no matter how endless. In Greece, the rather free and animated compositions usually represented fabulous animals, while in the East, the main emphasis was on regularity and symmetry, with flowers, geometry, and animals: griffins facing one another, leopards forming circles — always very rich compositions in brilliant colours. These large wall hangings were accompanied by less important works for daises, canopies, tents, doorways and carpets.

TAPESTRY TECHNIQUE
Low warp — High warp

It is a fairly simple matter to make a tapestry, at least in principle, and the method has changed little, if at all. As distinct from industrial products, which can always be improved and made more quickly and more cheaply, work which is handmade calls for the same procedures, comes up against the same problems, and uses the same tools, as those which have been established over the years, and have only varied very slightly from time to time. The present-day method of weaving is basically no different from that of the Coptic tapestries and the whole tradition of Eastern tapestries.

There are two kinds of tapestries, one of which is known as high warp (when the sheet of threads forming the warp is placed vertically in front of the tapestry maker, and the two frames are worked by his or her arms). The tapestry is a low warp tapestry when the sheet of threads is stretched horizontally and the alternation is worked by the tapestry maker's arms and feet.

The pedals are used to separate the sheet of threads.

Separation of a wide sheet using the whole hand.

LOW WARP TAPESTRY

In low warp tapestry, the warp yarn is attached to a horizontal frame mounted on a strong wooden or cast iron support.

The heddles are fixed below the horizontal curtain (via rods attached to a pulley itself attached to the pedals). Warp threads are connected to two wide pedals which rise and fall to separate the odd and even threads. The operator uses his or her feet alternately to work the two pedals ("pedal tapestries").

The cartoon is attached to the loom beneath the warp, so that the operator can see it between the threads and follow exactly the same procedure as for high warp.

There is substantially no difference between work carried out by either process. Low warp work is quicker and leaves the operator's hands free. High warp work takes longer and is therefore more expensive.

To finish a tapestry: when the tapestry is very wide, the threads are finished off by a weaving process.

If the cloth is narrow, the tapestry is finished off manually, with buttonhole stitch, and the edges are also turned down and sewn.

Then the tapestry is stretched, moistened and pressed (by a specialist firm).

The shuttle is introduced into the sheet of threads, using the right hand.

Shuttles on the loom.

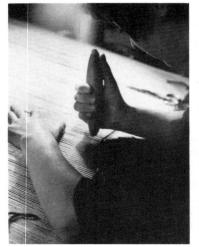

Beating-up, using the comb.

The tapestry maker pulls the thread vigorously.

Separation of a small sheet of threads.

Position of the tapestry maker on the bench.

Action of the pusher after each passage of the thread.

The pedals and pulleys (under the loom).

Action of beating-up using the iron or copper pusher.

HIGH WARP TAPESTRY

A high warp tapestry loom comprises a large vertical frame supporting two large cylinders, one at the top and the other at the bottom. The yarns forming the warp are stretched and wound onto the cylinders, which are like two huge bobbins. The spare warp is wound on to the top cylinder. A considerable amount of space is occupied by this type of loom, and the cylinders and yarn make a heavy weight, so the uprights and supports are made of very heavy timber or cast iron, and are fixed to the floor and ceiling.

The yarns used are cotton, and sometimes flax, but rarely wool, and form a vertical curtain in front of the operator. The threads must be moved apart to enable the shuttle with its coloured wool to move in and out between them to form the weft and therefore the design. A long glass tube known as a *crossing rod* divides the threads into two sheets. The front threads are odd: 1, 3, 5, 7, etc.; the rear threads are even: 2, 4, 6, 8, etc. Each thread of the rear sheet is attached to a cord ring (*heddle*), and all the heddles of the same size are fitted into a long rod (*heddle rod*) — a piece of wood which is parallel with the cylinder and situated above the operator (thus, high warp).

In weaving, the travel of a coloured shuttle is called a *pick*. It starts from one end of a colour (matching the colour on the shuttle) and extends to the other end of that coloured patch. Work is always performed on a portion of the sheet of threads, never on all of them, so that a number of operators can work side by side, the only spacing necessary being to allow for their arm movements. Their feet operate only one set of heddles (2 heddles) or two sets at the most (set of heddles: wood supporting the heddles: 1 heddle for the left foot and 1 heddle for the right). In ordinary weaving, one pick is enough to enable each coloured sheet to rise by the height of one thread.

In a tapestry, two picks are required to perform the same work, since the warp thread must be entirely covered (back and front) by the coloured weft thread.

Work starts at the bottom. The thread must be moved in a curve. If it is moved straight, the warp is not covered and the work is pulled in at the edges. The thread must therefore have a longer free travel than the width of the work, and it must not be stretched in relation to the warp. In this way, it can weave itself around the warp thread.

First operation. The sheet of odd threads and the sheet of even threads are kept separate by the crossing rod. The operator moves his wool-loaded shuttle through this free corridor. This first passage from left to right over the whole width of the coloured sheet forms half a pick. Once backwards and forwards produces a line.

Second operation. Using his left hand, the operator pulls the heddle rod towards him, thus bringing the whole rear sheet forwards, and then he moves his shuttle from right to left in the corridor thus formed. A combination of these two travels forms one pick, and the work advances by the thickness of one stitch.

In fact, the operator is forming a design in several colours, and he raises only that mass of warp threads which corresponds to the space which he intends to cover with any particular colour. In other words, the design progresses by horizontal rows each having the thickness of one stitch. If one row comprises 2 cm of blue, 10 cm of black, 3 mm of red, etc., the operator will change his shuttle every time he comes to a new colour, and cover exactly the required length with his weft thread. After each half pick, he uses a *pusher* to beat up the half pick against the sheet already woven and, when the woven sheet reaches about 0.5 to 1 cm, he uses the *comb* very heavily over the length of the sheet.

For very fine details, beating-up is performed thread by thread, using a *pricker*.

In high warp, the beating-up is done with a fork-like instrument with long teeth.

Passing the hand through to separate the warp threads.

At les Gobelins studio. High warp.

SEWN "TAPESTRY"

Obviously, high and even low warp tapestries cannot possibly be carried out by an amateur on his own, but there are interesting "sidelines" which require less equipment.

First of all, pieces of felt or any other material can be attached by either invisible or very obvious stitching to a fabric backing. You can vary not only the colours, but also the texture of the materials themselves (dull, brilliant, fine or coarsely woven, spangled, plain or with motifs), producing a decorative effect with the contrasts. Stitching and embroidery can be used to enrich and emphasise the design. This is long, difficult work, because these various materials have different thicknesses and tensions. However, in the hands of an expert, the process is rich in variety and personal possibilities; it forces you to simplify and stylize, and enables large-scale high-class work to be performed.

NEEDLEWORK TAPESTRY

Needlework tapestry (needlepoint or petit point) is easier and suitable for small and medium size work, such as chairs and armchair backs, sofas, cushions and carpets.

We call this technique needlework tapestry, even though it is more properly embroidery — a design needle-stitched on a backing of material specially and elaborately prepared for this purpose, namely canvas, in which the warp and weft threads are woven quite loosely. In "Penelope" canvas, which is the one most often used, the threads are grouped in pairs and are therefore easier to count.

You can design your cartoon yourself. It can be carried out in gouache, in colour. Before starting work, you must purchase your wools and make sure that you can obtain all the colours you have selected, otherwise you must simplify or modify your design in accordance with what is available. When the composition has been completed, you take an accurate tracing of it and transfer the outlines of the drawing to the canvas, using a felt pen. The main tones are marked out, and the colours are indicated with a tone of watercolour or highly fluid gouache. You can also mark out the canvas, dividing the surface into compartments, count the threads, and introduce a stitch at intervals to obtain points of reference. All that remains to do is to work the design by covering all the surface of the canvas with very dense wool stitches.

In a true tapestry, the weft stitch forming the design is horizontal. In petit point tapestry, it is oblique. However, there are many other stitches; you can combine them, or invent new ones, or you can use the elementary cross-stitch which has always been taught to schoolgirls.

In this way, any composition can be executed, and the translation of the design into stitches is a very useful exercise. Of necessity, the curves are broken up into straight lines, forming steps. But the resulting deformation is not disturbing, and may not even be visible in a large design, although it is more noticeable with a smaller motif and a larger stitch. Canvas can be bought by the metre, in different widths. If it is a large piece of work, it is performed in several pieces which are then assembled, or else work is performed on a small loom, with the canvas well stretched on a wooden frame which you can buy, or even make yourself with a little skill.

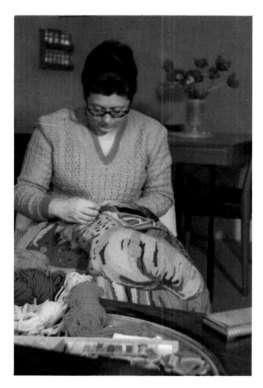

HOOK—STITCHED TAPESTRY

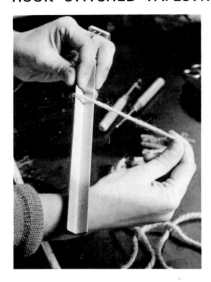

A design is first painted, using the available wool colours (a range of samples can be obtained from large stores or wool shops).

The design is drawn on tracing paper, with the colours demarcated accurately.

The drawing is then transferred to the canvas, using a felt pen.

Strands of wool are cut, using a small wooden bar. As far as possible, the strands of wool must all be of the same length. Holding the wool evenly tensioned, it is wound evenly around the small bar without leaving any space. Then the wool is cut along the length of the bar to obtain pieces about 7 cm long. In this way, several colours can be prepared in advance and kept in plastic bags.

To start the work, the edge of the canvas is folded, leaving the two first rows empty (when the work is completed these two first rows will be overcast with wool), and the folded canvas is worked for 4 rows. This system ensures a firm, attractive looking edge.

A strand of wool is bent exactly in half around the hook. Holding the two ends in your left hand, you push the tip of the hook into the first square (at the bottom left of the work), bringing it out again in the second square. Working from left to right, you continue this stitch in each square, taking care to change the colour in accordance with the felt pen outline. The second row is resumed on the far left. The hook is introduced into the second square i.e., the one where the hook came out in the first row. You continue this way until the 4 last rows, which are worked folded, like the first four.

Finally, the edges of the tapestry are overcast, and the projecting strands of wool are evened out with large scissors.

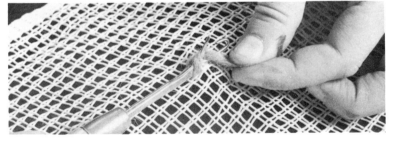

Original French text by
Dinah Relange
Fabric painter.

Painting on fabrics

Fabrics: 100% animal; 100% wool; 100% silk or wool/silk mixture.
Colours: aniline.

MATERIAL AND EQUIPMENT

— A fairly high table, so that you can work standing up; preferably 2 adjustable trestles and a large plank;
— a special frame;
— aniline colours;
— glue for setting;
— specially prepared fabrics (bleached and deglossed);
— glassine paper (florist) cut into 20 x 20 cm squares;
— white glue;
— 90° methylated spirit (from the chemist's);
— "C" or "F" spirit (from the chemist's);
— rubber gloves;
— absorbent cotton wool.

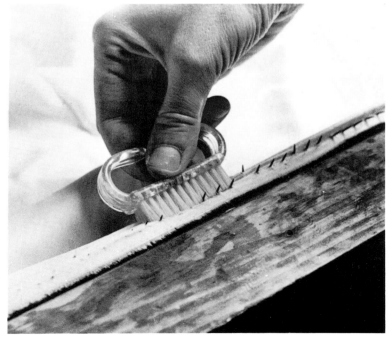

Stretch the fabric to be painted lengthwise over the frame (never attach the selvedge with nails); insert the nails using a small brush (such as a nailbrush).

Tightening the frame after stretching the fabric.

DESIGN

Shape the glassine paper into a cornet and glue the corner forming the tip, so that the cornet cannot open up during the work. Fill in the cornet about 2/3 with glue for setting. If the glue is a little too compact, heat it slightly over a water-bath; if it becomes too hard, dilute with "C" or "F" spirit.

Close the cornet properly at the top, to keep the glue in.

Cut the lower end of the cornet to make a very small hole, so that glue comes out only under the pressure of your hand.

Then draw on your fabric the design which you have prepared, using the cornet, which emits a thread of glue for your outline. This thread, which should be as regular as possible, serves to isolate the colours from one another. As the glue becomes used up, fold the cornet at the flared end to prevent air bubbles from breaking the line of glue, which must be absolutely continuous. Allow the glue to dry for about a quarter of an hour before filling in the colour. As soon as the outline looks dull, it is dry. It must not stick to your fingers when touched, and should be about 1 to 2 mm wide. Practise using the cornet of glue on newspaper before starting on the fabric.

APPLICATION OF COLOUR

Pour your colour into a glass.

Spread the selected colour using a cotton pad which you fold in four to make it firm. You will notice that the colour automatically spreads as far as the limits of the outline.

If you wish to obtain a few very fine lines of colour, you use a brush, but always between two outlines of glue.

To deal with large surfaces, pass your impregnated cotton evenly and rather quickly over the fabric, parallel with the selvedge. Once you have started this you must not stop, or "haloes" will appear.

Glue cannot be used with certain thick woollen fabrics. On these, apply the colours very lightly and allow them to spread naturally.

Once the fabric has been painted and has dried properly, take it to a specialist firm to have it fixed.

N.B. — *You can clean the painted fabrics with the special products intended for delicate fabrics and taking the usual precautions. At the first washing, rinse thoroughly until the water becomes clear.*

PROPORTIONING THE COLOURS

The colours which you buy are highly concentrated. They must be diluted in at least the following proportions:

50% pure colour,
40% methylated spirit,
10% water.

When working, add as much of the mixture of 4/5 alcohol + 1/5 water as is required.

PRACTICAL HINTS

Always wear rubber gloves when working, since aniline colours stain the skin and you will find them very hard to remove.

For the sake of safety, do not place a glass filled with colour on the frame, as you may be tempted to do, since it might get upset onto the fabric; place the glass on the table.

Never put your fingers on the fabric while it is drying, since a "halo" would appear immediately.

If the colour overflows the glue framing edge, the reason is that either the glue setting edge is not dry enough, or it is too fine and the colour can get through.

To finish scarves: roll-hem or fray.

Original French text by
Raymond Joly
Chief engraver at the Paris Mint.

Medals

"Don Quixote charging the windmills", by R. Joly (copper repoussage).

A medal faces its designer with the most difficult problem of all: a composition within a circle.

The maximum amount of thought must also be expressed in the minimum amount of space. This means that the general idea must be presented in concentrated form, and a language of allusions, symbols and suggestions must be adopted. Of course, the maker must comply with heavy technical demands, as professional engravers are well aware.

There are two kinds of medal: struck and cast.

For cast medals, it is advisable to make the model the same size as the final product. If the model is too large or too small, the medal must be reduced or enlarged, which is not always an easy matter since mechanical reduction or enlargement has standard limits, and, more particularly, the scale of an object alters its appearance, possibly away from the intention of the designer. Enlargement on plaster sometimes requires two successive phases, and the first phase must be retouched before starting on the second.

For struck medals, there are four main techniques by which the model can be produced:

1 Direct cutting in steel.
2 Direct cutting in plaster.
3 Modelling.
4 Metal repoussage.

DIRECT CUTTING IN STEEL

Whether they are cut in sunken or raised relief, the original striking instruments are made to size by the artist himself, then machined and hardened. When the engraving has been performed in raised relief, the relief is deepened, using a punch, to obtain the tool for sunken relief striking (die).

Generally, the engraver works, not on the medal, but on what are called the *steels* i.e. the tools with which the medals will be struck. The medals will be given the imprint of the striking tools by the rams of the presses.

There are three ways of making the striking tools:

1 By direct cutting of the steel, using drawings.

2 By means of a reducing lathe, starting with models cast in bell bronze from plaster models supplied by the artist.

Reducing workshop.
Reducing lathe.
Cast iron or galvanized reductions from 1.2 mm to 100 mm.

3 By reproduction machines, using resins or templates (zinc moulds).

Before examining the theory of each of these processes, one general comment is called for. Even though machines are used, engraving is nevertheless a manual skill. Whatever the approach, circumstances may repeatedly arise in which the engraver must intervene with his manual instruments, either to facilitate working on a machine, or for finishing purposes. Although a necessarily very brief summary does not emphasise this aspect, it is well to remember it.

The main field of manual work is obviously *direct cutting,* which we shall deal with first.

It is the oldest procedure and calls for a long apprenticeship, since the quality of the work depends on the drawing skill of the engraver, and also on his instruments. The instruments are a personal matter, since the engraver makes his own tools. He cuts up steel bars (3 to 10 mm in square section) into approximate lengths of 16 cm for etching tools, 12 cm for gravers, and 5 to 6 cm for punches. The pieces of metal thus prepared are lengthened by forging, and are then filed to give them the required shape; finally, the tools are hardened and tempered.

Etching tools are then given a fine finish by being ground to a point. A satisfactory engraving can be produced only with tools which are impeccably sharpened. We shall not go into detail about the innumerable types of engraver's tools. They can mainly be divided into three categories:

— etching tools (needles), for cutting the metal,

— gravers, for modelling the metal,

— punches, which stamp the engraving.

These three classes of tools are used by striking them with a small hammer, more heavily in the case of etching needles and punches. There are round, flat, and pointed etching tools. Medal engravers' etching needles must not be confused with those used by copperplate engravers, which are simply held in the hand and pushed. However, all engravers of sunken relief sometimes use pushing tools like those of the copperplate engravers. We use a tool called an "échoppe" (burin), which has many different shapes and sizes, and is used for finishing, which cannot be done by the hammer-struck needle.

Using all these tools, the engraver produces the striking instruments. He takes a cylindrical steel whose diameter is a few centimetres larger than that of the medal to be struck. A steel surface is very cleanly prepared. The engraver transfers his design to the surface by tracing. Then he starts cutting his subject directly in sunken relief, working from the back. From time to time, he uses a wax imprint to check the progress of his work, which is called a *die.* Some engravers cut their medal not in sunken, but in raised relief. In that case they use a *punch,* not a die.

The second process for making striking tools is *reduction by a reducing lathe.*

The master craftsman, H. Dropsy, stated in a paper which he read at the session of the Académie des Beaux-Arts held on the 24th October, 1958, that in 1729 La Condamine demonstrated to the Académie des Sciences a machine for making all kinds of regular and irregular outlines, and also a machine for cutting various kinds of "rosette". In 1749, in his book *The Turner's Art,* P. Plumier refers to this invention aimed at reducing a section, and seems to be as yet unaware of the copying lathe. Towards 1880, the blade which engraved the steel, and which could not perform the work all at once, was replaced by the *milling cutter* which, by its rotary movement, ensures more accurate and quicker performance.

At that stage, the machine was complete and became more and more widely used (Fig. 1).

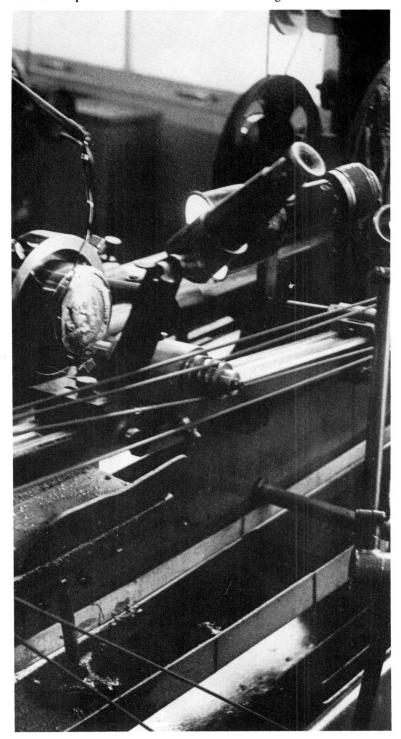

Reduction workshop. 12 reduction lathes.
Reduction of a punch after high relief casting. Sunken relief reduction can also be performed after a sunken relief casting.

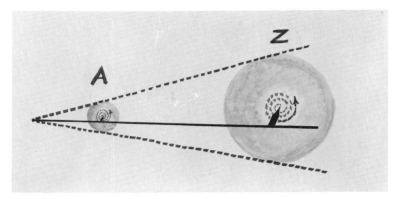

Fig. 1.

The principle is as follows: with the model situated at the most open part of the angle, the steel can move from *A* to *Z;* the more closely it approaches the model, the closer it is to the model's size. The reduction ratio is therefore inevitably limited. The best solution is a 1 to 2½ or 3 ratio; the ratio must not drop below 1 to 10 or 11. On the model, a steel touch-needle bears against the model and follows all its contours on the surface and in depth. On the steel, a milling cutter rotates and cuts the steel.

The weight of the bar which bears the touch-needle and the milling cutter causes them to descend gently, converting the circular movement motivating the steel models into an elliptical cutting movement; the starting point is always at the centre of the model.

Fig. 2 gives you some idea of the problem.

The milling cutter and the touch-needle are always conical. On the one hand, if the draught is inadequate, the design will be widened on reduction in the case of raised relief, and narrowed down in that of sunken relief. On the other hand, the milling cutter and touch needle cannot penetrate the model if the letters are too high and close together. Reductions can be carried out on models in either sunken or raised relief. If sunken relief is reduced, the result is a striking tool which is ready for hardening and use. If reduction is performed in raised relief, the result is a punch, and sunken relief must then be produced on the punch.

In the first case (reduction with sunken relief), time is therefore saved; this is the process usually adopted for urgent jobs. However, there is some risk of breakage, so it may be necessary to make a new set of tools from scratch. This means redoing a fairly lengthy job — a point which must be borne in mind if an order is to be completed by a particular date.

The reduction lathes work continuously on a job, since any interruption requires a fresh run as the part where the lathes stopped retains the traces of stoppage. Average runs take 12 to 24 hours, and on average, 2 to 3 runs are required, depending on the depth or height of the medal's relief.

The last of these three processes is *the use of reproduction machines.* The engraving workshop of the Paris Mint has two kinds:

A) A variable height parallelogram (KFI Deckel). This machine enables a model to be reproduced in its original dimensions, the two points A and A' being fixed, and F (milling cutter) and T (touch-needle) moving on the surface and in depth. The engraver probes the model with the

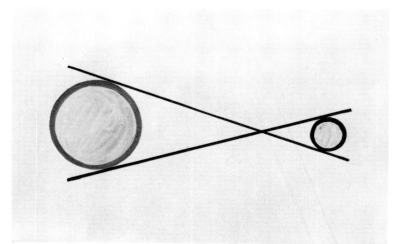

Fig. 2.

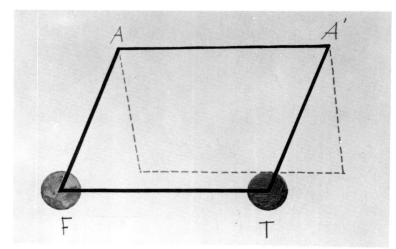

Fig. 3.

Daniel Flourat.
"Direct cutting" medal struck to commemorate the opening of the Rance tidal power station.

J.-C. Dieudonné.
Medal modelled for a town.

Sylvain Bret.
"Direct cutting" medal – "Heads of Grain" – for the Agriculture series (maize, wheat, barley, oats).

touch-needle, and the milling cutter reproduces the modelled forms on the steel (Fig. 3). This machine is adapted for 1 to 1 reproduction.

B) A pantograph (GK 12 Deckel), which allows high precision work, but with which a 1 to 1 ratio is impossible (Fig. 4). For enlargement purposes, the position of the steels and the models is inverted. It is often used with tem-

Fig. 4.

plates, which are a sunken outline on zinc of the required engraving, or with resins taken from the original medals.

All the processes described above can be used for carrying out engravings in either sunken or raised relief. If it is a case of reduction in raised relief (punch), to which several references have been made, we must now obtain the sunken relief which of course must strike the medal. To produce the die, the instrument for striking a medal in sunken relief, the pre-hardened raised relief (punch) is introduced into the other steel to give it its positive modelling. This forms the fourth and last important point of the present description: *bottoming.*

Obverse

Reverse

Maurice Charon. "Direct cutting" medal. "St. Olivier".

If you push your fingers into a paste containing round suspended particles, you will notice that the particles are displaced on either side of the point at which the pressure is exerted (Fig. 5). The same phenomenon takes place in steels, which are made up of highly flexible particles which slide against one another unless the steel has been hammer-hardened. The finger which you push in is the equivalent of the hardened punch which has the high relief engraving from which the unhardened steel cylinder will take the sunken relief imprint. The difficulty of bottoming lies precisely in ensuring that the steel remains flexible. This is why a start must always be made from the centre. If contact were to be first established over all the edges, there would be a zone of air trapped between the two steels at their centres, and nothing would be able to move. The machine would probably be broken. It is therefore necessary that:

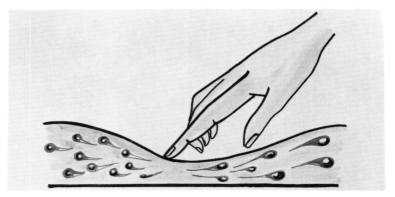

Fig. 5.

— the engraving must be designed in accordance with these needs;

— the steel to receive the imprint must be so prepared that the actual section to receive the imprint does not take the form of a horizontal circle, but has a camber whose outline must be adapted to the relief of the engraving. The fact is that the imprint is not obtained all at once; a varying number of strokes of the ram are required to obtain all the details of the engraving. Moreover, between every two strokes of the ram, bottoming must be assisted by working the steel of the sunken relief as the work progresses:

a) by heating the steel, so as to release the compressed molecules and restore flexibility to the metal,

b) by hollowing out those portions which are too resistant and prevent the model making the imprint properly.

Referring to Fig. 6, you will note that the part Z requires about the same clearance at Z' around the bearing parts at the base of the inadequately bottomed relief. If, instead of taking an imprint, a raised relief (punch) is produced on a sunken relief, you will see that it is a difficult, if not impossible, matter to obtain a model which is only slightly raised at the edges, and with weak relief at the centre. The centre is always attacked first, so that it hardens and drives the molecules outwards. As in the case of Fig. 5, the particles slide more and more towards the edge, and the engraving is said to "move". There is nothing that the engraver can do about this; the volumes never flow back, and everything goes to the sides, like a fruit which bursts when it is squeezed.

Obverse

Pierre Rodier.
"Direct cutting". Homage to engraving.

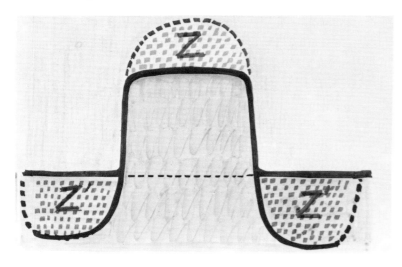

As you may imagine, the engraver's trade requires real training and a lot of patience, attention and persistence. Quite apart from all the artistic qualities which are also desirable, it requires more than inspiration to engrave a model for a coin or a medal. It is a slow, painstaking job which cannot allow anything slipshod.

Reverse

Pierre Lécuyer.
"Direct cutting" medal. Homage to engraving.
Produced specially to reward the holders of the C.A.P. engraver's certificate. The tools and the magi symbolize the schools of apprenticeship (knowledge and research).

Engraver's studio. Jean-Claude Dieudonné.
Remaking a service die from the historical collection.

DIRECT CUTTING IN PLASTER
(or possibly wood or any other material)

Before discussing medals obtained from a shaped model, we must point out that there are also artists who engrave either in sunken or raised relief in plaster in the same manner as that just described for steel.

However, although this work is close to that of the steel cutter, both in spirit and the effects which it produces, we again come up against the problems of the technique of producing the modelled medal. Reducing lathes must inevitably be used to produce the striking instruments, so that the model must be made at least three times larger than the medal to be struck. (Obviously, this does not apply to a medal which is to be cast the same size as the plaster.) The need for the model to be three times larger arises only in the case of a medal which is struck — i.e. where production tooling is used.

MODELLING

To produce a model for medal-making purposes, a round or rectangular base of hard material is used for each face, and covered with a very thin layer of plastiline. Sculptor's tools are used, namely roughing chisels and scrapers.

After the subject has been outlined on this wax-modelling base, the subject is built up in very thin layers, using pellets, always taking care to maintain an adequate inclination at the outlines of the subject to allow demoulding without the risk of sticking. This need to maintain draughts also meets the demands of the conical touch-needle of the reduction lathe which, as it passes over the model, cannot describe angles which are insufficiently open, and which will subsequently be produced as a deformed image at the other end of the apparatus.

When the wax model has been made, it is moulded in plaster.

The result is a sunken relief which may be retouched if necessary, or completed. It is easier, for instance, to engrave letters as a "negative" in the sunken plaster relief than to model them in wax. When engraving them, they can be taken slightly beyond the traced outline, since any excess relief can be eliminated when the positive version is made. It is therefore preferable to make too many marks than too few in the sunken relief; in the latter case, a fresh sunken relief would have to be produced to remedy the inadequacies.

The final raised relief must have a small flat edge of about 1 cm on the outside, in order to facilitate the stoppage of the touch-needle of the reducing lathe, which would otherwise merely drop off. The raised relief is cast in bell cast iron, and then mounted on the lathe to produce its reduced version, in the form of the steel striking instrument. If the model is in sunken relief, of course, reduction also produces a sunken relief in the steel.

Clearly, before any striking or bottoming operation is attempted, the steels are hardened and destressed.

METAL REPOUSSAGE
(For instance, copper, silver)

To perform repoussage work, you must already have practised the art of using the chisel.

First of all, the outlines of the subject are traced with a small chisel and hammer on a sheet of metal, thus causing the outlines of the subject to appear on the back of the sheet.

The sheet is turned over onto a soft material (heavy cement or sand). Using planishers or ball-shaped tools, the metal is struck with a hammer to obtain the reliefs. A great deal of practice is needed to produce the model of one's subject in reverse in this way; if the reliefs are raised too quickly, there is not only the risk of cracking the metal sheet (which is about 1 mm in thickness), but it may become impossible to reduce the relief obtained, since metal hardens when it is hammered. To restore its elasticity, it is heated to red heat; when it has cooled again, the molecules have expanded — it is *tempered*. This tempering is absolutely indispensable in repoussage operations, since otherwise the metal twists in all directions and can no longer be worked. Sometimes a repoussé medallion must be tempered 6 to 7 times before the desired effect is achieved.

To give a final finish to the work, the repoussé medallion is glued to a chiselling cement, and work is resumed on the obverse, still using a small chisel and a hammer, to define its outlines and volumes clearly.

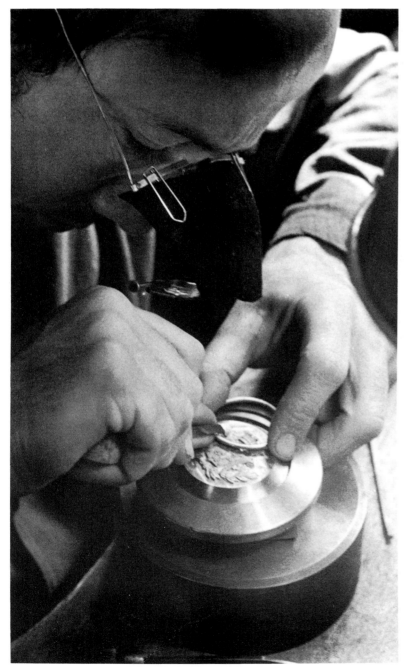

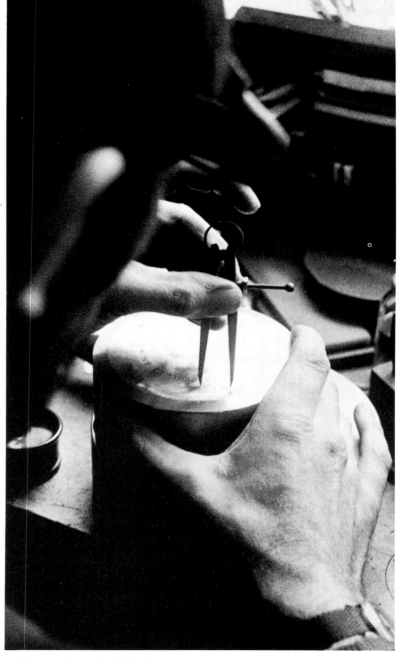

Engraver's studio. Daniel Ponce.
Using a punch to engrave the arms of the town of Sully-sur-Loire.

Engraver's studio. J.-L. Coppin.
Locating and striking a text for the reverse of a medal.

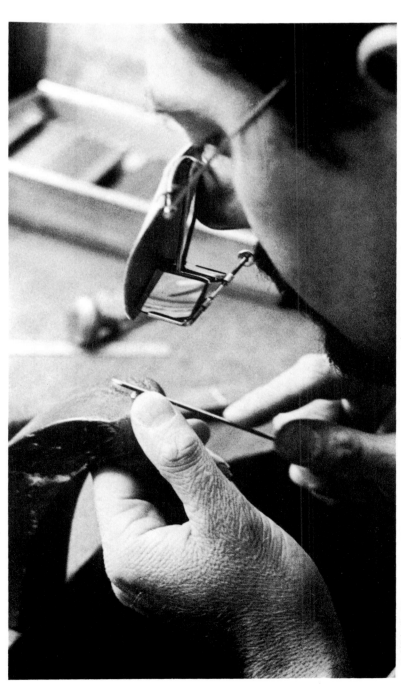

Engraver's studio. Sylvain Bret.
Finishing and retouching a commercial guarantee punch.

Engraver's studio. Marcel Couture.
Striking an alphabetic punch for the text of an embossed official seal.

Engraver's studio.
Alphabetic blocks for striking the text on medal dies.

When the work is completely finished, the plaster moulding is carried out; the sheet is slightly oiled and the plaster is cast. When it has set, it can very easily be detached, so long as care is taken to maintain an inclination at the outlines of the subject (giving it draught). The sunken relief thus obtained can be retouched or engraved; from this stage onwards, the technique is the same as that described above as regards modelling: the moulding of the final relief, the bell metal casting, the reducing lathe, etc.

When you have had a little practice with these modelling and repoussage techniques, they are very attractive to work on, as it becomes apparent that it is not necessary to over-emphasise the relief to give an impression of volume. In medal-making, everything is a question of transposition; you just need to know how to determine the relative proportions.

Apart from the first technique of direct cutting in steel, which produces the tools in their final sizes, the striking instruments must be engraved mechanically. The artist's models must therefore be produced at least three times the size of the final medal, since this is required by the reduction lathe.

When producing models which are larger than required by the medal, the artist must constantly imagine his work in its final size, and be accustomed to the effects produced by a reduction in scale.

Reduction can be performed in sunken or raised relief. In the case of a reduction in raised relief, as in the case of direct cutting using a punch, a bottoming must be performed. Moreover, technical means are constantly evolving; for instance, for some time the Paris Mint has used resins instead of bell cast iron for reduction in those cases where the model does not call for very marked raised relief.

Gouging a motif on sunken plaster relief.

Drawing a straight line with a ruler in sunken relief. 1 Plaster in sunken relief. 2 Ruler.

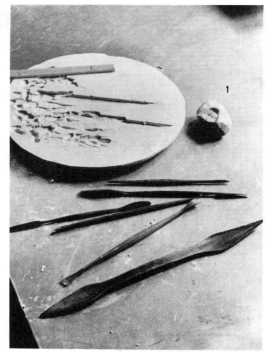

Plaster-working tools: spatulas and paring chisels. 1 Piece of plastiline for taking imprints.

Hammer — small chisels — coppersheet and heavy chiselling cement for repoussé work.

Tracing the subject on the copper to limit repoussage. 1 Tracing instrument. 2 Heavy chiselling cement.

Small chisel repoussage of the subject on the back of the copper, on heavy cement.

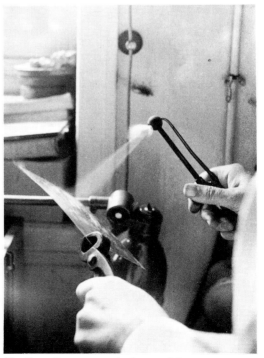

Heating the copper to be used in repoussage.

"Direct cutting" medal on steel for the 150th anniversary of the Savings Bank (reverse).

The Chief Engraver at his bench in his workshop.

Etching needle engraving.
M. Raymond Joly, Chief Engraver of the
Paris Mint.

Using a finishing tool (échoppe).
M. Raymond Joly, Chief Engraver of the Mint, at his workbench.

Engraving with a small chisel.
Reverse of the "direct cutting" medal by Benjamin Rabier.

Weingarten 110-stroke electro-pneumatic press.

Finishing phase of a silver gilt medal. (Closing the block.)

Finishing phase of a silver gilt medal. (Opening the block.)

Friction presses for striking small gold and silver medals.

Left foreground: vertical stroke press. Stroke rate: 60 strokes per minute. Power: 200 tonnes.

Right background: Muller hydraulic press. Power: 400 tonnes.

A medal maker possesses an important trump if he has mastered all these techniques. He can play on them as on the different keyborads of an organ, in accordance with the spirit which he wishes to express. Some subjects will be better dealt with by modelling than by direct cutting, or else are best engraved in plaster, or derived from repoussage. The art of the medal maker is one of suggestions and symbols. Suggestion must play its part in the physical sense as well as intellectually or poetically; sometimes grander effects are obtained by using very simple means than with complicated, heavy modelling. The most difficult thing is knowing when to stop: you have to trust a sort of instinct which prevents you from going too far.

In addition to technical knowledge, a medal maker must also have a synoptic mind, imagination, and a lot of feeling and enthusiasm.

You don't model with roughing tools, but with your heart. The best subtlety is not to be too subtle.

Original French text by
Mlle Claude Nassiet

Copper repoussage

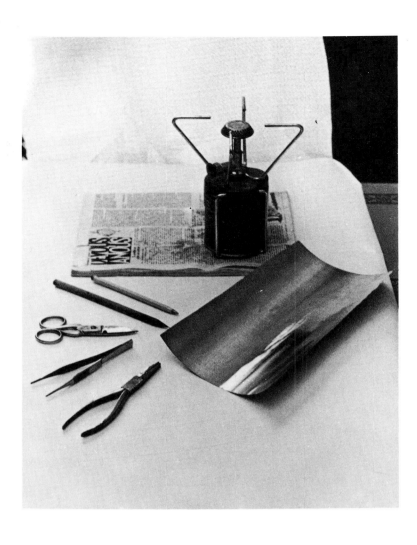

EQUIPMENT AND MATERIAL

— A sheet of red copper (foil) or brass 1/10 mm thick;
— pliers to hold the copper;
— scissors;
— a metal instrument with a rounded tip (the tip of a used ball pen);
— a tipped instrument of wood or bone;
— a small heater (e.g. a camp stove);
— newspaper thick enough to support the copper during the work;
— a colourless varnish;
— white wax;
— polish suitable for copper.

METHOD OF WORKING

After preparing a design, draw it on tracing paper.

To make the work easier, heat the copper by holding it with pliers over the flame of a heater (either a gas, spirit, or camping stove), so as to soften the copper. Bring it to red heat. Since it cools very quickly, it can then be worked.

Wipe the copper with a soft rag to remove the blackening produced by the flame. Heating the copper results in irridescent oxidations, which can be put to good use.

Cut out the required shape, using scissors (if the copper is left with jagged edges, they can be flattened with a mallet or filed).

Then trace your drawing in reverse on the back of the copper, so that the right side of the copper, which will be in relief, will reproduce the drawing correctly.

To make the drawing sharp, go round those reliefs which are to be emphasised on the obverse (relief) side of the copper plate, using the fine wooden tip.

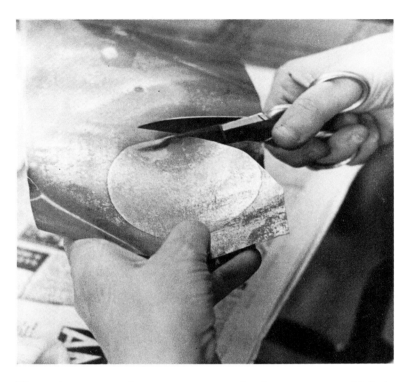

Place the prepared copper on a wad of newspaper which is flexible enough to yield with the copper, so that the tip which forms the relief does not encounter any resistance.

If you want the copper to be shiny, you must clean it with acid, rinse it thoroughly and rub it with one of the usual products for polishing copper. It can also be varnished or waxed. On the other hand, if you want to use the effects produced by fire, pass the copper over the flame again and clean it with a polish suitable for copper.

If the sunken portions are very deep, they must be filled with a filler of your choice, to prevent the relief from being crushed. (Clear cast embedding resin would be a suitable filler, or melted wax, such as candlewax or beeswax.)

Then carry out the repoussage in accordance with the drawing, i.e., push the tip in hard enough to hollow out the copper (you can produce scorings, dots, lines, etc.).

Original French text by
Denis Roche
Art journalist.

Screen printing

INTRODUCTION

The technique of screen printing originated in the Far East and came to Europe in the 19th century, when it was used exclusively for fabric designing. It subsequently went out of use and only gradually reappeared in the second half of the 20th century, primarily as a cheap method of reproduction. Its use in industry is slowly becoming more widespread; it is now commonly used in the manufacture of everyday items such as watch faces and dashboard panels as well as in advertising and in the design of the vast majority of plastic containers. But although American artists have been using screen printing for nearly forty years, it is little more than ten years since it gained recognition in Europe as an autonomous and original medium.

Among the most popular screen prints are those of artists like Vasarely, and it is no accident that the first artists to use the technique systematically were, like him, disciples of a geometric style of art, since the two principal characteristics of screen printing are clarity of outline and homogeneity of colour. Nowadays, screen printing is recognised as an original process in the same way as engraving and lithography.

But it is only an original process if the artist himself produces the matrix (in this case the screen) and does the printing (or at least supervises it) throughout the entire process.

Screen printing has three advantages over other forms of printing:
— the necessary materials are relatively cheap and light to use. You can buy elaborate machinery, but a simple set-up will still give you excellent results.
— it produces clear outlines and thick, even layers of colour.
— there are many different procedures, which will enable you to achieve an infinite variety of effects.

A silk-screen acts in a similar way to a stencil. A stencil is a perforated sheet of cardboard or thin metal through which ink or paint can be applied in the exact shape of the perforations. A silk-screen is basically a piece of material on which the shape or shapes to be printed are outlined; the area outside the outline is then blocked out so that the printing ink can only pass through the material inside the outline, thereby printing the appropriate shape onto the paper.

EQUIPMENT AND MATERIALS

The principle of screen printing is simple; the equipment you will need is also simple and will take up little space. Some artists even start off by making their own screen out of an old window frame hinged to the kitchen table!

Here is a list of the basic materials you will need:

A wooden or metal frame.

A piece of nylon or polyester of between 8x and 20x.

A staple gun.

A cutting tool.

A fine brush.

A pair of scissors.

An ink rubber.

A roll of sticky tape.

A rubber-bladed scraper.

A set of hinges.

Liquid filler (can be soluble in spirit, alcohol, or water as long as it is not dissolved by the particular pigment to be used in the printing).

Drawing gum, for the positive direct method.

Stencil film, with a transparent backing, for the indirect method. This is often sold with a special solvent.

A baseboard (blockboard or chipboard are ideal).

Some ink. (White spirit will act as a solvent for all oil-based inks.)

It is much quicker and easier to make a screen print than any other kind of print. There are three stages involved: 1 *preparing the screen* (though it is possible to buy ready-prepared screens), 2 *treating the screen*, 3 *printing*.

Work area and direct method of treatment.

PREPARING THE SCREEN

Originally, meshes were made of silk. Nowadays, nylon or polyester is almost always used. Depending on the weave, the mesh can have up to 40,000 openings per square centimetre. The ink passes through these openings and onto the paper, so different fabrics and different weaves will produce different effects.

The mesh is stretched over a wooden or metal frame. It must be glued onto a metal frame and either glued, tacked or stapled onto a wooden one. There are also self-adjusting frames which incorporate mechanical stretching devices, and some specialist shops sell frames which are already stretched with different fabrics and at different tensions. Once the mesh has been stretched, the screen must be made watertight so that the printing ink does not seep through any gaps between the mesh and the frame. This can be done by sticking lengths of sticky tape over the edges of the mesh where it meets the frame and coating it with a layer of liquid filler. Finally, before you start, you must remove any grease marks from the mesh by rubbing it lightly on both sides with a detergent solution. Ordinary household detergent is perfectly adequate. Once you have rinsed and dried the mesh, the screen is ready for use.

As we have said, the principle of screen printing is similar to that of stencilling. Each screen must therefore be for one colour only, and include all the shapes you want to print in that colour. You must also bear in mind that there is a whole variety of different inks which you can use, both opaque and transparent. The latter can be superimposed in order to produce an even wider range of colours.

TREATING THE SCREEN

THE DIRECT METHOD

Both this method and the indirect method involve printing straight from the design. The image does not have to be inverted as in engraving or lithography. The technique is based on the use of two essentially dissimilar substances, one which is soluble in water and one which is soluble in mineral spirits or alcohol, so that by using the appropriate solvent, one of the substances can be removed without removing the other.

Negative treatment. This is the simplest method. Dip your brush in the liquid filler and block out the area outside your design. You can either work from scratch or else draw the outline of your design very lightly onto the mesh before applying the filler. Alternatively, since the mesh is transparent, you can place your master design underneath it and paint directly round it.

Positive treatment, using drawing gum. This method produces more accurate results but requires two separate operations.

Firstly, you must paint or draw your design onto the mesh using latex-based ink or drawing gum. This time, of course, you must paint over the areas which you want to be printed. When this is dry, apply a thin layer of filler to the whole mesh (i.e. cover the design as well). This should be done using a rubber blade or coating trough. When the binder has dried, take your ink rubber and rub hard over the areas where the filler covers the drawing. A thin film should come away leaving the filler blocking only those areas of the mesh where there is no drawing gum.

There are many possible variations on this method; you can, for example, use lithographic ink or litho crayons instead of drawing gum. In this case, you would need to use a water-soluble polyvinyl acetate as a filler, and a cloth soaked in benzine instead of a rubber. Other possible resists are gum arabic and melted wax. It is also possible to combine various different methods.

Blocking out the mesh.

Indirect method: cutting out the stencil film.

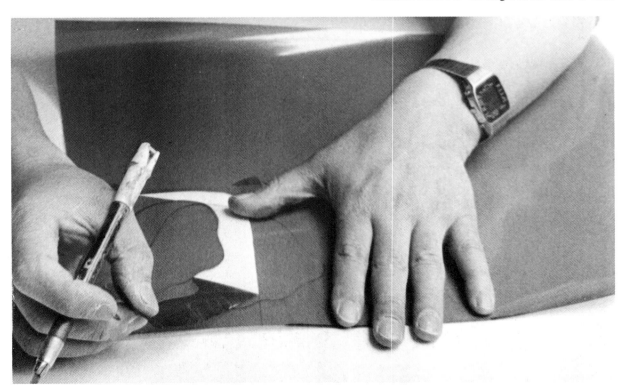

THE INDIRECT METHOD

The disadvantages of the direct methods is that they do not produce absolutely sharp outlines or give a completely accurate rendering of very fine lines. You can get round this difficulty by making cut-outs, or stencils, which will give you much more accurate results.

Take your cutting tool and some stencil film, which should have a translucent paper backing rather like tracing paper, and cut out the shape you want to print. You can either work freehand or follow a master design placed underneath the film, or else you can draw the design directly onto the film first. The accuracy of the final print depends entirely on the precision of your cutting out. The stencil is then placed against the underside of the mesh, through which it is impregnated with the special solvent that comes with the film. The solvent, which should be applied in thin layers, partially dissolves the film so that it sticks to the mesh and blocks the fabric. The paper backing should then be removed and the area of mesh outside the stencil blocked out with liquid solvent.

Finally, it is worth mentioning that there are further possibilities open to you with the use of photographic stencils. When the screen (or screens in the case of a polychrome print) has been treated, you can proceed to the printing stage.

PRINTING

You can print onto any of several media — paper, fabric, metal, plastic, etc. — and you can make as many copies as you like. The screen is attached to a baseboard by a set of hinges which allow it to be raised and lowered. During printing, it should be flat against the baseboard; at other times, it should be wedged or propped up at an angle of about 30°. The baseboard should be smooth, flat and solid, but also impervious to the inks and solvents being used; blockboard or chipboard are ideal.

Inking the mesh.

Printing.

You can buy more elaborate screens which are specially designed to prevent the paper from sticking to the mesh after printing. Alternatively, you can buy a spray-on glue such as is widely used in advertising; this is only slightly adhesive and acts for a limited time, but it is just enough to hold the paper down when the screen is raised. The next thing to do is to register the position of the paper on the baseboard in order to ensure that each successive print is identically aligned. Place your master design in the required position under the mesh and mark the board around the bottom corners of the paper. Then, to prevent the paper from slipping off the registration marks, build little barriers along them using card or layers of masking tape.

Even when the screen is lowered into the printing position, the mesh should not be in contact with the paper: pieces of card should be stuck under the corners of the screen to ensure a gap, or snap-off, of about 1/2 cm which will prevent the paper sticking to the mesh during printing. The snap-off should not be altered during printing because it causes a slight distortion of the mesh which must remain constant throughout the entire process. The instrument which is used to draw the ink across the mesh consists of a rubber blade of varying thickness and flexibility attached to a wooden handle. Support the screen in the raised position and place a sheet of paper on the baseboard in line with the registration marks. Pour some ink into the well at the hinged end of the screen and spread it across the full width of the mesh. The ink should never be used straight from the tin, but always thinned with white spirit — to a greater or lesser extent, depending on how bright a colour you want.

The screen should then be lowered into the printing position. Place the rubber blade behind the pool of ink, tilt it towards you and draw all the ink right across the mesh, maintaining a firm and even pressure. This forces the ink through the mesh and onto the paper. With practice, you will discover the ideal angle at which to hold the blade (between 30° and 35°) and the best speed at which to draw the ink across the mesh. Then draw the surplus ink back to the well, holding the blade at a lower angle, and raise the screen to the rest position. Finally, remove the sheet of paper and put it to dry. Drawing the blade lightly across the mesh prevents it from clogging while you position your next sheet of paper.

The whole process must be repeated for each sheet until you have the required number of copies. If you want to overprint in another colour, you will have to prepare and treat another screen.

Your prints will dry best in a slight draught; as they dry, the colours will fade.

Position of the hands during printing.

Original French text by
Jerôme Feugereux
Art publisher.

Printing

Title page of "L'entreprise de Naples par Charles VIII" by Octavien de Saint-Gelais, printed in Paris in 1499. (Woodcut and movable type.)

We can hardly spend a day without handling something which has been printed: a newspaper, a magazine, a book, a leaflet, or even a tin or a packet of some kind or other. Sooner or later, most of us also find ourselves involved in printing, either in the course of our work or on behalf of a club or society. An artist will be even more likely to make use of printing; for his very first exhibition he will need to produce invitation cards and posters, and, later on, he may well want to illustrate a book or even write a book himself about his work.

Different chapters in this book will have introduced you to the different methods of reproduction by printing: wood engraving, line engraving, lithography and screen printing. These four techniques form the basis of all types of printing both in industry and in the arts, but they have undergone such changes over the centuries that it is sometimes hard to believe that letterpress developed from wood engraving, gravure from line engraving, and offset from lithography, and that screen printing follows the same principles whether it is being used for artistic or industrial purposes. In the following pages, we shall describe briefly the history of printing, as well as the corresponding development of paper, and then look at the four different techniques, with particular emphasis on letterpress and offset — the former for historical reasons and the latter because of its contemporary importance. We shall then consider the advantages and disadvantages of these two techniques and, finally, describe the various stages in the printing process, without forgetting the importance of choosing an appropriate type of paper.

HISTORY

While the monks of medieval Europe were still diligently copying out texts by hand onto parchment (animal skin specially treated for writing) in their efforts to spread learning and knowledge, the Chinese had already known the secret of making paper for more than a thousand years (105 A.D. is the official date of the invention of paper), and had been printing texts from woodcuts since the end of the 8th century. The earliest known printed book dates from 868, and movable type was invented in 1041, also by the Chinese. It was only much later, thanks to the Arabs who had taken Chinese prisoners, that the paper which was necessary for printing (parchment was rare and consequently too expensive) came to Europe: the first records of the use of paper date from the early 13th century, but it was not until the middle of the 14th century that the first printing works were set up. The first European woodcut was made in 1370, the first wood-engraving in 1379, and 1437 saw the invention of letterpress, which represented the culmination of all previous developments, and which is still in use to this day. It was Gutenberg who had the revolutionary idea of engraving the letters of the alphabet onto blocks of metal and then, using these as moulds, casting an unlimited number of identical characters. He had to find a metal which was suitable both for melting down and for printing. Steel was too hard to melt and lead too soft to print with. The ideal alloy was found to be a mixture of lead and antimony.

Gutenberg's legacy to mankind was an unprecedented potential for spreading ideas.

From that day to this, hardly a generation has passed without some important innovation being made in either the techniques or the organisation of printing. Here are a few notable dates:

1496 — Etching invented.

1521 — The French National Library established as a copyright library, which means that at least one copy of every publication must be housed there. There are now some half dozen such libraries in Britain.

1796 — Lithography invented by Senefelder.

1839 — Invention of photography, which was to have far-reaching effects on printing.

Throughout the 19th century there was a continuous stream of developments and innovations in printing machinery.

None of the other mass media — records and tapes, radio and television — has yet challenged the supremacy of the printed word as a vehicle for new ideas; in Britain alone there are millions of books printed every year, not to mention the hundreds of thousands of other commercial and non-commercial publications, with circulations ranging from a few dozen to several million.

A 16th century printing works.

LETTERPRESS

In the five centuries after Gutenberg, professional printers considerably developed his basic techniques, each producing a special design to meet their own particular requirements. Although letterpress was for so long the printing method par excellence, it has gradually yielded its supremacy, and particularly so in the last ten or fifteen years, to offset.

As a method of composition, hand-setting has virtually disappeared nowadays and is still used by only a few printers The compositor, having chosen the appropriate typeface and body size, builds up each line of print on a *composing stick*, taking one letter at a time from the *case* where they are arranged in compartments, or *boxes*, of varying sizes according to the frequency of their occurrence in the language.

As early as the 19th century, this method of typesetting, which is only really suitable for small publications, began to be replaced by machine-setting. Linotype (invented in 1884) enabled a whole line to be set at once by casting it out of a single metal bar, or *slug*; the technique was highly successful, particularly in newspaper publishing, until quite recently. In Monotype (invented in 1887), each character is cast separately and the technique is still used today for high quality work (collectors' books, etc.), since it is cheaper than hand-setting and the printing is often superior (all the characters are new). Many other kinds of machines were invented over the years, but most of them have now been consigned to the back of the workshop, if not to the scrap heap.

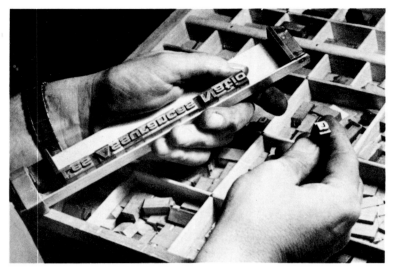

Composing stick.

Case.

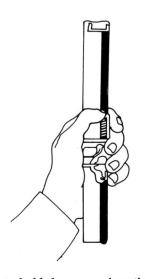

How to hold the composing stick.

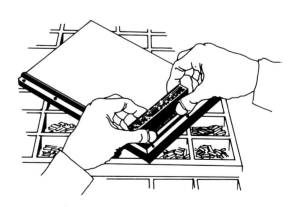

The completed lines . . .

. . . are placed in the galley.

The first book illustrations were either wood engravings, printed at the same time as the text and using the same principle (a fine layer of ink spread over the areas in relief), or metal engravings, printed separately. The discoveries of the 19th century (photography, electricity, advances in chemistry, etc.) led to great advances in speed, if not always in accuracy, of reproduction. Photogravure is a technique by which any document can be reproduced in one of two ways: in lines if it has strong contrasts between black and white, or by means of a *screen* (a series of tiny dots all the same distance apart but variable in tone from pure black to pure white) if it has several shades of grey.

The screen size is given by the number of parallel lines to the inch, so a 100 screen has a hundred lines to the inch, and a thousand dots to the square inch.

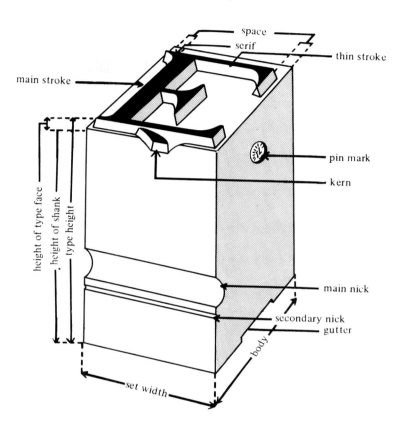

The screens most commonly used are the following:

— 32 for large posters;
— 50 for rotary-printed newspapers;
— 80 for flat-bed printed newspapers;
— 100 or 120 for ordinary publications;
— 133 or 150 for high quality work (on art paper);
— 175, 200 or 300 for extremely fine work (only used in offset).

Posters are often printed using a fine screen, and are then enlarged for reproduction.

Half-tone print, 133 screen.

32   **50**   **65**   **80**   **100**   **175**

OFFSET

Though based on the same principle as lithography, namely the antipathy of grease and water, offset has the considerable advantage of using cylinders which print at a much greater speed than letterpress or lithographic plates, with their relatively slow to-and-fro motion. Offset also uses mainly photosetting, which further increases the speed at which it can operate. These advantages have enabled offset virtually to monopolise the printing market.

Over the last few years, there have been such rapid advances in the techniques of typesetting, or, to be more precise, phototypesetting, that methods vary considerably even from one printer to another. The most sophisticated systems in common use are linked to a computer with a video screen: simply by typing the appropriate codes onto a keyboard, the compositor, or operator, as he is called, can carry out, not only the typesetting, but the making up as well. With letterpress, to change a single letter meant starting all over again; with phototypesetting, the body size and typeface of an entire book can be altered simply by typing out a code. Some systems even allow the spacing between letters or their angle of slant to be changed.

In letterpress everything is heavy and cumbersome; in offset, both the type and the illustrations are developed on film which is easily made up and easily stored.

Phototypesetting machine with keyboard and screen.

1 Suction box, 2 Margin tabulator, 3 Impression cylinder, 4 Blanket, 5 Damping roller, 6 Inking rollers, 7 Ink trough, or duct.

GRAVURE

Line engraving did not undergo the same developments as wood engraving or lithography; forcing ink into the hollows on the plate and then wiping it off the surface are operations which are too complex to allow for advanced mechanisation, even though attempts were made in the 19th century to mechanise the process (for printing lines in school notebooks, for example). But the development of gravure did involve a change from plates to cylinders. The cylinders are etched to varying depths corresponding to the tone of the image; although the variation in depth is only a few thousandths of an inch, it means that rich, deep blacks, and consequently strong contrasts, can be produced. The considerable cost of etching the cylinders limits the technique to the printing of prestige publications (such as fine art books) or magazines with large circulations.

Chrome cylinders after etching.

COMMERCIAL SCREEN PRINTING

Screen printing is acquiring an ever increasing, though still relatively small, share of the commercial market, thanks to its ability to print on a wide variety of materials (fabric, plastic, glass, metal, etc.) as well as on objects of various shapes (bottles, etc.).

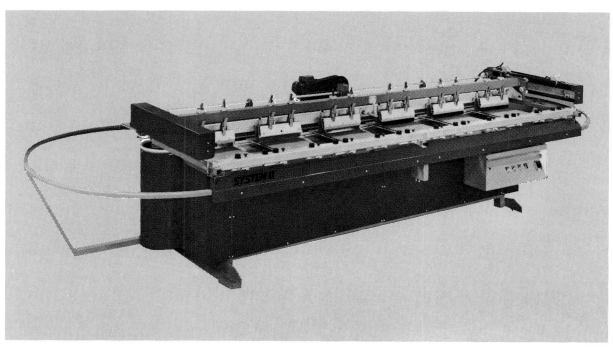

Commercial screen printing.

PRODUCING A PRINT

If you want to have something printed, you must first choose the process (basically either letterpress or offset) which is best suited to the type of print you want, and then find a printer who has the right kind of machinery.

The choice between letterpress and offset depends on several factors, including the following:

— a respect for tradition will make you choose letterpress, even though it is now possible to produce a print of comparable quality using offset;

— good letterpress printers are becoming increasingly rare and there may not be one near you;

— offset wastes a considerable amount of paper at the beginning of each run (several dozen sheets for a black and white print, several hundred for a colour print), so if you only want a few copies you would do better to use letterpress, especially if you are using expensive paper.

Even when you have chosen your process, you will find that not every printer will have a suitable set-up: some only have elaborate machinery which would be uneconomical for a short run, while others have small machines which would take too much time to do a long run. Once you have chosen a suitable printer, you must find out what format his machines are (or alternatively choose your printer according to the format of his machines) and, if necessary, alter the size of your original design so as to make the most of the equipment available. Finally, your choice of paper will also depend on the size of your design and the format of the machine: the paper should always be slightly larger than the design to allow room for the claws on the machine. There are many different kinds of paper and your choice should be governed by personal preference as well as by financial considerations, both as regards the weight of the paper (in grammes per square metre) and its finish (gloss papers give better contrasts but matt papers are often preferable for fine art prints). Your printer will be able to help you with your choice of paper, as well as with any other problems that you might have — provided, of course, that you give him a clear idea of what you are aiming at.

Once you have chosen your process, your printer and your paper, you must give the printer either camera-ready artwork, or, if he is to do the typesetting for you, a design which is as accurate as possible and a neat copy of the text: any corrections which have to be made can be very expensive.

In the case of illustrations, you will need to make proof copies on the same paper as you want to print on, as there can be considerable variation from one paper to another. Once you are using the machine, and particularly if you are printing in colour, you must try to waste as little time as possible; if you take too long, you may be charged more than the original estimate.

Printing a proof copy on a letterpress machine.

PRINTING IN COLOUR

Most of the above information has been concerned with black and white printing, but you can obviously also print in colour; in fact, your printer will give you a colour chart with a variety of colours to choose from.

To heighten the contrasts in a modelled design, you can make a two-colour print: the photo-engraver will produce two facsimiles using different screen sizes, one with strong contrasts for the full tones and the other with weak contrasts for the half tones.

Finally, as in screen printing, you can superimpose layers of colour in order to produce a multicoloured design; the usual practice is to make a four-colour print, which is based on the principle that the three primary colours (red, yellow and blue) can be combined to produce all the other colours. Colour filters are used to isolate the primary colours, and black is added to strengthen the contrasts. The whole process can now be carried out on a scanner, which operates using laser beams. After touching-up, when necessary, the proof is given to the customer for any final corrections. The definitive print is made either on a machine which prints one colour at a time or on one which prints the four colours in one run.

Offset printing machine, showing the rollers.

Retouching a cylinder.

Red   Yellow   Blue   Black   Four-colour

Wooden characters.

Glossary

COLOUR WASH

Monochrome: a painting which is done in various shades of the same colour, often with black and white as well for highlights and accents.

ENAMELS ON COPPER

Champlevé: this technique involves making cavities in the metal to receive the enamel.

Cloisonné: this technique involves separating the different areas of enamel with copper or silver wire.

Flux: this is a transparent, colourless enamel which adheres well to metal.

GOUACHE

Impasto: using thick paint.

OIL PAINTING

Blending: the process whereby colours gradually merge together when the paint is fresh.

Chiaroscuro: the balance of light and shadow in a painting.

Craquelures: small cracks caused by the movement of the ground and dried paint.

Dull spots: matt spots which appear as the paint is drying.

Glaze: a layer of almost transparent paint which modifies the colour underneath.

Patina: the appearance a painting assumes in time.

Pochade: a generally small painting done at one sitting.

Scumbling: a thin film of colour which is laid over a paint surface to modify it.

Support: the canvas, cardboard or paper on which one works.

Touch: the way in which the brush is handled, applying greater or lesser quantities of paint to the surface.

PAPER

Quire: 25 sheets of paper.

Ream: 500 sheets of paper.

Sizes:					
	A1	594	x	841	mm
	A2	420	x	594	mm
	A3	297	x	420	mm
	A4	210	x	297	mm
	A5	148	x	210	mm
	A6	105	x	148	mm
	A7	74	x	105	mm

PRINTING

Character: a single letter, or figure.

Composing stick: a stick which compositors used to fill with individual letters to make up a line of type.

Folio: the figure which indicates the page number.

Imposition: the arranging of pages on a plate, in such a way that they will be in the right order when the printed sheet (usually a sheet contains 16 or 32 pages) is folded.

Linotype: a typesetting machine which sets complete lines of type.

Lower case: small letters.

Monotype: a typesetting machine which sets each letter individually.

Offset: method of printing where a rubber blanket comes into contact with the paper.

Ozalid: a photographic proof of the arrangement of pages on a plate.

Plate: a metal sheet onto which the contents of a number of pages (usually 16 or 32) is transferred by photographic means. The plate is then attached to the printing machine, and is the source of the printed impression.

Upper case: capital letters (refers to the way individual letters used to be arranged in the compositor's wooden case).

STAINED GLASS

Grisaille: a design on glass produced using iron oxide.

WATER-COLOUR

Brio: a term used to describe the spirited execution of a water-colour.

Dryness: a fault on water-colour, due to insufficient quantity of water. The resulting effect is meagre and lacking in impact.

Running: a term used to describe colour that bleeds, or runs, over the areas it is intended to cover.

Singing: a water-colour can be said to sing when its colours harmonise in a manner which is pleasing to the eye.

Wash: paint. The term is used because of the nature of the diluting medium, water. To say that a water-colour is mainly washed means that it is painted in broad areas rather than with fine brush strokes.

Working with water: this is to have your brush always sufficiently full, so as to maintain the necessary degree of moisture, which is such an essential characteristic of this medium.

WOOD ENGRAVING

Champlevé: making depressions in a surface to leave a pattern visible.

Contour: to outline the drawing with a knife.

Rout: to scoop or gouge out wood, leaving the drawing standing proud.

PARIS ABC SCHOOL OF ART

This volume of TECHNIQUES is the work of a team. It was originally published in France, and was produced by Jean Feugereux from an idea by Jeanne Socquet. The original layout was by Claude Nadel.

The book was written with the help of:

Avati, Camille Berg, Nicole de Brus, Henri Cadiou,
Rodolphe Caillaux, Robert Cami, Pierre Castelnau,
Yvette Cauquil-Prince, Jack Chambrin, Michel Chaumet,
Michel Ciry, Pierre-Eugène Clairin, Lucien Coutaud, Jacques Courreye,
Georges Dayez, Georges Delplanque, Jérôme Feugereux, Lucien Fontanarosa,
Jean-Paul Froidevaux, Andrée Gavens, Paul Girol, Miléva Guita, André Hambourg,
Marc Havel, Raymond Joly, Jacques Le Chevallier, Daniel Legros, Philippe Lelièvre,
Albert Le Normand, Sophie Leroux, Riccardo Licata, Jacques Loire, Mme Lozach,
Marko, Myriam de Monneron, Claude Nassiet, Henri Plisson, Dinah Relange,
Denis Roche, Claude Schurr, Mme Nicolas Untersteller,
Vieira Da Silva, Claude Yvel, Zao Wouki.

Photographs of the techniques are by Philippe Guérin and Claude Poilbarbe.

The book was translated into English and published by
The Linguaphone Institute, London.

© Ecole ABC de Paris, 1971.
English translation © Linguaphone Institute Limited, London, 1982.

Printed in France by Gibert-Clarey

Linguaphone Institute Limited, London
207 Regent Street
London W1R 8AU